AWARD WINNING AUSTRALIAN ARCHITECTURE

AWARD WINNING
AUSTRALIAN ARCHITECTURE

NEVILLE QUARRY

CRAFTSMAN HOUSE
G+B ARTS INTERNATIONAL

Distributed in Australia by Craftsman House,
20 Barcoo Street, Roseville, Sydney, NSW 2069
in association with G+B Arts International:
Australia, Canada, China, France, Germany, India,
Japan, Luxembourg, Malaysia, The Netherlands,
Russia, Singapore, Switzerland, United Kingdom
United States of America

ISBN 90 5703 20 15

Design: David Pidgeon Design
Cover Photograph: John Gollings
Printer: Toppan Printing Co., Singapore

AWARD WINNING
AUSTRALIAN ARCHITECTURE 1981-1995

This book is essentially an illustrated compilation of buildings that have won National Architecture Awards from the Royal Australian Institute of Architects, since the inception of the national programme in 1981.

The Royal Australian Institute of Architects' national awards are celebrations of excellence in architecture. For architects, the awards are a chance to show off, enjoy a bit of ego-boosting and vindicate their own endeavours. For perceptive members of the public, these awards provide an insight into what the architectural profession values as outstanding work. Awards are both a response to and a stimulus for the prevailing culture. Award winners set standards to which others may aspire and against which all may compare.

To be considered for the national awards, a building must have already been an award winner in the annual awards programmes conducted by the local Chapters of the RAIA, in each State and Territory of Australia. The local awards juries have a similar composition to those of the national, but with different members. Any national award winner has passed, in effect, through two selection processes, one State-based, one nation-based. (Two exceptions to this requirement are the International Award, in which nominations are made directly to the National Jury, and the Queensland Chapter programme, which first judges regional winners before selecting State awards.)

The list of award winners, then, may be taken to represent the choices and values of the architectural establishment of the day. A review of the awards indicates that the architectural establishment is not always conservative, prim or unadventurous in its judgements.

Many established architects take pride in the notion that they can recognise outstanding qualities even in radical and idiosyncratic designers, and in emerging as well as in mature talent.

The structure of this book provides a record of the award winners and a contribution to architectural discourse, with essays relating to each awards category as commentary on the processes of assessment.

The list of award-winning buildings, their locations and their architects, together with the evidence of photographs, drawings and the verbatum reports of the juries, should provide some insight into the reasoning and subjective feeling behind each award.

In the double page spread for each award-winning building, the upper heading identifies the building, the lower heading names the architects.

To what extent are awards captive to fashions? Do the awards create trends which otherwise would never have happened, or might have quickly died out? What impact do awards have upon architects or the community? Is the allocation of awards by reference to criteria that are constant, durable and reliable, or are they subjective and erratically dependent upon the happen-chance selection of jurors, who carry their prejudices? How accurate are the awards as a reliable reflection of real architectural quality and the ethos of a particular period in time? In retrospect, have some deserving buildings missed the award accolade, and have some award winners failed to pass the tests of physical sustainability, lasting functional efficiency and fluctuations in the perception of style?

Before coming to their own conclusions about the worthiness of the RAIA awards system and of particular awards, readers should first consider the evidence presented in this book.

The awards communicate to architects and the public which recent buildings deserve attention and reflection. Any personal final judgement must ultimately be the result of directly experiencing the building and reflecting upon that experience.

So read well, but then get out there and look.

RESPONDING TO ARCHITECTURE

It is not actually necessary to know anything about architecture to experience its pleasures.

People who claim to know nothing about architecture may still declare their opinions about buildings. It is proper that they should. Often the opinions are deeply felt, the result of direct experiences of architecture. It is also proper that their opinions can be compared with those of people who are actually engaged in architectural practice. Knowledge can help to deepen individual experiences which can then be compared with those of other people. As a result of further reflection upon why one architectural experience was more satisfying than another, future experiences may be enhanced. Learning goes on.

Spoken and written communications about architecture range, in order of ascending significance, from gossip, anecdote, opinion, and discourse through to the critique. Gossip consists of snippets of information, not readily verifiable and not professionally relevant, usually intended to damage someone's reputation. Anecdotes are little narratives about minor incidents, that may be entertaining, but not particularly educative. Opinions are personal responses to a situation, without necessarily implying any general scope. A discourse is a discussion about causes and effects, sources, influences and implications. The critique is a discourse which makes comparisons, draws deliberate conclusions and provides a rationale. Discourses and critiques lead to understanding by comparing the familiar with new sensory experiences, and by comparing the particular subject with a set of theoretical principles (authoritative criteria), or an exemplary model (a paradigm), or a body of work accepted by the establishment as representing best practice (a canon). The RAIA National Architecture Awards constitute a canon, based upon published criteria, in accord with established parameters.

COMPARISONS

Architects tend to value uniqueness, and are prone to seek in any project an inherent or imposed speciality which makes it unlike any other. Consequently, comparing one project with another risks futility, for the creative fascination is in finding the points of incomparability.

A common platitude says that you cannot compare apples with pears. Well of course you can, on the basis of them both being fruit. Properties of freshness, colour and piquancy, for instance, can be validly compared throughout the genre. How might works of architecture be compared? By size, cost, complexity, originality, aesthetic qualities, social relevance, ecological sustainability? Any comparison is valid within its own terms, provided the terms are steadfast, clear and honest. If a group should decide that architecture is all about the concealment of plumbing, that's a proposition to be debated. But there is not much point in the covert plumbers trying to converse with another esoteric group which insists that architecture is a manifestation of chaos theory. For an effective degree of communication to exist a number of beliefs must be shared, or at least held to be relevant.

The comparative basis of the RAIA awards begins with the building type, based on use and date. Buildings that have similar uses are presumed to share sufficient similarities so that plausible comparisons can be made: Public Use — Sir Zelman Cowen; Residential — Robin Boyd; Urban Design — Walter Burley Griffin Award. Buildings which are being brought back to prior condition or being adapted to new uses have two different categories: Conservation — the Lachlan Macquarie, and Recycling — the President's Award. The Commercial, Interior Architecture, International, Special Jury Awards and the Citations for Access and the Environment are self-explanatory.

The awards categories are not precisely definable. Their boundaries are blurred, their territories negotiable. The temptation is always to extend and refine the description of types and consequently enlarge the number of awards. Their number has increased since the awards programme began. For every possible sub-category special pleas can be made by vested interests, but expansion of categories becomes absurd when extended too far — a thousand types with a thousand winners? The solution is to have just sufficient awards to differentiate, without swamping the system — and enough for the architectural profession to be satisfied. Currently there are eight categories for awards, and two for citations. To grapple with ten is not too large a task for a jury or an audience.

CRITERIA

For the sake of its own awards, the RAIA adopts the stance that architecture is what its corporate members practice. This limitation may seem chauvinistic and authoritarian. Of course, there are genuine examples of architecture by those who do not belong to the RAIA, and significant built works have come from people who are not architects at all. Rather than searching the universe for all possible claimants, the RAIA restricts its own annual awards quest to an identifiable set of participants. The RAIA has evolved, from initiatives in its Chapters, a detailed set of criteria which all juries must consider:

Relationship of the building to its site and context
Functional layout
Consistent and complete expression of the concept
Structure, construction, materials and services
Contribution to architectural development
User and client satisfaction

Clients are asked to respond to the following questions:

Did the finished building meet the brief?
Does it continue to service the needs identified in the brief?
Are the occupants happy with the created
   living/working environment?
Were the budget/item limitations complied with?
Do you consider the building is worthy of a
   state/national award?
Environmental performance/use of energy
   (Environment Citation criteria)

CRITIQUES OF CRITERIA

The RAIA Awards criteria are useful as a guide to assessment, since they provide a range of headings under which critical discussion can be consistently focused. They direct attention to specific topics. These topics are significant issues, but strictly speaking are not criteria, for they lack the embodiment of a standard that should be provided within a criterion. As they stand, the topic headings offer insufficient indication and no scale for differentiation, only an admonition that the issues must be seen to be addressed. The jury relies, in the end, upon its ingrained professional judgement. A criterion is a standard upon which a judgement may be based, an established goal to be met. A standard, or test, implies a scale of measurement. There are many items on the RAIA awards criteria which cannot be calibrated, although they can be referred to and addressed. For example, there is no meaningful definition for site and context relationships, but this does not mean that these relationships are unattainable or unrecognisable. Structure, construction, materials and services are areas of concern, not criteria. Calibration is not essential for informed commentary. The RAIA awards criteria are not measurable standards, but serve as principles which should be observed in the design of all buildings, and somehow particularly well in award-winning buildings. Those buildings which have reached the national level of consideration, after the accolade of a State award, are likely to exceed competency in all the issues that can be separately charted. Whether the outcome is a commonplace work or a masterpiece, it could still be argued that every single building ought to satisfy the RAIA criteria anyway. A checklist which required a numerical score against each item would be one solution not to be wished upon any jury, even if by some miracle the percentage weighting of each separate criterion was acceptable. Nor would I advocate some kind of mad matrix of elements in a labyrinthine algorithm as a basis for identifying excellence. There are no easy formulae. So what do jurors do, habitually, to escape the impasse of never-ending ideological conflict? They resort to remembered sensory experiences of architecture, to concepts, criteria, paradigms and to the canon of previous award winners. This is a hybrid process, based on peer review, combining criteria referencing with comparative and normative evaluation.

JURY DYNAMICS

The RAIA awards jury is selected and chaired by the Immediate Past National President of the RAIA, which pretty well ensures that no uncontrollable radical will buck the system. The criteria upon which the selection is based are listed under item 13.5.3 in the *RAIA Policy Book:*

Eminent architects widely respected within the profession.

Architects with a broad-based knowledge of architecture and ability to judge a range of architectural styles, project types, scale and contexts,

Recent RAIA award recipients.

Gold Medallists.

Senior office bearers of the RAIA.

Members of other juries.

An individual able to bring a unique and/or specific perspective to the jury.

Consideration of continuity of jurors from one year to the next may be an additional factor in jury selection.

When appointing non-architects or 'laypersons' to RAIA juries, consideration should be given to persons who have a prominent public profile such as members of the media or those with a similar public standing.

The emphasis is upon respected experience, maturity of judgement and eclectic tolerance. Consequently, very recent graduates or practitioners who are not already known for their buildings, publications or RAIA service are not likely to be included. This is the nature of any peer selection process; peers cannot select colleagues until they know more about them. I have heard arguments that this denies the 'young' a voice. Age is only a bar insofar as it mitigates against opportunities for prior recognition. The jury consists of five people, four of whom are architects, one not. This is enough to counterbalance any biased point of view dominating the assessment, and not so many to make the logistics of taking the jury to any part of Australia too awkward or expensive. It has been my experience, on three national juries, that after the jury is selected, the RAIA does not interfere further, other than to ensure that the RAIA National Awards criteria are brought to the jury's attention.

Whenever architectural juries gather, whether for the RAIA National Awards programme or for architectural competition deliberations, they experience similar group dynamics. In the preliminary skirmishes, individuals test each other's strength of purpose, range of ideals and tolerance limits; not necessarily in power plays intended to establish dominance but out of a concern to estimate whether a consensus is likely to be reached promptly or whether mavericks will prolong the deliberations. Politeness usually reigns in these early stages, as propositions and counter-propositions are tentatively put. Individual jurors may have difficulty in accepting a building that speaks an architectural language which is not their own habit, or which is antipathetic to how they believe society should be or appear to be. Amazing perhaps, that despite the different prejudices and perspectives each juror brings to the task, a consensus frequently comes fast. Efforts are made to recognise the validity of values which need not conform with one's own, but have appropriateness and vivacity. Behind closed doors, architects can be incredibly open to a wide range of architectural approaches, admiring things that are well done, even if not of their own persuasion. In public, exerting their egos, architects may be less inclined to show generosity or appreciation of others' work.

Architects are quite at ease with adjudication. They have all done it before, many times, as students, receiving critiques from their architecture teachers. A behavioural model is recalled — devastating critic confronts abashed student. Jurors are in the staff position, the submitting architects are in the role of students. Sometimes, individual jurors revert to antiquated staff roles, acting out the more cruel and destructive patterns they once found hurtful but now relish when on the delivery end. This retrospective revenge-displacement is not abnormal. Jurors tend to repeat the jury process they went through as students. Of course, some architects have embraced fresher learning procedures since their adolescent experience, but most bring to bear upon contemporary judgements the principles and practices that they absorbed while in their past architectural education. Architecture schools have to accept the heavy burden that what is taught there, in regard to critical method, may be all that is ever learnt. After graduation, architects do not always reassess their critical strategies. They may lose interest in theory, polemic and didactic discourse. A cosy intellectual torpor may settle in. Challenges other than the assessment of colleagues' work are likely to take priority in the lives of active practitioners. Getting the job and doing the job are difficult enough tasks. But just as architectural practice ought to evolve concurrently with maturity of experience and constructive reflection upon mistakes and achievements, the critical evaluation of architecture ought to be a continuous life-long learning process. Phenomena that are not evaluated are seldom understood. Every architect should be able to claim an understanding of architecture and defend that understanding with intelligence and feeling.

Meanwhile, back in the typical jury, after the personal shadow-boxing phase is over, jurors may ask 'What are the criteria, anyway? We can't assess properly unless we have relevant criteria'. Such a plaintive cry, more wistful than anticipating resolution, is assuaged by revealing the RAIA National Awards criteria, formally adopted in 1994. Prior to this, the criteria were more or less accepted as based upon those circulating in State Chapters for their own awards, or else the jury might make some desultory attempts to construct their own for-the-time-being criteria, before admitting that the time needed to pursue these thoroughly would exceed the time allowed a jury for visiting buildings throughout Australia. By this stage of deliberations, a jury is probably beginning to realise that the discussion of criteria is interminable, and that the process of shortlisting contenders must be faced without further delay. There will be too many award submissions passed on from Chapter programmes for the jury to visit, so normally the next step is for the jurors to make their own shortlists. Shortlists are compared. The jurors rely upon the submissions before them, and the observations of any members who have actually seen the buildings under review. The arguments are engaged for and against the inclusion of projects which happen not to have received instant consensus. This is a crucial period. Those submissions not surviving the cut have, of course, no hope of winning. The argument revolves around theoretical, practical and sensory contexts. Juries develop their own emphases on one or more of these contexts, or perhaps try to balance them all.

Theoretical contexts include the explicit criteria, and also personal intellectual mindsets and emotional bias. One person may have the Romantic disposition, which prefers aesthetic expression, complexity and earthiness; another the Classical disposition, which prefers discipline, simplicity and serenity. Different image paradigms may be held: the swirling curvilinearities of Borromini or the suave proportionalities of Palladio; the dynamic splinters of Zaha Hadid or the cool manoeuvres of Jean Nouvel. Inclinations towards minimalist abstraction or metaphorical association, or various positions in between, will emerge in discussion, and be debated. One person's theory may reckon architecture is foremost a community service, another may claim architecture as an autonomous art. Such oppositions are not to be solved in a single jury session, so compromises must be made, or an eclectic realm accepted. In practice, the jury takes on board the RAIA criteria, percolates them through the experience of the panel, makes comparisons and comes to conclusions in a consensus arrived at by debate.

PRAXIS

Architects know that the final design of a building is subject to many constraints. Often, the initial conceptual sketch, pure as a paradigm, cannot survive the competing interests of the developing brief, including restrictions on space, cost and construction method. In assessing possible award winners, the jury will seek to understand how a building has overcome, or been vanquished by, practical and circumstantial requirements.

The context of practicality is in some ways the most obvious — does it work, does it fulfil the need for which it was built, will it last? The answers are not so easy to determine. Evidence is needed of practicality in terms of occupants' response, durability of the building fabric, serviceability of building mechanics, and cost. Invariably, the clients' responses to questionnaires that are required with architects' submissions are supportive and replete with praise, but there is not usually available a comprehensive post-occupancy user evaluation, so a detailed assessment of how a building contributes to its occupants' comfort and productivity needs a more thorough and time-consuming effort than the jury is able to muster. During the jury visit, it is possible, nevertheless, to get a reasonable impression of functionality. Because the buildings being inspected for awards are usually freshly constructed or refurbished, the building fabric has not yet been ravaged by time, although experienced observers may foresee where problems are likely to occur. The mechanics of the building, the working parts such as lifts, doors and air conditioning can be checked by direct involvement — it is hard to mask operational inadequacies. Cost enters into the judgement, but it must be related to the intentions of the project. Buildings that are lavish need not be extravagant and cheap buildings need not be gaunt. Whether an impracticality can be traded off against a courageous aesthetic, is a compromise that each jury has to resolve in its collective wisdom.

SENSIBILITY

The initial and spontaneous sensory experience of the physical phenomena of architecture carries into memory. A building that cannot be recalled as a pleasurable experience or, worse, cannot be recalled at all, can hardly be influential. A vivacious work of architecture can snap through a theoretical fog, appealing directly to the emotions, short-circuiting logic and critical analysis. Award winners invariably have a vivid intensity — the power of a searing image penetrating the retina into the brain, generating positive thoughts about the ability of human beings to transcend the rationalist cycle of cause and effect. All the senses are invoked during the appreciation of a building, beginning with the distant approach and continuing through the entire transit of its interior. The journey involves time and space; tactile, thermal and acoustic sensations; memories and associations; the whole repertoire of personal past experience and future hopes. These personal apprehensions are emotional and subjective. But although some perceptions perhaps operate subliminally, they are not entirely arbitrary, not just random guesswork, not ignorant of causal connections and human empathy. Photographic images alone do not convey the full range of architectural sensations, although they may hint at it. Juries visit the short-listed award-nominated buildings for an intimate confrontation with reality.

ATTRIBUTE TRANSFER

Invoked by architects as attribute of buildings, the qualities of creativity, intelligence and passion are easy to perceive, impossible to quantify. The cerebral and emotive mechanisms that are involved in responding to particular elements or configurations are not simple to pin down and not readily understood. No doubt we transfer to the material assemblage of building those attributes which really belong to a personality. By some mental infusion, qualities that adhere to human individuals are read into architecture. From the architectural work we infer the architect's most profound personal values and compare these with our own. When there is congruence, we acclaim the work.

DEFINING ARCHITECTURE

Architecture, in common with other human concepts like music, religion, culture, sport and politics, has no agreed definition which includes all necessary items within the concept and excludes all pretenders. If there was an absolute definition, perhaps there would be no point in further commentary. There is no lack of attempts at definition. Here are a few samplings:

You employ stone, wood and concrete and with these materials you build houses and palaces; that is Construction. Ingenuity is at work. But suddenly you touch my heart. You do me good, I am happy and I say: 'This is beautiful. That is architecture.'

(Le Corbusier, 1923, *Vers Une Architecture/Towards a New Architecture*, Architectural Press, 1946.)

...architecture does not really exist. Only a work of architecture exists. Architecture does exist in the mind. A man who does a work of architecture does it as an offering to the spirit of architecture... spirit which knows no style, knows no technique, no method. It just waits for that which presents itself. There is architecture, and it is the embodiment of the unmeasurable.

(Kahn, Louis. 1964, in Latour, Alesandra, ed., 1991, *Louis Kahn: Writings, Lectures, Interviews.* New York: Rizzoli International Publications.)

Architecture, like other arts, produces 'culture capital', by which people display their upper class status through their tastes and possessions. One can hardly consume more conspicuously than through architecture.

(Cuff, Dana. 1991, *Architecture: The Story of Practice.* Cambridge, Mass.: The MIT Press.)

One could say, in desperation, that architecture is whatever you think it is. To continue the debate, however, there must be some community of subscribers to your proposition, otherwise it may remain esoteric and incommunicable. This is not to suggest we need an architectural definition by opinion poll; rather that the important thing to recognise is the common understanding of the group involved in the discourse. In connection with the RAIA National Architecture Awards, the group involved in the discourse is the jury for the year.

Each jury is different, so it could be expected that assumptions and criteria fluctuate over the years. But, as will be seen from the jury reports which follow, there are some underlying consistencies.

My personal inclination is toward Le Corbusier's definition for, even if subjectively opinionated, it identifies a response — heartfelt happiness — which for him is a necessary indicator in order to recognise architecture.

His definition contrasts ingenuity and beauty and in effect leads to a distinction between architecture as design and architecture as art.

A work of architecture may be recognised as being well-designed when it is perceived as a purposeful and coherent response to the circumstances, constraints, compromises and contexts of a set of problems which require a building for their solution.

A work of architecture may be recognised as being a work of art when it is sensed as an intense intellectual and emotional expression of aesthetic values.

When a work of architecture is both well-designed and aesthetically expressive, it deserves reverence and applause.

Applause may be manifest in public opinion, declared personally or communally through the media. Those buildings which are charged with meaning and expression to the highest intensity are those that are most deserving of the RAIA awards. The highest intensity is that which is revealed by works of architecture that have gained, over time, the accolades of the architectural profession.

INAUGURAL COMMENTS: 1981

In giving these awards, the Institute has reached a prominent point in its history; coming to terms with its national identity and its desire to promote high standards of architectural design to the general public.

We are honoured that Sir Zelman Cowen and Robin Boyd's family have agreed to the awards bearing their names. Both have contributed greatly to the profession and this is now recognised for posterity.

In these buildings we see the result of the design process being conducted to the highest standards. The clients have determined to achieve the best possible results out of their need for a building; the architects have applied outstanding skill and talents in producing the designs and the builders have ensured that the design intent is manifest in the completed works.

Michael Peck, President, RAIA, 1981.

The idea of Australian National Awards for architecture has floated in and out of the consciousness of RAIA National Councillors for almost as many years as the Institute has existed as an entity. It has been raised on numerous occasions at National Council meetings but has been reluctantly dismissed as impractical because of the heterogeneous nature of the awards system in the various Chapters of the Institute and the problems of timing.

It is difficult enough to get agreement from State to State on many of the day to day matters with which the Institute has to deal; how much more difficult to get agreement on awards for architecture across the nation.

Nevertheless a National Awards system and an awards publication have been achieved; not without stress, strains and a great deal of commitment from all Chapters. The achievement is remarkable and provides evidence once more that despite the surface differences which exist there is indeed a common bond amongst architects across the country.

This year there is evidence of work firmly in the mainstream of the Modern movement, the gradual acceptance of ideas coming under the generic if sometimes misleading title of 'Post-Modern', and a stream flowing from the greater social concerns of recent years involving participation by the public and the users of architecture.

Sir Zelman Cowen as Professor, Vice-Chancellor and Governor General — and as client — has shown a remarkable knowledge and understanding of architecture. He has spoken many times to architects and has many friends amongst architects.

Robin Boyd was Australia's foremost architectural writer and critic and a social commentator; his work commanded the attention of the Australian people, helping to bring about a revolution in attitudes to the design of the environment in which we live.

The two men were friends and Sir Zelman was a client of Robin Boyd's. It is appropriate that their names should be linked in the two national awards made by the RAIA.

Peter Johnson, Vice-President (Information) RAIA, 1981.

Sir Zelman Cowen Award for New Buildings	1981-95
Robin Boyd Award for Residential Buildings	1981-95
Lachlan Macquarie Award for Conservation	1982-95
President's Award for Recycled Buildings	1985-95
Commercial Architecture Award	1988-95
Interior Architecture Award	1988-95
Civic Design Award	1988
Walter Burley Griffin Award for Urban Design	1990-95
ACI Award	1982-87
Special Jury Award	1992-95
International Award	1991-95
Citations	1994-95

1981 CANBERRA SCHOOL OF ART

DARYL JACKSON/EVAN WALKER

1982 QUEENSLAND ART GALLERY, BRISBANE

ROBIN GIBSON

1983 EDUCATION BUILDING, EAST PERTH

CAMERON CHISHOLM & NICOL

1984 NATIONAL SPORTS CENTRE SWIMMING HALLS, ACT

DARYL JACKSON

1985 YULARA TOURIST RESORT, AYERS ROCK, NT

PHILIP COX & PARTNERS

1986 CADETS' MESS, AUSTRALIAN DEFENCE FORCE ACADEMY, ACT

DEPARTMENT OF HOUSING & CONSTRUCTION
AND ANCHER MORTLOCK & WOOLLEY

1987 JOINT AWARD

DINNER PLAIN ALPINE VILLAGE, MT HOTHAM, VICTORIA

PETER MCINTYRE, MCINTYRE PARTNERSHIP

RIVERSIDE CENTRE, BRISBANE

HARRY SEIDLER

1988 BRISBANE AIRPORT TERMINAL

AUSTRALIAN CONSTRUCTION
SERVICES AND BLIGH ROBINSON

1989 NEW PARLIAMENT HOUSE, CANBERRA

MIYCHELL/GIURGOLA & THORP

1990 BRAMBRUK CULTURAL CENTRE, HALLS GAP, VICTORIA

GREGORY BURGESS

1991 ADELAIDE TROPICAL CONSERVATORY

RAFFEN MARON

1992 MELBOURNE CRICKET GROUND SOUTHERN STAND REDEVELOPMENT

TOMPKINS SHAW AND EVANS/DARYL JACKSON

1993 STIRLING STATION, NORTHERN SUBURBS TRANSIT SYSTEM, PERTH

FORBES & FITZHARDINGE

1994 KAKADU VISITORS CENTRE, NORTHERN TERRITORY

GLENN MURCUTT AND TROPPO

1995 SWALLOWCLIFFE SCHOOLS, DAVOREN PARK, SOUTH AUSTRALIA

SA DEPARTMENT FOR BUILDING MANAGEMENT (DBM)
CONSULTANCY SERVICES; PROJECT ARCHITECT: PATRICIA LES

Projects within this category must be of a public or institutional nature, being either new buildings or substantial alterations to existing buildings and generally fall within Classes 3 to 9 inclusive as defined within the Building Code of Australia 1988 (BCA). The buildings should be of a non-commercial nature and exclude, for instance, the offices of a public corporation or an arm of government. However this category would include hospitals, churches and schools.

RAIA Awards Rules, March 1991

SIR ZELMAN COWEN AWARD

FOR PUBLIC BUILDINGS

THE PUBLIC ARTEFACT

No jury is likely to want to rewrite the definitions of classes of buildings given in the Building Code of Australia, or develop some new regimen of rigid classifications for taxonomic dispute, but it is clear that buildings intended for public use have some special prerogatives. The essence of public buildings is that any person may enter them. An architectural consequence is that an entrance should be easy to find and inviting, not obscure or repellant. Once across the threshold, however, members of the public might be required to pay for further admission. This charge is often exacted as a means of financially defraying the costs of a staged event — sporting, musical or theatrical, or for the maintenance of a displayed collection of cultural artefacts. In some cases, deeper entrance is restricted so that casual or unofficial visitors do not distract shy workers from their task of serving the public efficiently, without interruption. Thus there are political and cultural agendas involved as well as the delights of architectural progression. Just how far into a putatively public building anyone is allowed to proceed could be used perhaps as a measure of the extent of democracy in a nation. In totalitarian states, public buildings are often identifiable by the barbed wire and armed guards out the front.

In any society, it is probable that the public, unless persuaded otherwise by innovative propaganda, will seek the comforting reassurance of a familiar environment within their public buildings. One might suppose, then, that the aesthetic preferences of the public would be conservative, or even reactionary. This is not always so. In a society that is open, evolving and prepared for unpredictability, the public may applaud architecture that challenges established conventions and shifts cultural expectations in new directions. The Sydney Opera House is an outstanding example of how, despite political turmoil and interrupted development, an unfamiliar and radical expression of architectural form has become so publicly acclaimed that it is now an irrevocably Australian symbol or icon. The label 'icon' is becoming diminished in importance through overuse. Although an icon may still be taken to mean revered and sanctified, in the jargon of a non-religious activity it can also mean a symbol on a computer screen.

THE PUBLIC PROGRAMME

The social programmes reflected in the Sir Zelman Cowen winners may illustrate how significantly architecture illuminates the cultural landscape. Four of the Sir Zelman Cowen winners can be grouped into a sub-category of culture: Canberra School of Art, Queensland Art Gallery, Brambruk Cultural Centre and, representing horticulture, the Adelaide Tropical Conservatory.

Three winners accommodate tourism: Yulara Tourist Resort, Dinner Plain Alpine Village and Kakadu Visitors Centre. Sport has two winners: National Sports Centre Swimming Halls, and the MCG Southern Stand Redevelopment. Education appears to have two Sir Zelman Cowens, one in Perth, the other in Adelaide. The Education Building, Perth, however, is not a school but the headquarters of the State education administration (wonderful interior, if only the State schools were fitted out so well). So it is really only the Swallowcliffe Schools which carry the scholastic banner. Transport has realised its dynamic potential with two winners: Brisbane Airport Terminal and Stirling Railway Station. Among the others, the military gets a civil medal for the Australian Defence Force Cadets' Mess and, as one would hope for the pinnacle of political accommodation, so does Canberra's new Parliament House.

Brisbane's Riverside Centre might seem, because of its substantial office tower, to have wandered over the borderline between the public and the commercial categories. Nevertheless, anyone who has been in Brisbane on a weekend, when the Riverside ground level plazas are throbbing with market stalls, eating and meeting places, will appreciate what a vital contribution this architecture makes to public urban life. Here, as in the northern precinct of the QV1 Building, Perth, Australians and overseas visitors coexist in cosmopolitan, multi-cultural activities. Within the Sir Zelman Cowen Awards, what does this roll call of subcategories suggest about Australian public architecture or about Australian culture as a whole? The sample is small and probably too diverse for exhaustive generalisations. Still, a few observations might be chanced. From the 1980s to the 1990s a drift in architectural form-type is perceptible. Earlier, impressive, stand-alone set-pieces such as the Queensland Art Gallery and the Perth Education Building are geometrically precise and self-contained, orthodox mainstream modern monuments, the epitome of the second phase of modern architecture, limned by Robin Boyd in *The Puzzle of Architecture*, in 1965. Smaller in scale, more organic-looking, looser in arrangement and more obviously resilient to people are the later Brambruk Cultural Centre, Stirling Station, Kakadu Visitors Centre and the Swallowcliffe Schools. Did the sense of architecture really change over the decade or did juries simply become weary of the mighty blockbusters? As a counter-current, Yulara Tourist Resort and Dinner Plain Alpine Village, also early winners in the 1980s, were non-monumental, sprawling and picturesquely dispersed on their sites. The Adelaide Tropical Conservatory is a concise set-piece and the new MCG Southern Stand does not lack monumentality. All of these buildings are stimulating to their inhabitants. So the suggestion of a general movement towards more relaxed atittudes in the design of public buildings is not entirely substantiated by the evidence of the awards.

THE CULTURAL CONSTITUENCY

Does the number of winners in each sub-category suggest priorities in Australian culture? The order of award frequency is culture, tourism, sport, transport and administration. Could this hierarchy suggest that excellence in architecture is more likely to be sought by cultural than, say, administrative agendas? Tourism is now intrinsic to Australian culture. Whether we moan about the intrusion or not, tourism is the nation's largest overseas income-earner. So is tourism a public institution, within the terms of the Sir Zelman Cowen Awards, or should tourism's buildings be in the Commercial category?

The underlying intention of Friendly Beaches Ecological Tourist Development, like that of Yulara, was to earn money by luring people into culturally desirable ecological pathways.

Sport is really not excluded from culture, but is subsumed by it. The architectural act of providing facilities for sport spectators involves concerns of comfort, commerce and culture. Such functional fulfilments as good sightlines and dry seats are a necessary but not sufficient condition for sports architecture projects. For a nation that no longer suffers from the cultural cringe, and that is also sport-obsessed, one might have expected a scintillating range of sports facilities amongst which there would be a large number of award winners. Perhaps the stimulus of the 2000 Sydney Olympics may yet be an inspirational catalyst.

Many buildings are eligible for more than one category. Consider, for instance, the Powerhouse Museum. Part of this complex would fit the Lachlan Macquarie Award for Conservation; part would fit the President's Award for Recycling. The Museum has a civic presence which could make it eligible for a Walter Burley Griffin Award. The enterprise is trying to survive by being more commercial. The facility is in a public building. Of many plausible awards in 1988, the Powerhouse received the President's and Interior Architecture Awards, and a Commendation in the Sir Zelman Cowen category. Another example, RMIT Building 8, winner of the 1995 Walter Burley Griffin award, could equally have been considered under the Sir Zelman Cowen or the President's Award, for it is a public building, with the lower floors recycled from a previous, not very old, building designed by another architect.

No doubt RAIA National Awards juries, in selecting from public works, bear in mind the dilemma of public impulses that seem contrary — towards the security of mediocrity on the one hand, and towards the thrill of the unexpected on the other. Every new building is bound to be innovative to some extent. An architectural jury is more likely to veer towards exploratory rather than hackneyed outcomes in the belief that, rather than merely respond, architecture can transform an existing culture by indicating possibilities beyond banal stereotypes.

JURY REPORT

In its juxtapositioning of buildings and open spaces Daryl Jackson's and Evan Walker's Canberra School of Arts is, ironically, a model of the Canberra style of 'open' urbanism itself. The individual buildings and courtyards which constitute the complex are arranged along a straight line circulation 'spine' generated from the central axis of the old Canberra High School which to date has been home for the Art School. Outside of the site itself this axis connects to further axes in the form of streets at both ends. Jackson and Walker have acknowledged its importance by concluding it with a symbolic 'back door' adjacent to the School of Art's gallery at the Ellery Crescent end.

The simplicity of this whole arrangement, carefully created to relate to new buildings, old buildings and open spaces, contributes significantly to the school's character.

The inclination of the architects to clarify rather than obliterate extant conditions provides a clue to the explanation of the architectural forms themselves.

The old High School is an exemplary Art Deco style building which constitutes a part of what small architectural heritage Canberra has. In addition there are smaller 1950s- and 1960s-styled buildings on the site. The way in which these forms have been absorbed and yet not dominated by the new buildings is a measure of their importance to the whole design. Walls of painted brick (with relatively small window openings) terminating in parapets are an example of clarification of the old High School architecture. The only concession, incidentally, to the latter's rich horizontal mouldings is a single recessed string course at approximately entablature height. Likewise the windows and doors are squarish and divided into smaller squarish sections; they are windows to look at as well as look through.

Clarification of form, combined with a deliberate restriction of materials and colour to simply white walls, white framed glazing and brick paving, has engendered a restrained, understated architecture which is almost certainly the subtlest imaginable response to the particular situation.

This same restraint is exercised internally in a range of accommodation, which includes workshop teaching spaces, lecture rooms, offices, residences, gallery and common rooms. Many of the workshops are open to views in from the circulation spine or courtyard spaces, reinforcing the feeling of 'community'. Finishes inside vary appropriately from hard metal and concrete in many of the workshops to modest beige carpets and tan paint accents in more formal areas such as library and lecture rooms.

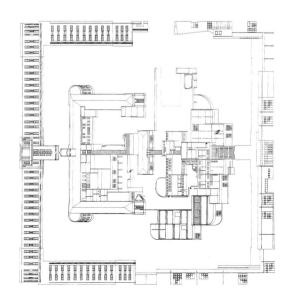

SIR ZELMAN COWEN AWARD 1982

QUEENSLAND ART GALLERY, BRISBANE

ROBIN GIBSON

JURY REPORT

In the judging of the Sir Zelman Cowen Award, the choice came down to two buildings — both designed some time ago, one however just finished, and the other completed in 1976. One is firmly in the mainstream tradition and is a worthy product of that tradition. The other broke new ground in its time in the design of commercial office buildings.

The selection committee's decision was a difficult one and was ultimately influenced by the fact that the award is meant to be for recently completed buildings.

The Sir Zelman Cowen Award has been made to the Queensland Art Gallery, designed by Robin Gibson, and a Commendation has been made to the American Express Tower, Sydney, designed by John Andrews.

The Queensland Art Gallery was opened in June 1982 as one of five major buildings of the Queensland Cultural Centre. A brochure about the centre states: 'The Cultural Centre is not a temple for a select few where culture is worshipped: it is a series of exciting environments where the entire community can be involved in the celebration of a vast array of cultural events'.

Robin Gibson has said that it is a place where barriers are broken down and where there is a constant interchange between the art world and the public: a living gallery.

The design successfully resolves the conflict inherent in art gallery and museum design — the battle between the art of the architecture and the art of the exhibits. The internal spaces are open, light and relaxed, inviting contemplation. Organised around a water mall, two rooms of galleries of varying height and size provide appropriate spaces for art works of different kinds and sizes.

There are spaces for fine objects, large high spaces for big art works and light airy spaces for objects needing contact with exterior light. The spaces invite exploration essential to the act of discovery, which is the excitement of a gallery. The use of water in the water mall is an appropriate recognition of the building site alongside the Brisbane River. The pools of varying kinds, some inside and some outside the building, with fountains, cascades and water surface patterns, and the sensitive use of water sound all provide an exceptional linking element visible from all the major galleries.

Throughout, the building materials have been used in a limited, related palette with discretion — sensibly and with elegant detailing. The character of the public spaces supports the function of displaying art objects — not a restriction or distraction.

There remains a lingering thought that there could have been a greater sense of contact with the river at certain points to complement the water mall's analogy.

The gallery has an openness, lightness and spaciousness appropriate to its Queensland location. A relaxed but appropriate place for the display of art, it works well, is a place of spatial contrasts, gives delight and has that depth which is so important to enduring architecture.

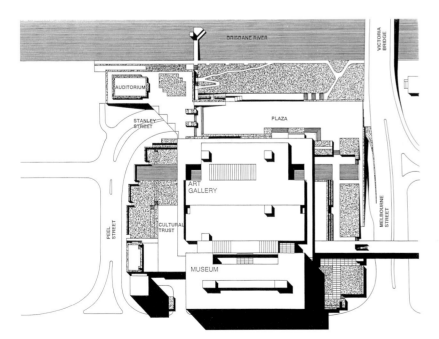

EDUCATION BUILDING, EAST PERTH

CAMERON CHISHOLM & NICOL

JURY REPORT

The basic premise adopted by the architect in the design of the Education Department Building was to 'demonstrate that today's successful buildings can only evolve when human needs, environment, energy and economic concerns are integrated in a simultaneous rather than sequential fashion'.

The National Selection Committee unanimously agreed that the architect has solved a very complex brief with a building of strong expression and consistent character. The translation of the client's requirements into a composition consisting of a series of internal courtyards creates local neighbourhoods, giving the building its intended human scale.

The Committee considers the external handling to be consistent with the intention to produce a building of appropriate scale for its site, with forms that achieve a balanced asymmetry, expressed in a technologically appropriate skin of tinted aluminium and grey tinted glass.

This building is commended for its attention to detail, its sense of place and for its statement that large buildings do not necessarily have to be tall or amorphous.

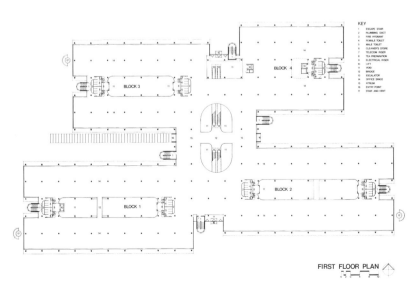

FIRST FLOOR PLAN

SIR ZELMAN COWEN AWARD 1984

JURY REPORT

The National Sports Centre Swimming Halls, sited in the base of the valley which forms the site of the National Sports Centre in Canberra, is a fine example of 'verification' in Daryl Jackson's terms. It is a building which clearly mirrors the activities within, and uses that mirroring to express a relationship to the immediate site context, and in a larger view to the Australian landscape.

By its strong colour and form it not only becomes the focal point of the address court on which it is located but becomes the mark by which its neighbours are 'read'. The placing of the building as a central element on the circulation spine further reinforces its visual domination, being passed through, or by, most users of the Centre.

The National Sports Centre is a National Capital Development Commission (NCDC) project providing facilities for the Australian Institute of Sport, and for the citizens of Canberra.

The Swimming Halls was the first building in the complex to be designed by Daryl Jackson, completing the central address court flanked on two sides by the National Indoor Sports Centre and the Gymnastics Hall, both designed by Philip Cox, and on the fourth side by the main centre access road.

The programme for the building required the provision of a 50 metre constant-depth training pool, and a 25 metre warm-up pool. Flexible spectator seating for 650 was required in the main hall for national competitions.

The siting was defined by the NCDC development plan, and provided for an east-west orientation of the pools, maximising the winter sun able to penetrate the long concourse where swimmers do dry land training, and where the coaches walk while the swimers are in the pool.

Further, the programme required that the building should respond sympathetically to the environmental context in which it was placed. Daryl Jackson defined that environmental context as 'the natural bush backdrop to the Sports Centre, the strong man-made earth forms, and the highly structuralist expression of the stadium and indoor sports building'.

Jackson responded to the environmental context by designing a building that adopted a reclining stature — a reflection of its function, and in terms of massing, as a means of relating to the surrounding buildings. The berms that surround the building are a continuation of the earth-related forms instigated by Philip Cox with the outdoor arena, and with the transposing of that imagery to the court which the other Cox buildings and the swimming halls surround.

The reclining stature also responds to the long low forms of the valley edge, and further beyond to the surrounding Canberra hills.

The passive expressiveness of the bull-nosed linear form provides a counterpoint to the highly visual 'activity' of the adjoining Cox buildings.

DARYL JACKSON

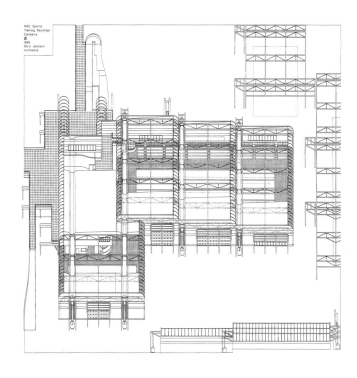

Philip Cox has referred to Daryl Jackson as 'the one mentioned most frequently' as an opposite number. It is interesting to bear in mind the long association and friendship between the two, when looking at the detail elements of the swimming halls.

In that respect, the reference to the exposed trusses of Cox's indoor arena (the 'activity' of the buildings) made by the truss penetrating the wall skin, post-tensioned to the earth mound, and the emphasis given to the rainwater heads and rainwater collection sumps are intentionally overstated. By the prominence given to those elements, they are clearly mimicking the Cox buildings with an almost tongue-in-cheek expression.

However, the elegance of the total composition of the Swimming Halls, that relies on both the expressed structure and the applied colour and form, make the apparent mimicry an integral link in the overall contextual relationship with the Cox buildings.

The taut skin of the building provides the new architectural element that defines the junction between the visually active Cox buildings and the passive Jackson building, the colours of the Swimming Halls having been deliberately chosen in the grey/green of the Australian bush palette.

The base of the building is dark green lightened off progressively towards the sky. Interspersed with the grey/green are bands of water green giving the 'clue' to the aquatic function of the building, albeit an obscure clue. The external colour bands are carried through to the interior of the building, the derivation of the colours being reinforced as one catches glimpses of the surrounding hills from the inside.

Jackson's Australian colour reference, and the use of the stripe as a device to express the linearity of the internal function, and as a mirror of the linear nature of the surrounding landscape, is justifiable. However, looking at more recent work of his office, there seems to be an emphasis on the stripe to express an architectural 'image', such as in the Australian Film and Television School, and in a far more subtle manner in the recently completed Singapore High Commission in Canberra. Therefore retrospectively, the contextual generation and impact of the stripe in the Swimming Halls is lost to an overriding interest in this particular architectural motif.

Undoubtedly by the use of colour, form and pattern, the Swimming Halls building develops an architectural expression which advances the exploration of the Australian idiom, enhancing, rather than at the cost of, the building's function.

James Grose

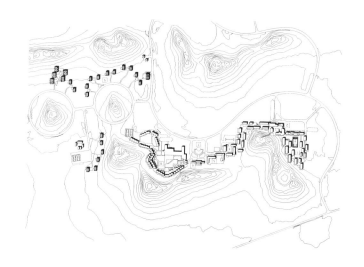

JURY REPORT

The hardest decision the jury faced this year was the Sir Zelman Cowen Award for non-residential work.

There were, in this category, 23 nominations which the jury culled to five finalists. All were of exceptional quality and most deserved the prize. After exacting examination, two seemed to tie for first place, Yulara and Number One Collins Street.

The intellectual decisions taken in the design of Number One Collins Street commanded great admiration but the project did not quite tip the scale against the total intellectual and emotional experience of Yulara.

The jury was dubious about the performance of some of the thermally transparent buildings of Yulara. It could not fully accept the orientation and sun protection of others. Some jurors were worried by the colour of the shading sails, and wondered what the Bedouin would have used.

Every jury member could imagine a different architecture for this arid place and delicate ecology different from the personal style evolved by Cox from his work in less extreme climates.

But overwhelmingly the joyous experience of this resort won out over its competitors. It is literally an oasis of architectural delights in the desert.

Experienced travellers will appreciate the thoughtful planning of the hotel rooms and hostel accommodation while campers will enjoy the way that bus tours are discreetly separated from the individual's tent. All visitors have been carefully provided for.

Glimpses through folds of sand dunes subtly introduce this township to the visitor. It finally unfolds with its soaring sails and rich colours borrowed from the desert, lending festivity to the scene.

A walk through the town reveals exciting architectural vistas and controlled views of the awesome desert. Glimpses of Ayers Rock and the Olgas as well as full-frame views are reminders of the *raison d'être* of the town. Even though the desert touches, possibly grasps its edges, the town gives a sense of security from the apparently infinite and ruthless desert.

The detailing cleverly satisfies the complex demands of building in this remote location. The visitor is left in no doubt about the high cost of fuel because of the vast array of solar collectors which roof many of the buildings. Sensibly no attempt is made to disguise them. In today's world, in a place like Yulara, they show as a 'natural' part of the development.

When fully occupied Yulara is the third largest population group in the Northern Territory. It is remarkable that this township has been created so skillfully and so rapidly.

It is a very worthy winner of the Sir Zelman Cowen Award.

CADETS' MESS, AUSTRALIAN DEFENCE FORCE ACADEMY, CANBERRA

DEPARTMENT OF HOUSING & CONSTRUCTION AND ANCHER MORTLOCK & WOOLLEY

JURY REPORT

The Cadets' Mess is a polished product of modernism; beautifully detailed and finished, sited to capture views, to consolidate the adjacent Parade Ground, and to fit harmoniously with its complex neighbourhood.

The building is the focus of the cadets in this military university, a place to relax, a place for refreshment and a place to unwind, in a campus which places a strong emphasis on the development of young military minds.

In human terms it is a welcoming building, which skilfully uses a stepping back and a stepping down to turn a very large building into a number of smaller and more intimate areas.

In architectural terms, this stepping down is reflected in quadrant windows — complete with bull-nosed sun screens — at the points of descent, which allows sun light and external views.

The stepping back is reflected in the building's cubist exterior, which suggests both high-tech and a philosophical strand in architecture with its roots in the Heroic Modernism of the 1920s.

The jury was delighted by the attention to detail, the internal harmony and the excellent internal planning, which shows the skills of the architect when faced with a complex and almost multi-purpose environment.

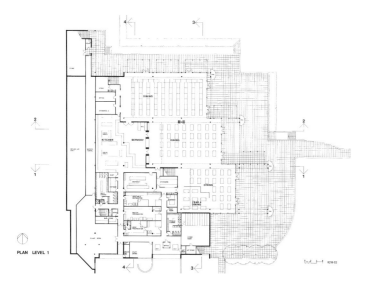

PLAN LEVEL 1

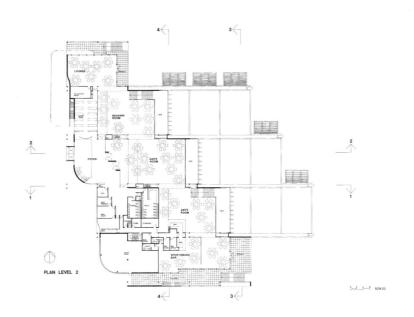

PLAN LEVEL 2

DINNER PLAIN ALPINE VILLAGE MOUNT HOTHAM

PETER MCINTYRE, MCINTYRE PARTNERSHIP

JURY REPORT

This project set about creating an entirely new ski village in the environmentally sensitive high plains of Victoria's alps. It is set just a few kilometres from Mount Hotham, and comparing the two settlements there is not difficult. The contrast is between the new and the old, between skilled planning and haphazard development, between understanding the environment and obliterating it.

This is not the case of a single home in the highlands. It is the far more dificult task of finding the site for a village which will eventually be the winter playground for 6000 people. The development there must continue to retain the perfection of that site and a measure of control over the owners of blocks, to ensure that the unique charm is maintained for the benefit of all.

The National Jury found this much more difficult to assess than a single dwelling. The concept transcends the boundary of single buildings and must also be considered in the context of its success in urban design and planning.

The concept is outstanding and reminds one of Robin Boyd's unfulfilled quest to see designed a community of buildings devoid of urban Australian ugliness.

It achieves much of what Boyd sought. The National Jury was very impressed with the achievement at Dinner Plain in terms of site planning, land use and servicing, and the quality of architecture.

A fertile vocabulary has been introduced to provide individuality within a controlled village design. There are occasional hiccups in this, and not all of the buildings reach the same heights of design quality. But these failings do not detract from the success of the whole, and may indeed show its humanity and guarantee its future as a people place.

Most of the buildings we inspected have been finished to the highest standard, using imaginative planning to make spaces of great charm and utility. Although small, the houses and lodges use windows, decks and raked ceilings to enhance the spaces and link with the native landscape

The construction is sound, the design imaginative with a touch of whimsy, all appropriate to a resort and a place of entertainment rather than a suburbia in the Snowy Mountains.

The use of reversed cavity walling allows great visual variety in external cladding. This sometimes goes a bit crazy — the Australian Ski Club building has a wilful exterior beyond justification on most grounds, but the quality and imagination of the interiors is remarkable. As with other projects which introduced what we called 'interior architecture', Dinner Plain has paid the highest possible attention to interiors, but has also managed to handle urban design, streetscape and environment in a beautiful area which deserves this degree of care.

The village includes an interesting variety of residential building types, including hotel, guest house, chalet, ski club, cluster housing and individual residences.

All developments are strictly controlled to a maximum of two storeys and employ a limited palette of environmentally appropriate materials. These include natural stone, stained timber cladding and galvanised or coloured steel roofing.

The architectural expression is relaxed and recreational and whilst there are glimpses of 'Doctor Zhivago' and 'Aspen Colorado', the character is essentially 'Australian'. Much has been done to retain the existing snow gum vegetation and the built environment has been sympathetically colour coded into the natural habitat. Within the strict constraints described, there is a great variety of architectural form and vocabulary, with the result that the development is both serious (in integrity) but also appropriately whimsical (in style) for a recreational community.

It is fruitless to attempt to describe or assess individual buildings in detail, as they are already far too numerous, except to say that individually they appear of a high quality of design but, more importantly, collectively are eminently cohesive, never dull, and combine to produce a powerful and appropriate image.

The imagery is reinforced by a sensitive design approach to elements of urban design. Well conceived street lighting, signposting, fencing and road definition are the matrix that cement together the individual structures.

The final word on Dinner Plain should go to those who visit, come summer or winter. It is fun and very hard to leave. The spirit captured here is unique in Australia. It is something precious and of great value as an inspiration to and place of relaxation for the community.

JURY REPORT

Among the architects who have shaped our modern Australian cities, Harry Seidler remains resolute in his aim to add a consistent human dimension to his high-rise projects. For Harry the use of a high-rise solution is justified by the provision of open space for people at the foot of his buildings. In this way he seeks to avoid the 'concrete canyon' syndrome and provide efficient and economical office space with excellent views and environments for tenants, while providing a community attraction for all those who do not directly use his building, but seek shelter in the city oasis he creates.

The jury was most impressed with this project. The impact of the project was not that Harry Seidler had done anything radically new with his own already well-honed skills, but that the scale and size of the project allowed his very simple clean-cut design approach to make an impact by its repetition over a large area and a number of small buildings at concourse level. The one thing that stands out about this building is its unique relationship to the Brisbane River. This is a refreshing change in a city which seems to have ignored its river.

In this case, the river is not only part of the building, but a focal point. Plaza areas link the building to the waterfront. A waterfall provides a visual link with the water's edge. Ferries, yachts and pleasure craft tie up at the piers, watched by people at the open air plaza restaurants.

There are interesting architectural solutions here too. The triangular shape of the building was dictated by the desire to provide as many office workers as possible with a view of the river.

The clean lines of the building are given a sense of texture by the addition of finely detailed aluminium sun screens on those sides of the building receiving a significant solar heat load. The angle of these screens, while fixed, varies in relationship to the angle of the sun on that part of the building.

Also in line with the architect's desire to have a relationship between his building and the tropical river environment, a number of sky gardens have been created at various levels of the building. The effect is very successful, both from the building users' point of view and from the external appearance.

Internally the building works well. Column-free space is created by linking the central core to a support structure at the outer edge of the building. The efficiency of this is apparent in a triangular building, rounded slightly at the points of the triangle. In construction terms it means that there is a great deal of repetition in the fabrication, leading to a very creditable three-year design and construction period.

This structural support at the perimeter of the building could cause restrictions in the front foyer area, but here the imagination and attention to engineering which is synonomous with this architect have come to the fore. By a skilful bringing together of beams into a web pattern, an interesting foyer area has been created. This has also lead to the creation of a three storey high-foyer area on the Eagle Street side, and allowed a lower foyer on the other two sides, one of which houses the Brisbane Stock Exchange.

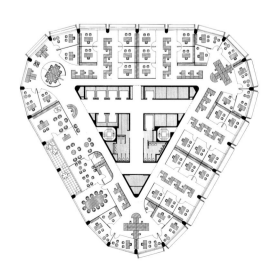

SIR ZELMAN COWEN AWARD 1988

JURY REPORT

This building has rendered all other Australian airline terminals obsolete.

Public acceptance has been high and its constant 24 hour-a-day use under the pressure of expo visitors has highlighted its success.

The layout is simply understood from the aircraft or car park side. It is convenient and a pleasure to use. It can also service the international terminal proposed to be built within the next five years.

Hopefully, those making decisions on that terminal will build on the excellence of this one and avoid the passenger-insensitive mistakes made in many Australian airports. This one is actually a pleasure to visit and, we imagine, a pleasure to work within.

Built on a reclaimed desert of inhospitable mud flat and sand, the domestic terminal is huge but never feels large. The scale is set by the aircraft and people — two extremes. One minute it is bursting with activity and the next dormant.

The building shell is a smooth, durable surface composed of modular panels allowing later changes, and allowing for the inevitable building movement on such an unstable foundation.

Internally it has a strength of character which seems to overcome the dangers of commercial chaos produced by shops, rental car booths and the like.

It is a landmark work of architecture and has been unanimously acclaimed by the jury as an airport by which all others may be judged.

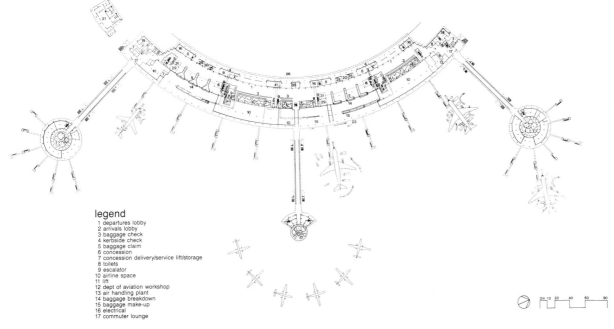

legend
1 departures lobby
2 arrivals lobby
3 baggage check
4 kerbside check
5 baggage claim
6 concession
7 concession delivery/service lift/storage
8 toilets
9 escalator
10 airline space
11 lift
12 dept of aviation workshop
13 air handling plant
14 baggage breakdown
15 baggage make-up
16 electrical
17 commuter lounge

0m 10 20   40   60   90

SIR ZELMAN COWEN AWARD 1989

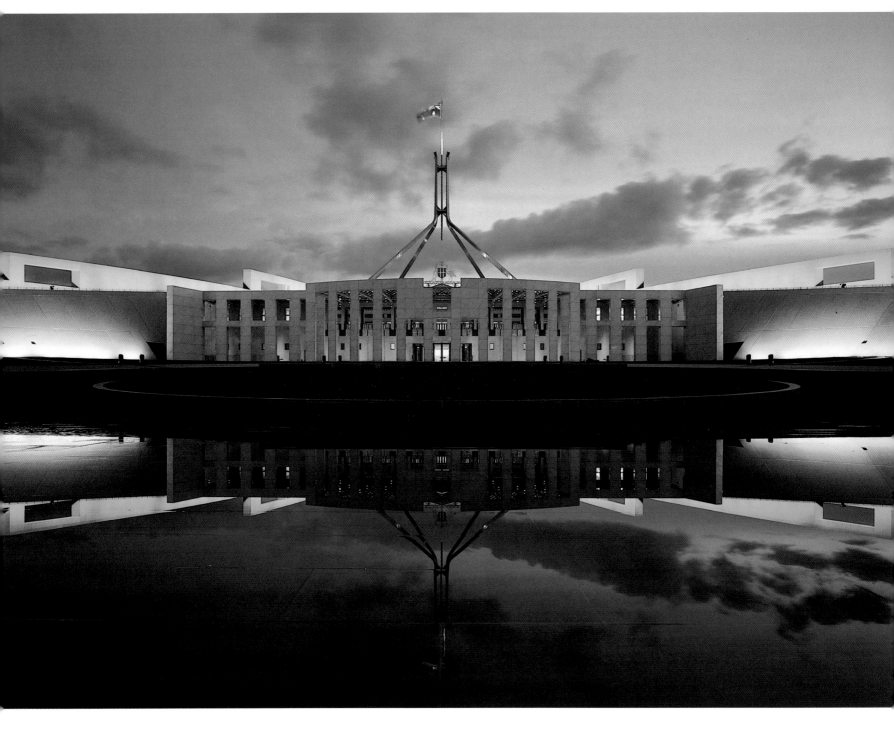

NEW PARLIAMENT HOUSE, CANBERRA

MITCHELL/GIURGOLA & THORP

JURY REPORT

This year marked the culmination of some eight years' work on the new Parliament House; an immense project that absorbed much expense and the best available skills in the architectural, consultant, construction management and construction fields. So much so that it could be said that it puts more modest entries for the Sir Zelman Cowen Award at a disadvantage.

Nevertheless, this is the premier ward of the Institute and is intended to single out a work of excellence. While comparisons between very different types of building are difficult, the jury considered that there were enough constants in the judging criteria to include this singular project in their consideration.

Already more people have visited the new Parliament House than most Australian buildings see in their lifetime. Not only this, it has an army of users. It is therefore not surprising that there are diverse views about the building, which is all to the good of the state of architecture in Australia.

It is likely that the personal reactions of individual members of the jury were equally varied, but they were unanimous in their view that the building be given an award for at least two reasons: one, for its brilliant conceptual solution to the problems of symbolism and the physical qualities of the site. Two, for the integration of the interior design, including furniture, furnishings and artwork, as part of the total architecture of the building. On these two grounds alone, it was considered the building was outstanding and worthy of the premier award of the profession.

In elaborating on the initial concept, one needs to take into account the difficulty of the symbolic and physical problems posed by the site.

As has been generally agreed, the need seen by Griffin for a people's place on Capital Hill superior to Parliament, was met superbly by the courageous decision to take a public grassed ramp over the building.

This symbolism was then emphasised by the enormous flag and a particularly successful device has been the careful faceting and finishing of the four legs to catch the morning and evening sun. Modern architecture is weak in effective symbolic gestures. The evening view for those entering Canberra along Northbourne Avenue can be so dramatic as to make one believe the building is the recipient of cosmic energy (would that it were: just imagine what that would do for our parliamentarians!).

The equally courageous decision to cut 20 metres off the top of Capital Hill has meant that the huge bulk of the building has been lessened. Whatever was said about the site, it was a difficult one and this difficulty showed in most of the competition entries. Now that the winning entry (of the new Parliament House competition) has been built, it has vindicated the view of the competition jury that this project, more than any other entry, lessens the dominating effect that is inevitable for any building sited on a hill at the centre of several avenues.

Regarding the integration of the interior design, furnishings and artwork, the building is unusual in that the artists and craftspeople were brought in early in the design. There was also someone to co-ordinate the selection of artists and artwork. It has long been agreed that such measures are necessary for a successful integration, but they rarely happen.

There is a consistency throughout Parliament House that is even more remarkable when one considers the plurality of contemporary Australian society and the divergence between its Aboriginal and colonial past.

Finally, the jury would like to commend the equally successful integration of building and landscape, due to the close and early collaboration between the landscape architect and the architect. This will, in time, ensure that the new House and its environs become a notable part of the established Canberra scene.

Roger Johnson

BRAMBRUK CULTURAL CENTRE, HALLS GAP, VICTORIA

GREGORY BURGESS

JURY REPORT

Set in Halls Gap in the Grampians, this building has been used for Aboriginal meetings with great success; moreover, it is attracting use by the mixed local community. It assuredly will be well received as the design was the result of a year's gestation period with the architect, Greg Burgess, working with a small group of elders, ideas being tested through the use of models. The result is an 'organic' building of great impact.

The building can be seen in many ways: the undulating two-toned corrugated iron roof as a feather of a bird or the carapace of a beetle; the curving ramp through the centre of the building as the serpent, and the central hearth as the traditional fire. The circular rooms pick up the form of stone dwellings found nearby. The most intriguing aspect of the interior is the glimpses out to the breathtaking ranges on either side. These glimpses are sometimes gained by looking first through other rooms or spaces. Views on the central axis line up on the two highest peaks. Huge ironbark poles, cypress pine cladding, undulating sills, ochre walls, and a controlled, almost gloomy light give the interior its character.

The history of the Aborigines in the Grampians was catastrophic, and this building is a memorial to terrible happenings as well as an indicator to a happier future. To capture such nuances and to reflect his clients' wishes so accurately, and on a limited budget, is a tremendous achievement by the architect.

Roger Johnson

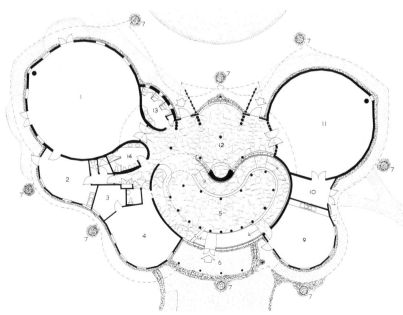

ADELAIDE TROPICAL CONSERVATORY

RAFFEN MARON

JURY REPORT

A message for our time perhaps: an artificial nature dependent for its survival on some of the most ingenious technology of man. A humidicrib ten stories high through which one walks on the simplest and clearest of paths. A cathedral of the new religion of tree worship. Easy enough for an architect faced with such a task, and a limited budget, to be overwhelmed by the dimensions of the technical problems, or to dismiss them as matters for engineers to solve. Here, on the contrary, we have a true fusion of themes, in which the technical cannot be separated from the symbolic and both enhance the two purposes of preservation and display.
Tom Heath

The Adelaide Bicentennial Conservatory is a magnificent structure and should be viewed as one of this country's most important buildings. Vital to the conservatory's success is the wellbeing of its exhibits, tropical rainforest plants. It is pleasing to see that most are thriving and many have doubled their size over 12 months. The walkway traversing the plantation provides a generous viewing path for crowds, while gentle undulations and resting plateaus accommodate the elderly and wheelchairs.
Helen Wellings

This conservatory, housing a tropical rainforest plantation, sits like a jewel on the edge of the Botanic Gardens. When landscaping is completed on the adjacent (train barn) site, it will look even better. It is a highly innovative solution to a highly technical problem of enclosure. It resolves all the issues of sun-penetration, maintenance of temperature and humidity, plant growth and pedestrian circulation, in a simple and purposeful way. The geometry for the enclosure, the sweeping curves of which appear complicated, is in fact a simple resolution of parts of cones. The detailing is impeccable and the building as a whole makes a beautiful and appropriate statement about its function.
John Morphett

A brilliant solution to a very complex design problem. This building needed to embody sophisticated services and specific climate needs, whilst being attractive to the public. It succeeds on all accounts.
Rob Caulfield

This is a most accomplished work and reaches an international standard. The glazed walls, part of a cone, form the major component, repetition being an important element in the building process, as well as making for a most economical structure. Technologically, it has incorporated systems developed by NASA but without resorting to such complication that would cause the failure of the conservatory to operate. Structurally, the system is direct, it is steel and concrete with access into the rook of this great 'hump back'! This work imparts an optimism: it does not rely heavily on the European model, and spatially it is a joy to walk within.
Glenn Murcutt

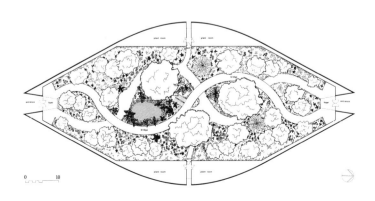

MELBOURNE CRICKET GROUND SOUTHERN STAND REDEVELOPMENT

TOMPKINS SHAW AND EVANS/DARYL JACKSON

JURY REPORT

This is a very large and gutsy building which directly and forcefully expresses its two main functions: spectator viewing and crowd movement. The task of getting 60,000 people to and from their seats has been particularly well handled. The bold expression of inclined ramps against the curved facade is most successful.
John Morphett

This is a heroic work of architecture, in concept and in execution. Its prime purpose is to give good viewing conditions for very large numbers of people watching sport. From this apparently simple issue, great complexities arise, not only providing shelter and excellent sight lines, but also in arranging the architecture to ease the tremendous surge of spectators from the points of entry to their places of observation and contemplation, and in fulfilling their demands for socialising in spaces for eating and drinking, without losing touch with the competetive dramas they have come to enjoy. The new Southern Stand satisfies all these functional requirements admirably, and it does more. It brings legibility and dignity to the process, and by the clever articulation of circulation and observation spaces heightens the experience of architecture and the sense of occasion.
Neville Quarry

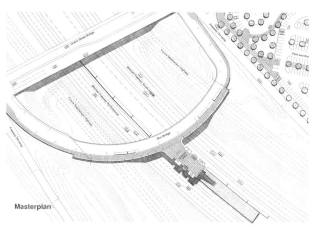

Masterplan

STIRLING STATION, NORTHERN SUBURBS TRANSIT SYSTEM, PERTH

FORBES & FITZHARDINGE

JURY REPORT

It cleverly satisfies all of the criteria, takes advantage of its orientation and mid-freeway position and responds beautifully to the speeding road and rail dynamics which are its framework.
Robert Cheesman

After an absence of significant railway architecture for many years, this suburban station builds on the tradition of the celebration of train travel. Not only is an exciting visual imagery created and the tight and exposed site well handled, but input by the architect has resulted in the repositioning of the original location for the station to better relate to the residential area it serves.
Anne Cunningham

Pedestrian movements from one transport system to the next are logical even for the new visitor and one feels at ease with the system. The bus interchange is quite beautiful, with its sweep across the rail link.
Glenn Murcutt

In a progressive programme for public transport, Perth has boldly built seven new railway stations as part of the Northern Suburbs Transit System. The most dramatic of these is at Stirling. Here the experience of commuter travel is exhilarating. City-bound passengers arrive at a sweeping, cantilevered roof crescent arcade, pass down through a ticket lobby lined with cubical amenity containers, then down by escalators, stairs or lift, moving through sets of butterfly roof planes en route to the platform. Along the way, the transparency of the enclosure and the visible precision of the steel structure give rise to contrary expressions of fragility and stability, and this enlivening sensibility is enhanced by the positioning of the railway lines and platform, mid-way between the paired traffic lines of a freeway.
Neville Quarry

The fine design lines of this structure belie its utilitarian role. It handles the transfer of commuters efficiently and comfortably in a most pleasing environment. It's light, bright, secure and illustrates a commendable new thinking in public architecture.
Maggie Tabberer

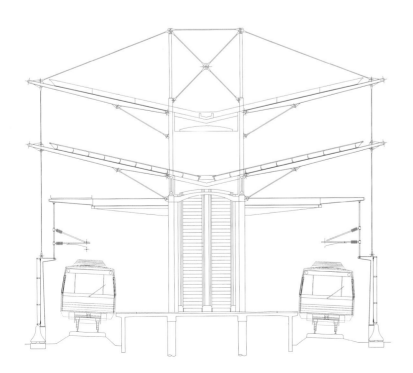

KAKADU VISITORS CENTRE, NORTHERN TERRITORY

GLENN MURCUTT AND TROPPO

JURY REPORT

This is a simple building, though not without a few idiosyncrasies (thank heavens). The building exhibits a freshness in its supposed lack of sophistication, and is one which sits easily with 'everyman'. It is highly professional and can set, or reconfirm, a direction of Australian architectural identity. It is at the front line.
Graham Bligh

This finely detailed, elegant, carefully articulated building lightly floats above its site with its thin-edged planes sheering a series of open and enclosed spaces. Skilful and innovative use of rammed earth construction, timber decking and posts, rocks and water and corroded steel suggest a strong affinity with the land.
Peter Crone

This marvellous building has a sense of always having been there, of having grown out of the land it sits on. It draws you in and leads you on and there is a reward at every turn. The signs are brilliant, witty and culturally sensitive, and the responses to the extremes of climate are beautifully simple.
Rebecca Gilling

People swarm eagerly through this building — it positively invites exploration. In this part of Kakadu, the bush reads as overlapping palisades of several species of spindly trees above a tattered ground collage of stringy grasses, shed bark, shallow gullies and bare ginger coloured soil. The Visitors Centre colludes in this landscape with architectural counterpoint — a variety of verticals: concrete columns, steel posts and peeled timber poles; a mix of wall types: flat grey or brown panels, shimmering corrugated iron, massive rammed earth and shadowy slatted timber screens and floors. The roof planes bound about in swooping curves and flying flats, over ample decks, covered ways and solidly enclosed exhibition spaces. The Centre exudes that kind of spontaneity which can only be achieved by a prior deep sensitivity of thought and feeling. The analogies with the place are evident, but refreshingly free of any self-mocking symbolism or phoney camouflage.
Neville Quarry

A total design, controlled from start to finish. The building sits within its bush setting by reaching out with spaces, roofs and paving. The layout is a walk through the bush; twists and turns add special interest to the journey. The use of natural ventilation, enhanced by screens, texture and colour, makes the building cool.
James Taylor

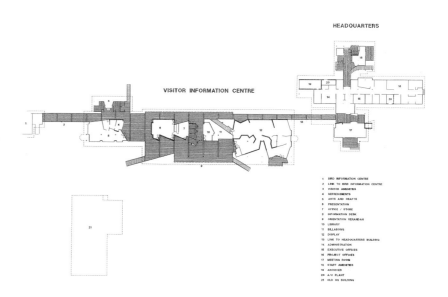

SWALLOWCLIFFE SCHOOLS, DAVOREN PARK SOUTH AUSTRALIA

SA DEPARTMENT FOR BUILDING MANAGEMENT (DBM) CONSULTANCY SERVICES — PROJECT ARCHITECT PATRICIA LES

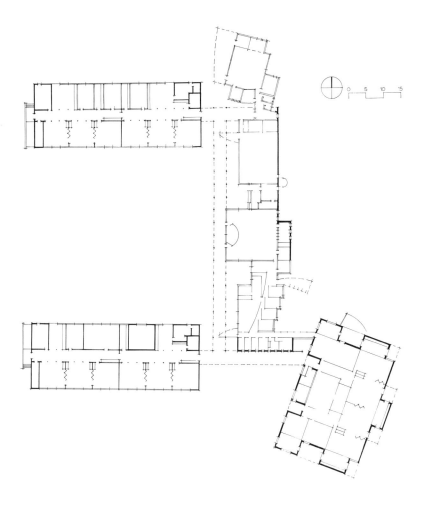

JURY REPORT

The new building links the replanned and refurbished wings of the original school, establishing a comfortable, welcoming scale and a joyful character expressive of the requirements of primary school children. The varied architectural components have been skilfully composed to form a cohesive, contemporary statement accentuated by the inclusion of amusing, eye-catching icons created by artists and members of the school community. The new identity of the school has been carried through in the design of a new emblem. A consistent control of detailing has been achieved throughout, from the decorative rainwater heads and elegant steel truss ends to the softly curved verandahs and covered ways. A most successful outcome of the association of a devoted architect, an enlightened client and a committed community. There is a clarity in the way the architecture has been derived from a detailed consultation process whereby the community has a sense of ownership. The project demonstrates the capacity of the architects to understand not just the physical but also the economic and social context in which they were working.

1981 **TWO HOUSES, MT IRVINE, NSW**	**1991** **JOINT AWARD**
GLENN MURCUTT	**TENT HOUSE, EUMUNDI, QUEENSLAND**
1982 **NO AWARD**	GABRIEL POOLE
1983 **SEA HOUSE, MORNINGTON, VICTORIA**	**GALLERY HOUSE, HAWTHORN, MELBOURNE**
PETER MCINTYRE, MCINTYRE PARTNERSHIP	DALE JONES-EVANS
1984 **RESIDENCE REDEVELOPMENT, EAST PERTH**	**1992** **CLARE HOUSE, BUDERIM, QUEENSLAND**
LOUISE ST JOHN KENNEDY	LINDSAY CLARE
1985 **HOUSE ON NSW SOUTH COAST**	**1993** **PALM BEACH HOUSE, SYDNEY**
GLENN MURCUTT	GORDON & VALICH
1986 **PIE RESIDENCE, PERIGIAN BEACH, QUEENSLAND**	**LYON/JENKIN HOUSE, CARLTON, MELBOURNE**
GEOFFREY PIE	HAMISH LYON, ASTRID JENKIN, CHARLES SALTER
1987 **WOOLLEY HOUSE, PALM BEACH, NSW**	**LARRAKEYAH MEDIUM-DENSITY HOUSING, PRECINCT 2, DARWIN**
KEN WOOLLEY, ANCHER MORTLOCK & WOOLLEY	TROPPO
1988 **HENWOOD HOUSE, PADDINGTON, NSW**	**1994** **BRANNIGAN HOUSE, ST LUCIA, QUEENSLAND**
ALEX TZANNES	BUD BRANNIGAN
1989 **GRACEVILLE HOUSE, BRISBANE**	**1995** **TOWNHOUSES AT 106-112 CREMORNE STREET, RICHMOND, VICTORIA**
DONALD WATSON	CRAIG ROSSETTI
1990 **'GRIFFIN' HOUSE, CASTLECRAG, NSW**	**HAMMOND RESIDENCE, POMONA, QUEENSLAND**
ALEX POPOV	CLARE DESIGN/KERRY CLARE, LINDSAY CLARE.

Projects within this category must be residential in nature, being Class 1 or 2 type buildings as defined by the BCA, including alterations and additions. Appropriate projects would include residential colleges, multiple dwelling units, public housing and retirement villages.

RAIA Awards Rules, March 1991

ROBIN BOYD AWARD

FOR RESIDENTIAL BUILDINGS

A MIRAGE FOR LIVING IN

In general, people's dwellings reflect the cultural habits of the community in which they are established. You can't escape your society. In particular, an individual's anxieties, ambitions and idiosyncracies are manifest in how a domestic environment is self-determined, or otherwise indifferently accepted. You can't escape your persona. Cultural habits may include mimicry as well as iconoclasm, nostalgia as well as prognostication. People who wish to demonstrate their upward social mobility or who lack belief in their contemporary culture, may be inclined to prefer traditional house forms, in the hope that such forms will suggest a powerful aristocratic past and a future dynasty. Hence the popularity of neo 'Federation' and 'Colonial' models in the family home market. In our violent and volatile world, individuals seeking a spurious heritage by association can hardly be blamed for snuggling behind the camouflage of historicism. To many of the public, much modern architecture is too abstract to be comfortable in body or mind, for it has no generally acceptable frame of reference, no tangible meaning or signification. In time, however, abstract Modernism collected its own associations, of 'progressiveness' and 'faith in the future', and so emerged as no longer abstract but self-referential, confident and appropriate for those who chose to look ahead. Nowadays modern architecture has extended its embrace to include the regional, the vernacular, the elitist, the esoteric and the kitsch, so that the use of the term 'modern' as a discriminator is hardly worthwhile.

WINNERS

In 1981, the first Robin Boyd Award for Residential Buildings went to two adjacent houses at Mt Irvine. These houses comprise simple compact shapes and sit serenely in the landcape. Here are no oversailing roofs, extended planes, exhibitionist structures, multiple transparencies or the zappy trappings of hectic mannerisms. Their affirmative presence reminds me of how Miles Davis, with no more than two exquisitely placed and timed trumpet notes, can make your spine tingle with the magical austerity of their impact. The interior of the Mt Irvine house, although not large, exhibits the modulation of natural light and volume that characterises wondrous architectural space.

Perhaps after this initial burst of exemplary quality, the next year's RAIA jury lost their nerve, or just failed to achieve consensus. Or maybe they simply regarded nothing submitted as up to an awards standard — a curious position since as only one award had so far been

made there was not a long list of exemplars upon which to make comparisons. No Robin Boyd Award was made in 1982. As a sort of compensation, the 1982 jury gave Commendations to three not-quite-winners: to architects Edmond and Corrigan for a house in the Melbourne suburb, Kew; to Falk and Gurry for a house at Point Lonsdale, Victoria, and to Peter Overman for a house and duplex in Applecross, Western Australia. Commendations went to architect Peter Elliott for Knox Schlapp Housing Development in 1985; Synman Justin Bialek for a House in Toorak; Cocks Carmichael Whitford for a house in Armadale, both in 1990; Raffen Maron for Public Housing in Adelaide, Nonda Katsalidis for a residence at St Andrew's Beach, Grose Bradley for the Newman house and Glenn Murcutt for the Magney house, all in 1992; and Stutchbury & Pape for the Israel House 1995; but in these years major awards were also given.

Not giving an award at all provokes the perennial argument of whether an award should be made to the best of the current crop, or only if there is one which reaches the standard according to the jury criteria. To add to the complexity, in 1991 there were two Robin Boyd Awards, in 1993 three and in 1995 two. There is a genuine difficulty in choosing between houses which are equally valid and outstanding, but which proceed from quite distinctive design assumptions, or between a single family house and group housing — each of which involve the same agenda of dwelling but different parameters. Resolution of the dilemma by introducing sub-categories is arguable, but begins to trivialise the process, as does too many equal awards in the same year. Once they accept the burden of the assessment role, juries ought to be courageously decisive and refrain from too many multiple awards.

The second Robin Boyd Award, in 1983, went to the Sea House by architect Peter McIntyre, on the Mornington Peninsula, Victoria. This seaside holiday house has an informal rambling quality, replete with alcoves, irregular spaces and picturesque massing. Although there is certainly no recidivist historicism here, I am reminded of the flexible, involving and intricate qualities of Federation houses — without any of the stylistic gimmicks which usually attend such moods. Any nostalgic overtones come from the sturdy imagery of functional nautical building.

In 1984, alterations and additions to a house in East Perth received the Robin Boyd Award. In scale and extent, this project is small; at the level of innovation and enticement it is grand. A fine example of suburban extension in blissful, disciplined, romantic mode.

Glenn Murcutt won his second Robin Boyd award in 1985 for a house on the South Coast of NSW. The Murcutt characteristics are here much evident — rectangular, in-line plan, external venetian blinds, extended eaves, sharp roof edges, a cross-section like the silhouette of a bird in flight, box gutter, large rainwater funnels above circular downpipes in their own exedra, and a resolute crispness in every detail. Murcutt's earlier Mt Irvine houses are demure, even sombre from the outside. In contrast, the South Coast house feels more like an extrovert, joyous fling. The envelope is audaciously flamboyant and the concave-to-convex ceiling swoop is a voluptuous *tour de force*. As an isolated object in a severe setting, it confronts the landscape. This is a far cry from the tired, overworked catch phrase of 'touching the earth lightly' that some commentators have sought to foist on every Murcutt venture, thus entirely missing the point of his design process, which is based on responding profoundly to the uniqueness of the site and the separate circumstances of each project.

So, after four years, the awards were widely spread with regards to type and location: farm and beach houses in NSW, beach house in Victoria, city house in West Australia. Over the next ten years, six Robin Boyd Awards went to houses in Queensland and one in the Northern Territory (or two if the Marika/Alderton house Special Jury award is added to the genre). How can it be accounted for, this tropical surfeit of awards?

UNCRITICAL REGIONALISM

'Beautiful one day, perfect the next' claims the tourist blurb for Queensland, ignoring all frames of reference except the weather. Can this be the inspiration for a regional architectural culture? The sub-to-tropical zones are thermally benign for much of the year. On the hottest and most humid days, reasonable comfort can be achieved by an effectively insulated canopy and bounteous openings to optimise natural air flow. Where cyclonic conditions have to be met, tying down the structure and fabric is as important as holding it up. The occasional cool nights are easily catered for — burn a few sticks of scrap timber, switch on a single-bar radiator for a little while, or put on a cardigan. Topographically, tropical houses are most comfortable on a hillside or by the beach, or in a location which offers both. Views of landscape expanding to the distant horizon provide that singularly Australian prospect — the unconfined boundary. Socially, the tropical pattern of living tends to informality. An architecture made for egalitarian entrance, loose enclosure and easy encounter seems to be the appropriate response to locale and social preference.

Apart from the portents of paradise, there is, behind the modernist tropical iconography, an accountable architectural lineage that can be traced. In Europe, in the 1920s, Gerrit Rietveld exploded the house shell into planar shards (but never dared the dynamic diagonal); in the USA, Frank Lloyd Wright burst the outside-inside barrier and welcomed the landscape; Rudolph Schindler set platforms on clusters of canted poles on Californian hillsides. In Victoria, Australia, in the 1950s and 1960s, Roy Grounds, Robin Boyd, Chancellor and Patrick, Peter McIntyre, Kevin Borland and later Daryl Jackson and others wrenched the vernacular into the extraordinary on the Mornington Peninsula and in the Dandenongs. On Sydney's North Shore, architects such as Bill Lucas, Peter Johnson, Allen Jack and Cottier, Ken Woolley and Philip Cox segued their palpable carpentry and earnest brickwork into craggy suburban bush sites. The traditional 'Queenslander' with its corrugated iron roof and latticed verandahs, not much inflected by fashion, continued to soar on stilts. This entire spectrum of architecture blended into an indulgent tropical cocktail, exuding its own distinctive flavour. Not by any means does all the architecture in the Australian tropics have a background allegiance to either Modernism or the naive colonial tradition. The dear old temperate climate, suburban paradigm of the tile-roofed, double-fronted brick veneer is ubiquitous still: stuffy, cramped and careless of place-relevance.

TROPICANA

The Pie Residence, described by the jury as 'in the spirit of Robin Boyd' indeed has a courtyard plan quite like Boyd's own 1957 house in South Yarra, and is similarly suave in concept, but much more regional in its functional relationships and architectural expression.

The Tent House reaches the ultimate in ingenious lightness of roof and mobility of wall enclosure, simultaneously delicate and sturdy.

The Clare House burgeons a quiet sort of drama from the most opportune materials and elements, endowing their commonplace attributes with a rare dignity and clarity.

In the Arcadian gentility of a Brisbane suburb, the Brannigan House captures outdoor spaces from within the site and integrates them in easy transition with the built space.

The Hammond House continues the Queensland elemental genre:

light steel roof braced to a timber structure, elevated platform floors, plywood and corrugated iron cladding, glass louvres and sliding slatted screens. The on-ground solidity of storage modules and the fly-away skillion of the carport roof are counterpoint, respectively, to the off-ground grace and the stable gable roof of the house.

The Graceville House is distinctly suburban, and deliberately takes its architectural influences from another earlier hipped tile roof genre — the roof as cloak, compared with the more usual Queensland metaphor of roof as umbrella. The house exhibits a splendid variety of spaces, held well in control by octagonal and square planning grids that mesh harmoniously. The jury said of this house, too: "Robin Boyd would have approved"; but I'm not so sure. Boyd might not have welcomed the confident sensibility of its suburban deference. I think it may have been too eclectic and lush for the patrician and purist Boyd.

BESIDE THE SEA

Again, the jury postulated the accolade "Robin Boyd would have loved it", for the Woolley House. An elementary description sounds like the Queensland type: sea horizon views, copious external decks, kitchen-dining-living in a single space, bedrooms on a lower floor, 'crow's nest balcony' at a higher level, corrugated iron roof, weatherboards, casement windows, lattice; so maybe this house had a stimulating influence which travelled north.

The Palm Beach House, although a much more compact conjunction of prismatic forms, shares with the Woolley house architectural qualities that almost, but not quite, slip into the tropical genre. Tropicality? No, the strong sense of enclosure as well as free-flowing space, definite places that are adjacent to one another but do not overlap, and flexible but distinctive planning within a functional zone palpably separate these Palm Beach houses from their northern compatriots. The whiff of a cold southern wind requires the possibility of becoming hermetic. Similarly, the Sea House, on the further fringes of Port Phillip Bay, is not far off the tropical pace, but enough, in an even more temperate climate than Palm Beach, to be unmistakably Melburnian in origin. Climate and sea proximity are the most vigorous factors in determining the form of these houses, but the metropolitan energy of the nearest urban centre has its side effects.

URBAN INTERVENTION

Four of the Robin Boyd Award winners address the issue of urban insertion, infilling a gap in a stretch of houses with boundary party walls, in established streets: Henwood, Lyon/Jenkin and Richmond Townhouses.

The Henwood House slots into a collective facade of typical Paddington terraces. Instead of aiming for genre replication, it draws on a wider concept of urbanity and is disjunct with the architectural detail of its neighbours, but compatible with the cosmopolitan nature of the street. The Lyon/Jenkin House is inserted into a street facade which is already polyglot, although heritage-listed, and adds the recent language of non-associative simplicity, which is eruditely close to the simple vernacular of the neighbourhood. The Richmond Townhouses, six in a row, disport emphatically framed first floor windows as a witty exaggeration of the suburban cliché, and establish a scale and street order that contrasts with neighbours, but suggests a new direction appropriate for other such urban interventions.

SUBURBAN HOUSES

Suburbia: a setting of independent houses on a carpet of subdivided blocks of land, individually owned. Excoriated by Robin Boyd in *The Australian Ugliness*, for being selfish with resources, careless of infrastructure and unconducive to sociability. The suburban house has remained, nevertheless, mythically desirable to generations of Australians, and with good reason. Until recently, the suburban house offered the owner an investment that was expected to appreciate. For singles, semi-attached multiples and nuclear families, the advantages, if affordable, are still clear: the free-standing house in a well-serviced older suburb enables the choice of private or community-oriented patterns of living, of solo exclusiveness or urban gregariousness. So long as daily consumables can be afforded, for citizens to have this sort of versatility is to have a privileged status, available in many other countries only to the very wealthy. Five Robin Boyd Award winners: the East Perth, Pie, Clare, Brannigan and Graceville houses, meet my definition of suburbia: independent house-objects, in sight of and proximate to other independent houses, with natural light available around practically the entire perimeter of the property.

The East Perth renovation presents no public street elevation for it is to the rear of an existing dwelling, which it extends physically and contextually. Its suburban emphasis is on developing a civilised back yard: a mini-utopia between the paling fences.

A different special case is the 'Griffin' House, in the Sydney suburb Castlecrag that Walter Burley Griffin established in 1922. Griffin's use of firm enclosure by sturdy masonry walls and flat roofs, and his ability to manipulate interior light and space was the inspiration for the 1990 Robin Boyd Award.

The Gallery House does not actually touch its boundaries, but inveigles the entire site into a sumptuous composition of interlinked pavilions and courtyards, engaging in a virtuoso display of enclosed and open, light and sturdy contrasts in an extensive compound-filling array of forms and spaces.

The Larrakeyah Army Barracks, Precinct 2, in Darwin, is a new mini-suburb of 21 detached and semi-detached houses. The difficulties are real: to achieve medium density with privacy in a tropical climate that demands copious air circulation, for a military clientele that is transitory but seeks a strong sense of home and identity during the term of duty. The difficulties are cleverly resolved and this is the only truly multiple housing suburban development to receive a Robin Boyd Award.

ARCHITECTS' OWN HOUSES

Nine of the 18 Robin Boyd Awards were designed by architects for their own or family-related use: Peter McIntyre; Geoffrey Pie; Ken Woolley; Gabriel Poole; Dale Jones-Evans; Lindsay and Kerry Clare; Hamish Lyon, Astrid Jenkin and Charles Salter; and Bud Brannigan. Shrewd site selection, thorough briefing and client empathy would be expected. With themselves as their own patrons and clients, architects' imaginations are unblocked, and in each of these houses, personal convictions are strongly expressed.

JURY REPORT

In a large paddock on the edge of a spectacular easterly view from the Blue Mountains, Glenn Murcutt has erected two houses that are of some considerable importance in the development of an Australian domestic idiom. The houses most immediately impress with what can be called a sense of place. Built in lightweight transportable materials for two Sydney families who farm the property, they are sited with great sensitivity to retain privacy for each, yet provide the mutual support of a visible neighbour. Both houses are built above the ground with minimum modification to natural topography, in the manner of barns or woolsheds. The simple forms of these earlier building types are further evoked by the forms of the buildings themselves. Both exploit that humble but ubiquitous material, corrugated iron, deploying it for walls, roof and water tanks, giving a considerable unity to the appearance of the houses and illustrating new possibilities for a common material at the same time.

The first house is the simpler of the two. It is essentially a steeply double-pitched roof over a narrow span, the whole extruded to a substantial length. Within the long rectangle a range of changes creates various spaces and accommodation.

The other house is more complex with a subsidiary section added to the basic rectangular plan. In this section are kitchen, bath and laundry with their own separate roof and skylighting. The whole eastern end of this house is one large verandah, which is roofed to eliminate sky glare but allow views of Sydney on the horizon.

One of Murcutt's concerns has been that the potential walls and roofs have to become a sort of variable membrane that can moderate the outside environment in a number of different ways. At Mt Irvine this preoccupation has evolved to a sophisticated level using nothing but traditional materials and methods. Large areas of insect-screened glass louvres are fitted with external timber venetian blinds that are tensioned to withstand high winds. This effectively turns the living areas of the houses into giant verandahs. No longer is the narrow and often unusable traditional verandah required — any part of these houses can become a verandah.

At $50,000 for 160 square metres each, these are not expensive houses and prove that good architecture need not be costly. They are frugal in their use of resources both in the initial materials and running costs. If we can overcome the official stigma that still seems to be attached to corrugated iron as a building material, these two houses must be recognised as a step forward in Australian domestic architectural development.

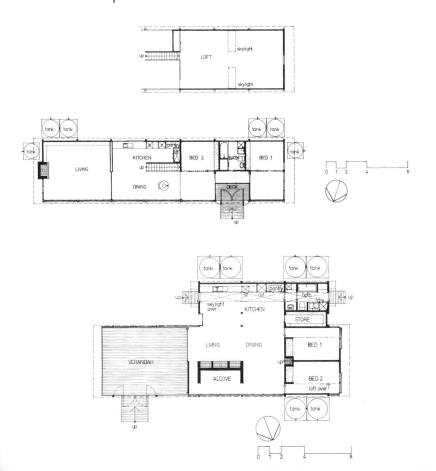

ROBIN BOYD AWARD 1982

NO AWARD

JURY REPORT

There is going to be some disappointment that the Robin Boyd has not been given this year and that, instead, there are three Commendations. It is not however a sign of declining standards nor of slackening interest, rather it is an indication that in housing, as in other areas of architecture, there is at present a state of ferment in which ideas are being conceived and developed. Some of them will, in due course, form part of the mainstream of architectural developments while others will be cast aside. This year's jury found experimental work taking place, especially in submissions from Victoria, where a group of vigorous younger architects are developing ideas which in part stem from the work of a middle generation of architects such as Edmond & Corrigan. These architects are not just accepting an architectural language passed on to them but are reaching out for new ideas, sometimes from the local context, sometimes from other sources.

Although the buildings in this category submitted for consideration by the National Selection Committee had received awards in their home States and although they revealed developments which will be watched with interest, none could be said to have arrived at a level appropriate for the Robin Boyd Award, in a national context.

In some States, older buildings have received named awards, having previously been considered for merit awards, or their equivalents, in past years. These buildings were not eligible to be considered, since the Robin Boyd Award is for buildings receiving an award for the first time in the year of the national awards. Thus generally it will go to a recently completed building — the award was deliberately intended to be for recent architecture.

SEA HOUSE, MORNINGTON, VICTORIA

PETER McINTYRE, McINTYRE PARTNERSHIP

JURY REPORT

This house built on an exposed cliff at Mornington on Port Phillip Bay, has a particular quality of immediacy of access that the National Selection Committee regards as unique. The building has a sense of the outdoors and there is an effortless relationship between the inside and the outside.

The Committee considers that the building sensitively respects the delicate environment, being sited and deriving its form in response to the ecological balance of the exposed site.

Internally, spaces are intimate and defined, yet by clever use of timber shutters can be held in a state of transition between the vast space of the sea and the composure of the timber indoors.

Externally the building reflects the gable seaside shack with a unifying sense of simplicity. The character expressed by the the use of stairs without railings, and remote small timber decks consolidates the relationship with the local vernacular.

The Committee praises the manner in which the building values its place and its deference to the environment, which precludes an imposed architectural dogma.

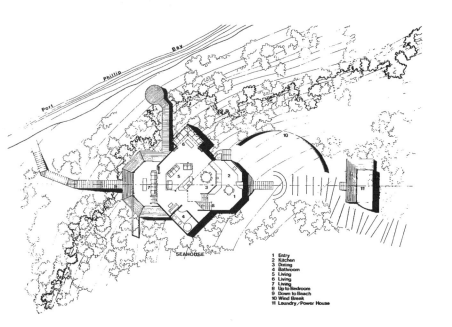

1 Entry
2 Kitchen
3 Dining
4 Bathroom
5 Living
6 Living
7 Living
8 Up to Bedroom
9 Down to Beach
10 Wind Break
11 Laundry/Power House

RESIDENCE REDEVELOPMENT, EAST PERTH

LOUISE ST JOHN KENNEDY

JURY REPORT

This residence directly addressed the problem besetting any architect of additions and renovations to a substantial old house. It is the problem of maintaining the integrity of the original without compromising the possibilities of the more transparent and extroverted architecture of a casual modern lifestyle.

The accommodation schedule for the addition was as follows: a family of two adults, three children, two dogs and puppies, three cats, canaries and a pair of guinea pigs; the addition was to make provision for three children's bedrooms and a play area, bathroom, kitchen, casual eating, casual living, laundry, swimming pool (with training lane).

The strategy adopted by the architect here is the controlled expression of the dichotomy between the old and new components: front, enclosed, introspective, static, formal; and rear, open extroverted, dynamic, informal. To resolve all these conflicts is no mean feat. It has been achieved through the fairly literal expression of the role of each component in the programme. The front of the house has been left largely intact retaining the formal qualities already existing.

Only the dining and sitting rooms have been opened to each other across the passage. A large 'hole' has been cut into the rear facade of the existing house along the line between the laundry and the kitchen. Within this space, the rather dynamic transition between old and new, between house and garden, has been expressed by a curving balcony to the children's mezzanine above. Outside this very large 'hole' is a spectacular conservatory. This is verandah-like, with glazed roof and wall. The timber detailing is redolent of the existing front verandah and it effects a marvellous relationship between the interior casual living and the garden, sky and water outside.

There is intimacy to the scale of these spaces such that someone in the pool, another on the timber deck and another inside can all be involved in conversation together.

A small stream cuts through the slate floor of the conservatory.

Careful retention of a very large palm tree has ensured considerable summer shade to the glazed roof. Retractable aluminium 'Verasol' blinds suspended upon wire tracks assist the tree. Given that proofs lay within the puddings' eating any concerned gourmands of architectural science will have to deal with the inhabitants' ecstatic regard for the space after nearly 12 months occupancy which included an autumn like a Sydney summer! In fact these clients are so well suited to their architect's whim and fancy that recently during the night of the wildest equinoxal storm on record they were seen seated, sipping champagne in the conservatory whilst 50 mm of rain was delivered upon the glass roof above and sheets of water shot straight over the gutter into the pool beyond.

Geoffrey Donald

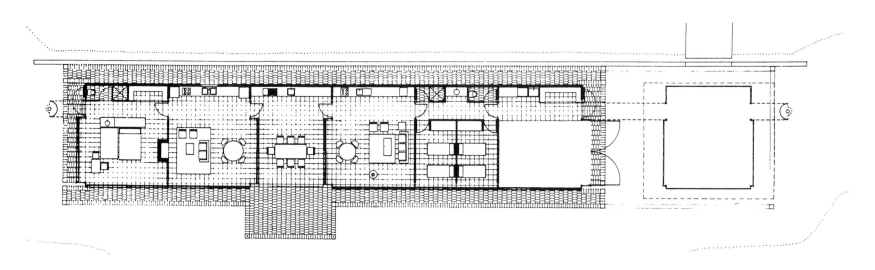

HOUSE ON NSW SOUTH COAST

GLENN MURCUTT

JURY REPORT

The house on the South Coast, by Glenn Murcutt, is a clear winner. The site could be Murcutt's most challenging yet. It is a gentle slope without trees or other prominent features to which a house might be visually tied. Yet it is deftly located in the right place and our architectural romantics have already said 'like a butterfly alighted' with wings tilted to the hill and the view.

The house turns its back to the prevailing and fierce sea winds. It opens its heart and mind to the magnificent coastal view to the north.

The jury was surprised by the bold use of steel in this harsh coastal situation, not just the corrugated sheeting but also the structure. However, here it is sensously curved, reflecting the roof shape.

Careful joining details, contemporary protective coatings, and the manufacturers, all give reassurance of longevity, and termites will be very disappointed.

The unusual planning requirements for the holiday house of the family of this client have been accommodated in a typical Murcutt linear plan. The client's desire that their permanent house should be redolent of the tent they had used on their site for many years, has been skilfully met. Perhaps this desire has been carried through at the expense of thermal qualities for a long cold winter and the sorts of facilities one usually needs in a country house like a vestibule for sodden rainwear and mucky boots.

The interior is finely detailed, polished, restrained and simply furnished. The butterfly curves of the roof are reflected in the structure and the ceiling. Ventilation can be controlled with ease and the homespun external venetians of Murcutt's earlier buildings are replaced by smart European products internally operated.

People will love or hate this house — it accepts no compromise. Murcutt's clients are amongst the 'love it' group and the building will bring credit to Australian architecture internationally.

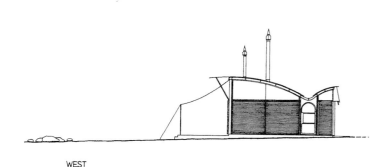

WEST

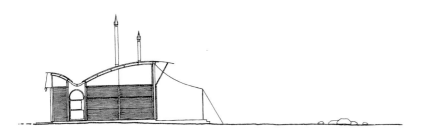

EAST

PIE RESIDENCE, PERIGIAN BEACH, QUEENSLAND

GEOFFREY PIE

JURY REPORT

The jury were delighted with this house, which brought comments of 'a house in the spirit of Robin Boyd'.

The house at Perigian Beach, Queensland, is a place for relaxation. It makes no demands but has a 'laid back' atmosphere inviting the visitor to cast away cares and indulge in a lazy stay.

The house is in a street of houses behind a sand dune ridge — a typical Australian suburban beach development. But this house fits in with its setting where its neighbours do not. The walls of greying natural Australian timber blend with the subdued colours of the native vegetation and are a background to splashes of mauve, Chinese red and electric blue. The bright colours are applied to windows, shades, handrails and the like in just the right quantity to give vitality to appearance but no more. The detailing is thoughtful, tidy and well built but does not demand reverence — only respect.

The house is planned to the slope of the site, its mature trees and its views. It allows the parts of the family to come together or disperse as they wish. It works beautifully for a family and its friends on holiday.

The house makes no dramatic breakthrough but it consolidates the Australian domestic architecture of the present in an excellent and unpretentious way.

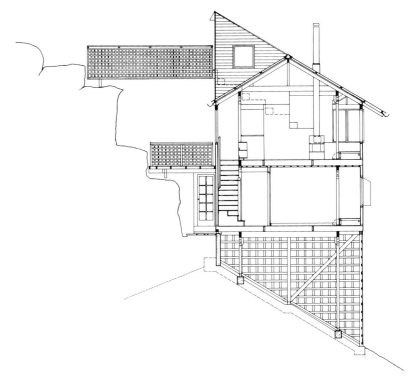

JURY REPORT

Here is a problem many architects love to wrestle with, and few succeed with quite such clarity.

The site is a virtual cliff face with much of the ground unstable soil and incapable of providing a reliable building foundation. Added to this there were many small trees clinging tenaciously to the site. To build on the block required careful thought on the type of structure and its positioning to minimise environmental damage and, equally importantly, the position and design of its foundations to ensure it stayed there.

The architect's solution has been to develop the themes he has used so successfully in his two previous award-winning houses. The house is a series of stairs and landings, all within a relatively small tower-like structure.

There are three separate levels matching three distinctive requirements. The lowest is structural and is screened by a very open form of wooden lattice. It provides a tall link between the ground and second or sleeping level. This is fully clad in timber with only small openings for the bedroom windows. The top level is the living area, with glass all round. The skilled use of timber and the open plan create a tree house feeling as you sit looking at the ocean and Barrenjoey Head through the tree tops. This living level also has a small mezzanine informal sleeping area on the way to the highest part of the house, where it links into the top of the cliff face.

It is possibly of more than passing interest to note that houses designed as weekenders should win the Robin Boyd Award four out of the past six times that the award has been presented. Perhaps it shows that architects are happier working in a peaceful setting? Perhaps also it reflects our basic desire as architects to work within more creative environments, and that these are not easily found in the Australian suburban environment.

The character is delightful, presenting a variety of spatial and environmental options: cosy rooms, 'crow's nest balcony', a sun terrace in a landscape environment, and the variable living room. All in all, a plan that makes the most of a very small site and leaves as much of it as possible for the fauna and flora that lured the architect and his family here in the first place.

Everything about this house is architecture taken to a logical conclusion given the constraints of the site and the nature of the house as a weekender. The site is an unusual one, even in Sydney, with a unique microclimate in a narrow and steep gully, sheltered from the cold southerly ocean winds and the harsh drying westerlies. Its northern aspect has been used to maximum advantage.

Ken Woolley's quiet imagination has made a lovely place, with care and deep thought to be found everywhere. The paint/stain junctions are considered, as is movement of timbers, ventilation and cleaning of gutters — all in a building which transcends its construction. Just like last year's winning house by Geoffrey Pie, it is safe to say that Robin Boyd would have loved it, but then it is also a place any sensitive person would love.

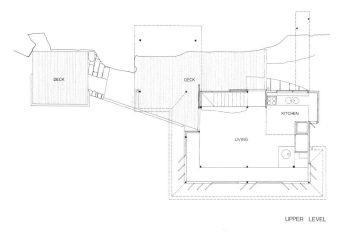

UPPER LEVEL

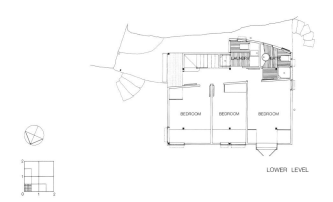

LOWER LEVEL

ROBIN BOYD AWARD 1988

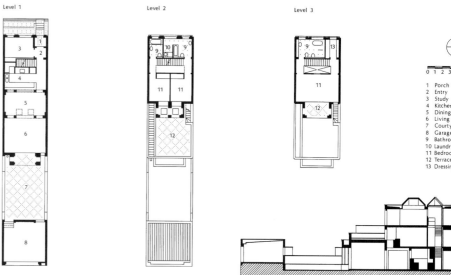

Level 1

Level 2

Level 3

N

0 1 2 3 4 5

1 Porch
2 Entry
3 Study
4 Kitchen
5 Dining
6 Living
7 Courtyard
8 Garage
9 Bathroom
10 Laundry
11 Bedroom
12 Terrace
13 Dressing

Section

HENWOOD HOUSE, PADDINGTON, NSW

ALEXANDER TZANNES

JURY REPORT

This is a building that councils and anyone interested in the revitalisation of inner cities should look at closely. Built to replace a fibro shed, this house is three storeys while its neighbours have two. It is modern while its neighbours are old. Yet it fits in well, without pretending to be an imitation historic house.

It shows that, when left to a skilled architect, infill housing can achieve charm and space in a tiny lot and still be built on a tight budget.

It is a marvellous balance; thoughtfully designed in context with its neighbours while breaking new ground.

The central skylit cross stair well is astonishing in a house of this size and is bathed in light, bringing it right into the heart of this modern terrace house.

The southern external wall is stepped so that, for most of the year, sunlight reaches the southern courtyard.

It is amazing how much has been fitted into this 5.5 metre wide house. It even has a generous ground floor ceiling height while fitting in two more floors still within the roof line of its two-storey neighbours.

The Henwood House is an exercise in planning and design that reaches levels of elegance and refinement rarely achieved in contemporary domestic architecture. It represents an approach that completely by-passes all new waves of style and expression and forthrightly achieves excellence in all fundamental aspects of design.

Deep within an area largely composed of lace-fronted terraces and controlled by regulations structured to create new imitations of the same, the Henwood House projects a subtle but distinctive individuality. Despite the additional storey, the parapet is kept in line with the silhouette level of its neighbours. This has allowed a lower site coverage than other terraces and, consequently, a larger garden area with more sunshine and more light.

There are lessons here for anyone wanting to live in the city. Lessons on the use of space, the internal planning and, above all, the sense of 'home' and shelter captured elegantly in a house that is fun.

The house is beautifully furnished and much loved by its owners. It is impossible to imagine ever growing tired of living in the Henwood House; indeed, its elegance and refinement would inevitably lead one to live an increasingly gracious lifestyle.

GRACEVILLE HOUSE, BRISBANE

DONALD WATSON

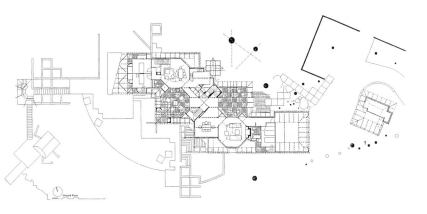

JURY REPORT

The brief called for the replacement of an existing house in a mature garden. The clients fancied a 'Walter Taylor' house (so called after the architect/engineer/contractor who built a number of substantial hipped, tiled-roofed houses in the vicinity). The design was to take better advantage of the riverfront site, be informal and be on three levels; parents upstairs and recreation on a lower ground floor down from the main ground floor.

Other requirements were for a boat house, swimming pool, cover for three cars, natural ventilation and central heating, and for the garden to be retained. The roof was to be without valleys and gutters in a defence against leaves on such a treed site. The house settles beautifully into the mature site, and the transition from garden to entrance to interior spaces supported with ever-present river views is truly delightful.

The house is skilfully placed to take advantage of views up and down the Brisbane River as well as just across it.

The plan is generally only one room deep for cross ventilation with views both ways and exploits the advantages of a northern orientation.

The precise positioning of the plan was determined by a number of axes established to take advantage of both view and particular trees in the garden. Each room has its own outdoor spaces adjacent (screened porches or terraces), and major rooms have skylights and/or glazed sections of roofing to admit reflected or (in winter) shafts of sunlight.

The house includes references to traditional Queensland housing, to Arts and Crafts design, and to South-East Asian building.

In several visits to the house, jurors, both state and federal, were unanimous in their desire not to leave. The house is much loved by the owners. Robin Boyd would have approved.

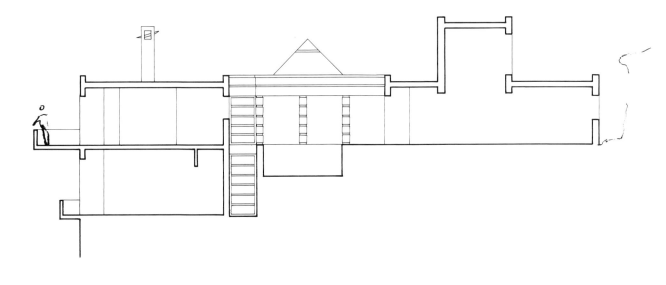

ALEX POPOV

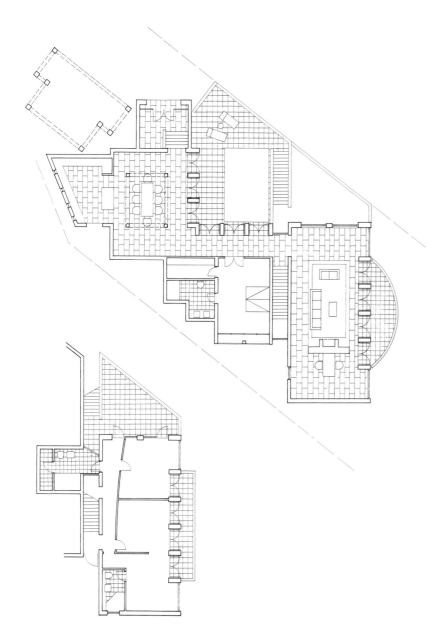

JURY REPORT

In spite of the fact that Burley Griffin's concept of Castlecrag has been largely destroyed by random uncontrolled suburbanism, it is a sheer delight to find that there are still people and designers who would wish to sustain his original concept. The Popov house does this brilliantly.

The architect has paid a reverent tribute to Griffin, but has in no way allowed this to interfere with the process of creating a beautiful and lovable building which responds to the needs of the client and the constraints of the site.

The house has been built behind an existing house facing the street on a steep wooded site sloping to the adjoining bay and facing south. There was a requirement, therefore, to capture the magnificent outlook of the site and, at the same time, to ensure that it was able to capture the sunny northern aspect. The house is informal and has managed to fit into the lifestyle of the clients in a way that enhances their living and working patterns.

Griffin used sandstone from the site to create some of his buildings. Sandstone and brick have been used here to echo those buildings. In doing so, the architect has shown a high dgree of design integrity. The rooms of the main floor level are beautifully integrated with the sunny terrace and the swimming pool.

The jury had some reservations regarding the energy efficiency of the house, but decided that the success of all the other elements was sufficient to ensure that this building should be recognised for the Robin Boyd Award.

JURY REPORT

A piece of fun design which responds to the client's own brief of a low-cost, easy to build shelter suitable for warmer climates. This building shows that a different range of living values and experiences can be achieved by reassessing the types of building materials used.
Robert Caulfield

This house is of the country, if not the wilderness; enclosure is reduced to the minimum; even the weight and rigidity of glass are rejected in favour of transparent and translucent fabrics; simplicity and the natural life are achieved by the most sophisticated and up-to-date means.
Tom Heath

A celebration of the alternative lifestyles in a beautiful rural setting. The architect has thoroughly explored a number of innovative solutions to providing the absolute minimum enclosure at minimum cost.

The design has a playful quality, emphasised by the little tented pavilions partly covering the decked areas. Some of the detailing is 'agricultural' and the kitchen-bathroom core is very tight and lacks the generosity displayed in the handling of the major spaces.
John Morphett

Situated just inland from the Sunshine Coast, this house for $50,000 is a challenge to housing in the north. Designed to met cyclonic onditions, the steel 'Coolclad Custom Orb', canvas and vinyl roll-up walled house is sited in what was a rainforest gully with outlook to some beautiful peaked mountains and distant views. With the walls lifted, the house becomes a shaded platform floating above the landscape.

The house is planned tightly with a somewhat nautical feeling. The structure is straightforward welded and cleat and bolt connections which rise from ground level on posts to the wall plate at door head. A ridge beam supports the inner canvas liner and another the outer vinyl fly, thereby achieving a double air-ventilated roof system.

TENT HOUSE, EUMUNDI, QUEENSLAND

GABRIEL POOLE

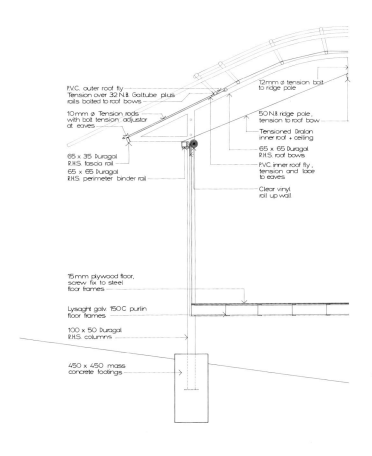

P.V.C. outer roof fly
Tension over 32 N.B. Galtube plus
rails bolted to roof bows

10mm ø Tension rods
with bolt tension adjustor
at eaves

65 x 35 Duragal
R.H.S. fascia rail

65 x 65 Duragal
R.H.S. perimeter binder rail

12mm ø tension bolt
to ridge pole

50 N.B. ridge pole,
tension to roof bow

Tensioned Dralon
inner roof + ceiling

65 x 65 Duragal
R.H.S. roof bows

P.V.C. inner roof fly,
tension and lace
to eaves

Clear vinyl
roll up wall

15mm plywood floor,
screw fix to steel
floor frames

Lysaght galv. 150C purlin
floor frames

100 x 50 Duragal
R.H.S. columns

450 x 450 mass
concrete footings

Whilst the vinyl and canvas elements need renewing from time to time, the costs set against repayments for a traditional building and its need for upkeep would appear to remain well ahead.

This house is without the need for mechanical heating and cooling. It is solar-powered and relatively low on energy in its making and running. It is a house which celebrates the north life and has a festive atmosphere which has been augmented through the fabric and coloured outside shades, which relate to the pinnacled mountains nearby. Although the shades embody such landscape connections, they are not as successful as the house proper.
Glenn Murcutt

It is with some excitement that one discovers the colourful Tent House, perfectly positioned in the hills outside Eumundi and alongside the Aboriginal sacred Mt Eerwah. From a distance its brightness and movement created by flags and flapping canvas give the image of a resting flock of parrots.

The Tent House has attracted a lot of public interest, not the least due to its low price. Some 250 orders have already been placed with the architect. Such demand indicates the need for attractive, affordable housing. Hundreds of thousands of families in Australia are forced to live in caravans and mobile homes; the latter cost around the same as the Tent House. While many people will view it as a holiday or 'retirement' home, the Tent House design should also be considered as a welcome alternative to these other forms of cheaper family accommodation.

It challenges councils' and the public's perceptions of acceptable standards and aesthetics. Hopefully, the success of the Tent House will provide an impetus for change and promote more flexibility and imagination in councils' interpretation of building design and materials specifications.
Helen Wellings

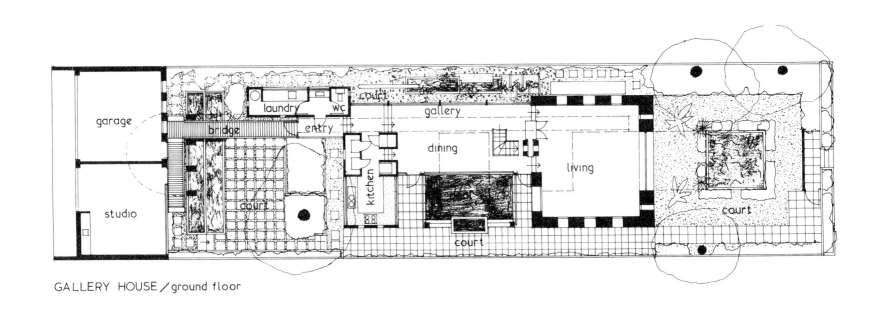

GALLERY HOUSE / ground floor

GALLERY HOUSE, HAWTHORN, MELBOURNE

DALE JONES-EVANS

JURY REPORT

An interesting solution to the problem of providing a good quality home on a site overlooked by flats. The relationship of indoor and outdoor spaces is good, but some of the materials used are gimmicky.
Robert Caulfield

This house is essentially urban: a cunningly defended environment which only appears to be open to the outside world. It displays a mannered, slightly perverse pleasure in the ornamental treatment of structure and in the play of unexpected vistas; each of those apparently decorative windows frames a different view.
Tom Heath

Looking at the photographs, one has the impression that there is too much going on — all the good ideas and historical references are fighting for attention. However, a visit makes it clear that the house hangs together very well indeed. Both internal and external spaces are very well organised, with some beautiful elements and clever detailing. The house has a seductive quality which is hard to resist.
John Morphett

Situated in residential Hawthorn, this house recalls Aldo Van Eyck's statement 'A leaf is a tree and a tree is a leaf' — this house is the city and the city is a house. It links the voids and spaces like a city street links the various buildings. This is a clever building.

To the north, sections of the building are glazed onto courtyards, with retained established trees working to shade the glass in summer and allowing sun penetration in winter. Moving through the house, one is made aware of the picturesque through vista, enclosures, solid, void. The spaces are complex, at times not entirely satisfying but always thoughtful. Detailing on the whole is very well considered, if at times a little ambitious.

Evidence of sagging edges emerges on the roof to the rear upper bed over the garage. Winter nights must be very cold in Melbourne and heat loss in this building considerable! Energy costs in maintaining a level of comfort could be high. Like the Tent House, it is innovative and makes a great deal out of a relatively ordinary, tight site.
Glenn Murcutt

Dale Jones-Evans succeeds in making full use of a long, narrow site, hemmed-in on one side by a block of flats and on the other by a Victorian house.

Garden courtyards, one of which features a 100-year-old mulberry tree, provide secluded retreats for contemplation. These domestic courtyards are pleasant and well-proportioned, forming natural links with specific zones of the house and meeting the architect's objective of an internal and external art gallery.

The eye is constantly reminded of this integration.

There's the clever use of a floor window overlooking a pool below, glazing along the corridor floor and a small bathroom window with a parallel mirror beyond, all providing images within images. But the glazing also serves to rob the house of warm air on colder days. The jury was concerned that the energy efficiency of the house for a good proportion of the year has been ignored.
Helen Wellings

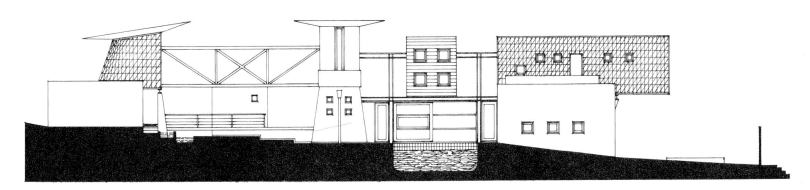

GALLERY HOUSE / north elevation

CLARE HOUSE, BUDERIM, QUEENSLAND

LINDSAY CLARE

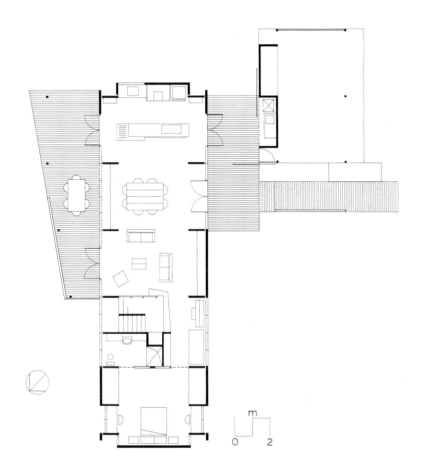

JURY REPORT

The house achieves an excellent integration of strong imagery, programme fulfilment, site responsiveness, structural intelligence, quality of construction and cost sensibility. In appearance, the house is crisp, instantly comprehensible and attractive. To gain the advantages of north orientation and an ocean view, the long, two-storey rectangular volume, under a gently curved roof, steps across the site contours. Entrance is directly into the handsomely spacious dining, kitchen and living room, from which the outlook is fully appreciable. Beyond an open stair well, parents' quarters are secluded. Upstairs is the domain for five children, with sleeping zones at either end linked by a generous common room, with excellent light and cross-ventilation. Setting back this common room floor from the external perimeter walls enhances the sense of double height volume. The Clare House has an abundance of architectural character, realised through unextravagant means.

Neville Quarry

This is a house in harmony with its environment and the large family that inhabits it. It's quality, from design to finish. It's also intelligent, economical and practical. Hopefully, its brilliant simplicity will influence future accessible housing design in this country.

Maggie Tabberer

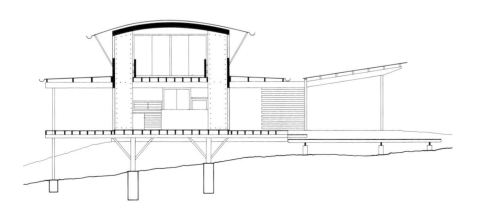

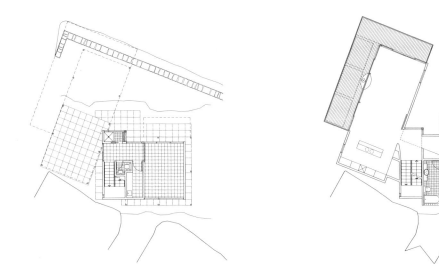

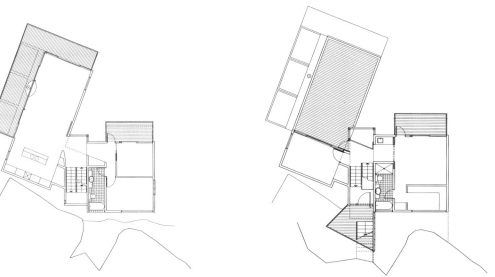

PALM BEACH HOUSE, NSW

GORDON & VALICH

JURY REPORT

This is a well executed and sensitive solution to a difficult site. The excellence and suitability in siting and form are starkly demonstrated by its contrasting, impolite neighbours. The interior spaces are delightful and take full advantage of the views, sea and sun.
Robert Cheesman

This deceptively simple house is an elegant and sensitive response to the challenge of locating a beach house in a prominent and environmentally delicate position. The town planning requirement restricting height has resulted in undue prominence being given to the rooftop car park but at the same time has contributed to the integration of the house within the hillside.
Anne Cunningham

Even though the site is steep, living spaces connect easily to the garden and access paths to the beach. The house is simply detailed, great care has been given to the fitout in the main spaces, while standard units are used for wardrobes and general cupboards.
Glenn Murcutt

The house is like three levels of stacked trays in two blocks, one askew to the other, so that the staircase, which connects both, presents in sequence a variety of outlooks to within and beyond the open-planned rooms, so contact with the exterior and the interior is integrated. In its dramatic landscape the house sits gently, not cringing in its context but compatible.
Neville Quarry

The spectacular 'sighting' of this house almost outweighs the considerable architectural achievement but not quite. Situated on a precipitous block, it commands the magnificent views yet harmoniously settles into the landscape.
Maggie Tabberer

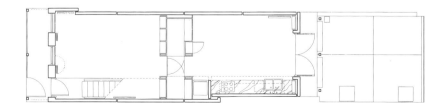

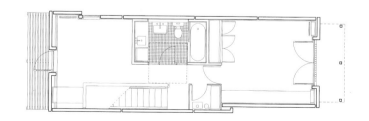

LYON/JENKIN HOUSE, CARLTON, MELBOURNE

HAMISH LYON, ASTRID JENKIN, CHARLES SALTER

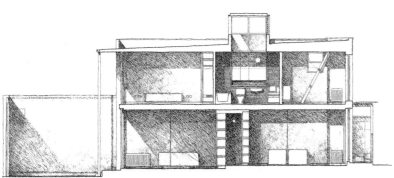

JURY REPORT

This new house in Carlton is on a parcel of land that measures only 4 x 18 metres and is part of a heritage-listed streetscape. It is excellently and economically executed, energy-efficient and offers a real and responsible lesson for backward-looking government.
Robert Cheesman

This is a particularly fine contemporary example of infill housing in an inner urban situation. The architect has sought to explore appropriate and low-cost methods of construction on a very tight site that would be applicable on other sites.
Anne Cunningham

Techniques incorporated in multi-storey buildings have been worked into this house. Precast walls on both side boundaries meant rapid progress to lock-up stage, an important consideration in Melbourne. This small terrace is carefully thought through. The detailing is good, materials well-crafted where it matters.
Glenn Murcutt

The discipline of keeping the number of surface finishes few, of maintaining simple proportions and clarity of natural lighting, of doing the obvious with great sensitivity and restraint, gives this tiny house a real presence, far beyond the prospect of its dimensions.
Neville Quarry

A brilliant 'little' house that skilfully utilises 'big' materials. The partnership of strength and finesse (concrete panels and fine finishes and fittings) provides a polished yet warm interior. It has clever and spacious storage and addresses the city noise factor and wins. At under $200,000 it should convey to all young home builders that good design and 'style' can out-distance dollars.
Maggie Tabberer

LARRAKEYAH MEDIUM DENSITY HOUSING PRECINCT 2, DARWIN

TROPPO

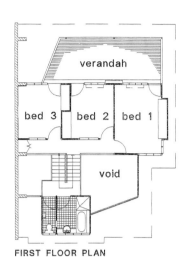

GROUND FLOOR PLAN

FIRST FLOOR PLAN

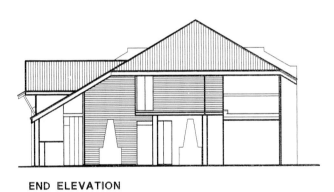

END ELEVATION

FRONT ELEVATION

JURY REPORT

This project advances energy efficiency in tropical housing into a medium-density context, without compromising essential climate or landscape solutions. Internally the design is neither precious nor pretentious, allowing relaxed living with tropical sensitivity.
Robert Cheesman

Troppo has shown that increasing density need not be at the expense of achieving good thermal qualities and an attractive, lively environment. In fact these qualities are considerably enhanced by the seemingly ad hoc siting of each house and the clever juxtaposition of low-maintenance materials. Troppo's hallmark of extensive use of louvres internally and externally is there, as is the split-level planning and mezzanine bathrooms. The high standard of landscaping, yet to mature, will contribute significantly to the area's privacy and microclimate.
Anne Cunningham

Generous upper level verandahs, courtyards and patterns of air movement all contribute to the open and relaxed lifestyle in which Darwinites are forced by climate to participate. This is a considerable advance on the run of buildings in our north, where most at best are replicas of our dreariest southern examples; so inappropriate for the tropics.
Glenn Murcutt

There are 21 dwellings, some detached, some semi-detached, designed for passive cooling, with cross-ventilation, ample roof shading and site locations that do not inhibit breezes, but also have the capability of being air-conditioned.
Neville Quarry

BRANNIGAN HOUSE, ST LUCIA, QUEENSLAND

BUD BRANNIGAN

JURY REPORT

This building shows that the architecture of the suburban house for everyman can be a place of joy and low cost... an example of high architectural resolution without clichés, trends or affects, quietly going about its own business.

Graham Bligh

This house possesses many fine qualities... the processional sequencing of open and closed spaces... the simple structural concept and restrained selection of modest building materials... it responds well to local climatic influences through cleverly designed windows and window walls.

Peter Crone

Nestled in a quiet street, this unpretentious house demonstrates what's achievable in a suburban context, on a controlled budget, using simple materials and sensitive design. While respectful of its neighbours, it is nevertheless a highly individual structure.

Rebecca Gilling

The Brannigan residence is an excellent example of relaxed modernism: it has a generous interplay of outdoor and indoor spaces, it overcomes the constraints of a suburban block by ingenious siting and planning and, with deceptive innocence, creates a domestic scenography of rare and compelling dignity, harmony and simplicity. There must be some fortunate chemistry between the subtropical regionalism and easy vernacular construction, infused with non-doctrinaire modernism, that has lead Queensland to evolve many unpretentious but precious gems of residential architecture, of which the Brannigan residence is amongst the best.

Neville Quarry

This is totally lost within its bush setting. Architect-owned and occupied, it is a personal house that answers their desired lifestyle. A very affordable residence which uses natural ventilation to the maximum.

James Taylor

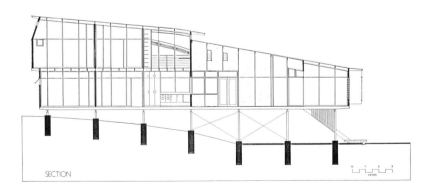

SECTION

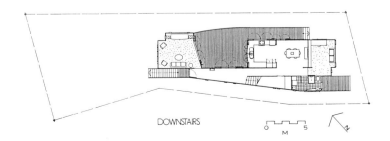

DOWNSTAIRS

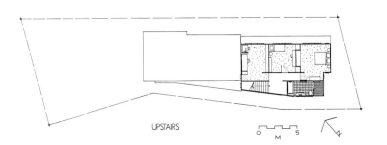

UPSTAIRS

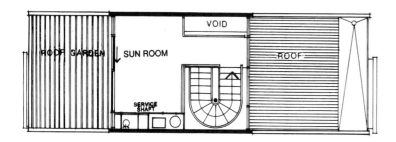

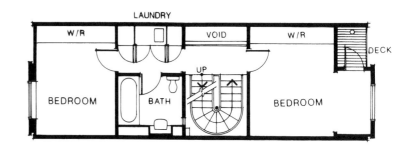

TOWNHOUSES AT 106-112 CREMORNE STREET
RICHMOND, VICTORIA

CRAIG ROSSETTI

JURY REPORT

The amenity and architectural quality provided for its low-budget price is striking... The highly resolved approach to detailing both internally and externally has led to a rich mixture of quite modest materials and details often far removed from the accepted market-driven options of other speculative developments. The process shows the architect's capacity to conceive a project, work out a syndicate to purchase the site, design and manage the project and end up owning a dwelling. This is a model for inner-city redevelopment and for individuals taking control of their accommodation needs.

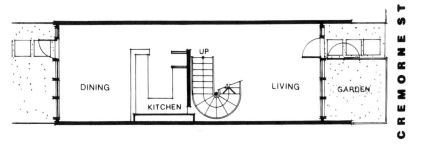

HAMMOND RESIDENCE, POMONA, QUEENSLAND

CLARE DESIGN — KERRY CLARE, LINDSAY CLARE

JURY REPORT

This is an expression of the philosophy of living with the Australian environment — neither dominating nor ignoring it — using the sun and the wind. The residence sits lightly on its platform above the ground. It takes maximum advantage of its site and aspect, carefully acknowledging both the site and the setting. Privacy, intimacy and openness are carefully considered. All this is properly conceived and achieved within a tight budget and within the costraints of working in a remote location which had to be self-sufficient. Its greatest contribution to Australian architecture lies in the creative and innovative use of standard elements and materials.

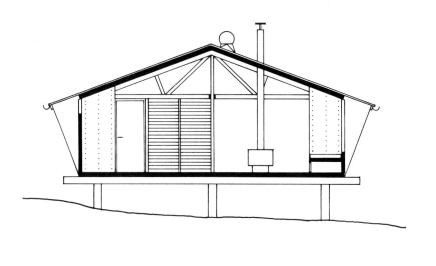

1982 MOOREE LANDS OFFICE, MOOREE, NSW

NSW GOVERNMENT ARCHITECT

1983 HARRISFORD, PARRAMATTA, NSW AND JUNIOR MEDICAL OFFICER'S HOUSE, PORT ARTHUR, TASMANIA

CLIVE LUCAS

1984 MELBOURNE CITY BATHS

KEVIN GREENHATCH

1985 EMERALD HILL FACADE AND VERANDAH, MELBOURNE

EUGENE KNEEBONE, VICTORIA MINISTRY OF HOUSING

1986 BIG STABLE RENOVATION, NEWMARKET, SYDNEY

TIMOTHY COURT

1987 THE MORTLOCK LIBRARY, JERVOIS WING, SA STATE LIBRARY, ADELAIDE

RON DANVERS WITH SA DEPARTMENT OF HOUSING AND CONSTRUCTION

1988 DUNDULLIMAL HOMESTEAD, DUBBO, NSW

CLIVE LUCAS, STAPLETON & PARTNERS

1989 JUNIPER HALL, PADDINGTON, NSW

CLIVE LUCAS, STAPLETON & PARTNERS

1990 LYNDHURST, SYDNEY

CLIVE LUCAS, STAPLETON & PARTNERS

1991 COMMONWEALTH BANK HEAD OFFICE, SYDNEY

AUSTRALIAN CONSTRUCTION SERVICES
PROJECT ARCHITECT: BARRY MCGREGOR

1992 HYDE PARK BARRACKS, SYDNEY

TONKIN ZULAIKHA HARFORD

1993 SANDSTONE RESTORATION PROGRAMME, SYDNEY

NSW PUBLIC WORKS DEPARTMENT

1994 THE GOTHIC BANK CORNER OF QUEEN AND COLLINS STREETS, MELBOURNE

PEDDLE THORP/HERITAGE ARCHITECTS: ALLOM LOVELL

1995 LUNA PARK MILSONS POINT, NSW

HASSELL MAHER/PAUL BERKEMEIER AND
McCONNEL SMITH & JOHNSON,
PROJECT ARCHITECTS: KEN MAHER,
PAUL BERKEMEIER, MARK WILLETT

This category applies to any built project which involves conservation and should be in accordance with the Burra Charter.

Evidence, drawings and/or photographs of the building prior to conservation/restoration must form part of the submission in this category.

Projects may be within any class of the BCA and though exhibiting changes of use should be predominantly entered for authenticity of the conservation/restoration work undertaken.

RAIA Awards Rules, March 1991

LACHLAN MACQUARIE AWARD

FOR CONSERVATION

FUTURE RETENTION

The case for retaining old buildings, when the conditions for which they were constructed no longer apply, is two-fold:

1. To conserve resources and keep an investment which is still capable of continuing returns. This can be determined by an energy and financial audit, a calculation in which the arithmetic may be impeccable. The predictions will be based upon economic assumptions which are truly unverifiable — until the future actually happens. An estimate of commercial value can be conjectured, nevertheless.

2. To provide citizens with a sense of their past, of memories of the causes and effects of events more profound than mere nostalgia, by maintaining the physical and contextual evidence of built forms. An estimate of social value can be declared. Appreciation of the past builds present confidence.

As both commercial and social entities, buildings embody cultural heritage. Even in the midst of the destruction of the 1939-45 war in Europe, some far-sighted architects were planning for reconstruction. Architects in Warsaw, aware that their city would be reduced to rubble, secreted away drawings of entire sections of the metropolis so that it could be rebuilt, post-war, exactly as it was pre-war. And this in part, was done. The new 'old city' is much appreciated by citizens and tourists, and generates income by simply existing. The post-war Stalinist architecture offers no such consolation to body or mind.

Since the end of the Second World War, in reaction to its tremendous carnage, many countries decided to safeguard their cultural heritage. In 1945, UNESCO sponsored a convention on the Protection of Cultural Property in the Event of Armed Conflicts. A further congress in Venice in 1964 established the International Charter for the Restoration of Monuments and Sites (ICOMOS). The current international directive on conservation is the Burra Charter, which aims to further the conservation, protection, rehabilitation and enhancement of monuments, groups of buildings and sites. The significance of an item or place destined for conservation is embodied in "its fabric and its setting, and in other evidence of its history, and in association with the community". The Burra Charter defines the processes that must be addressed in terms of conservation, maintenance, preservation, restoration, reconstruction and adaptation. Under these international conventions (to which Australia is a signatory), conservation is not narrowly conceived as only restoring a building precisely to its appearance at the time of its construction, nor to some singular time chosen out of a continuing history. Conservation encompasses intelligent and sympathetic modification. For some buildings, 'authentic' restoration is most warranted and is possible because research can establish the complete architectural condition of first completion. To keep later accretions as traces of an ongoing history, or to remove them because they defile the original, is a philosophical rather than a calculable judgement — depending on the relative iconic power of the original and the modifying circumstances.

MODIFYING CIRCUMSTANCES

In 1982, the RAIA instigated the Lachlan Macquarie Award, named after the Governor of New South Wales from 1810-1821. Governor Macquarie, among other enlightened actions, appointed Francis Greenway as first Government Architect to the colony, marked out plans for five towns in the Hawkesbury district, introduced building regulations and reduced the number of public house liquor licences.

Many buildings that have gained the Lachlan Maquarie Award had reached a severe state of dilapidation, or been so overwhelmed by insensitive accretions, that a future role for them was hard to imagine. The Moree Lands Office had been damaged by fire, the Big Stable by white ants, Dundullimall and Lyndhurst were wrecks, Harrisford House vastly altered and Juniper Hall fringed with a foreground of shops, the interior devastated by years of incongruous use and careless alterations. The Melbourne City Baths and Luna Park, Sydney, were facilities which seemed to be obsolete. The Mortlock Library, Adelaide, the Commonwealth Bank, Sydney, and the Gothic Bank, Melbourne, required their working conditions to be made compatible with current needs for air conditioning, lighting, computing, fire safety and hygiene, if their architectural fabric was to be continually useful. Although the shop fronts and terraces behind them had been considerably altered, the Emerald Hill verandahs still had just enough existing integrity to warrant restoration. Harrisford House and Hyde Park Barracks are the only two of the award winners which have been welcomed into a second life as museums. Juniper Hall and Lyndhurst are no longer dwellings but offices. Luna Park has once again found difficulties in establishing commercial viability. For most of the Lachlan Macquarie Award winners, however, continuity of use has prevailed. Special mention must be made of the tenacious and brilliant work done by architect Clive Lucas (subsequently Clive Lucas, Stapleton), for a string of five awards: in 1983, 1988, 1989, 1990 and 1992 (with Tonkin Zulaikha Harford).

The 1993 award was not for a single building but for a State programme for the restoration of sandstone buildings and elements in New South Wales, a task which embraces many projects.

The evidence is clear: given a community commitment and a political will to conserve fine examples of fine architecture, there are really no architectural conservation problems that cannot be overcome. Managing to get the funds for conservation and achieve a completed project which will be an asset rather than a financial drain, is the real headache.

AUTHENTICITY

The key criterion specified for the Lachlan Macquarie Award is authenticity.

Authenticity implies genuine concordance with the original. To have the attribute of authenticity, then, the original must be already known. So the first task of the conservation architect is to establish, with documentary records — which may be original drawings, photographs and observers' accounts — the architectural attributes of the original. This may not be too difficult when complete records exist — it just requires hours and hours of painstaking research and scholarship, but often the documentation is scrappy and sometimes hardly exists at all. So the conservation architect is obliged to make some inferences, by referring to other work by the same architect or similar architects of the same period, and to buildings of the same type. It is more than likely then, that the conservation architect for a particular project will be the most knowledgable and expert judge on the authenticity of the project. The awards jury will almost certainly be less well informed, so how can they judge better than the architect who is directly involved? The jury must resort to their individual experience of the period, the work itself and the documentary evidence presented by the conservation architect of not only the building in its original state (if ascertainable), but of the whole process of investigation, inference and conclusion that lead to the architectural decisions which were made in finalising the conservation design. Compromises are often necessary. Original material — perhaps an exotic timber or rare stone — may no longer be able to be supplied. The use of a paint pigment or metal alloy identical to the historical model may be too expensive to accept. The aim is for an achievable product closest in veracity as possible to the original, not necessarily exact in every detail but precisely compatible in mood, style and perception. In conservation work, architects must maintain rigorous integrity.

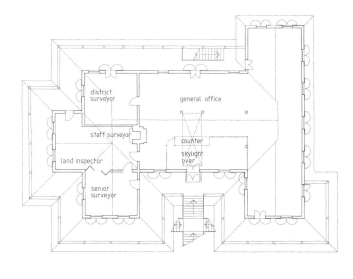

JURY REPORT

The Lachlan Macquarie Award is made this year for the first time, and it is fitting that it should go to the Government Architect of NSW, since that office has done so much in recent years to advance the cause of maintaining the heritage of old buildings owned by the NSW Government.

This is not an easy award to decide as there are so many different criteria which may be used to determine the extent and the nature of the restoration which has taken place. An award has been given for some years in some States for which the criteria have been somewhat general. In other States, multiple awards are given for different facets of work in this area. By contrast, this year the Victorian Chapter has made its judgements within the rather more strict criteria of the Burra Charter.

The jury found it difficult to differentiate between the different criteria used in the various Chapters but sought a standard of excellence which would cut across the boundaries established by the buildings submitted by various Chapters to suit their award conditions. It was impressed by the range and nature of the work going on across the country and decided to make an award and two commendations.

The award is for the restoration of the Lands Office in Moree in NSW. This has been carried out with considerable care in a manner which gives great pleasure to architect and layman alike, in a building constructed faithfully after a fire and adapted sensitively for continued use.

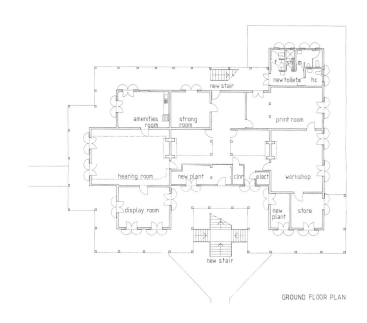

FIRST FLOOR PLAN

GROUND FLOOR PLAN

LACHLAN MACQUARIE AWARD 1983

HARRISFORD, PARRAMATTA

JUNIOR MEDICAL OFFICER'S HOUSE, PORT ARTHUR

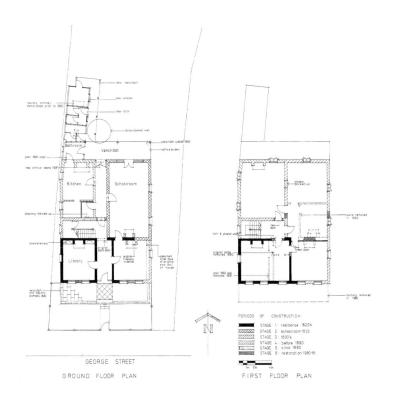

GEORGE STREET

GROUND FLOOR PLAN

FIRST FLOOR PLAN

PERIODS OF CONSTRUCTION:

STAGE 1: residence 1820's
STAGE 2: schoolroom 1832
STAGE 3: 1830's
STAGE 4: before 1890
STAGE 5: circa 1890
STAGE 6: restoration 1980-81

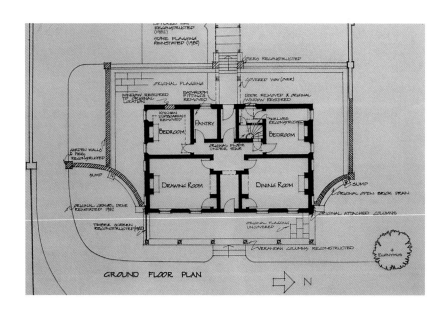

GROUND FLOOR PLAN

HARRISFORD, PARRAMATTA NSW AND JUNIOR MEDICAL OFFICER'S HOUSE PORT ARTHUR, TASMANIA

CLIVE LUCAS

JURY REPORT

The Lachlan Macquarie Award for 1983 is made to Clive Lucas for two restoration works: Harrisford, Parramatta, and the Junior Medical Officer's house, Port Arthur.

The National Selection Committee considers that Clive Lucas' approach to meticulous restoration by the use of original materials and techniques, and the restoration of the buildings to revert to their original uses overshadows other projects considered.

The success of restoration depends on careful research of the significant aspects of a building's life, and in the transformation of the restored building to a modern context through its new use, or in its relationship to the buildings and environment around it.

Understanding of a building's character and atmosphere is a critical process in restoration, and in these two buildings, Clive Lucas has successfully explored their histories to restore the dignity and sense of place of the two distinctly different buildings.

The Lachlan Macquarie Award 1983 is made to Clive Lucas in recognition of his skill, sensitivity and dedication to the discipline of restoration, elegantly expressed in these two buildings.

LACHLAN MACQUARIE AWARD 1984

MELBOURNE CITY BATHS

KEVIN GREENHATCH

VICTORIAN CHAPTER JURY REPORT

Kevin Greenhatch was commissioned for the City Baths project by the Melbourne City Council at a time when the baths were losing money and redevelopment of the site was an option. A detailed feasibility study however, showed that the fine old landmark designed at the end of the century by EJ and JJ Clark could be recycled and updated to provide profitable modern leisure faciltities.

Greenhatch's conversion embodies new construction and adaptation in the spirit of the original, and some restoration. It offers up-to-date swimming, gymnasium and squash facilities, with ancillary uses, a cafeteria and a sports clinic.

The jury applauded the close working relationship between the architect, client and Historic Buildings Council, and commented that this successful conversion proves that historic buildings only impose restrictions when the designers working on them are uncreative and insensitive.

EMERALD HILL FACADE AND VERANDAH, MELBOURNE

EUGENE KNEEBONE, VICTORIAN MINISTRY OF HOUSING

JURY REPORT

The Lachlan Macquarie Award is for conservation. The jury was very impressed by the work carried out in the first stages of the restoration of the Victoria Barracks, in Sydney, and looked forward to the time when the restoration of the whole complex might be submitted for the award.

The winning nomination, Emerald Hill in Victoria, also represented a situation where a government organisation took positive steps at conservation.

At Emerald Hill, the Victorian Ministry of Housing has conserved the fabric of a very large city block contrasting markedly with its neighbour, an earlier total demolition of a comparable section of the city and the high-rise precast concrete tower which now dominates it.

In the conservation of Emerald Hill, the Ministry has restored the inherent charm and character of the street facades and gained, with justification, popular acclaim. It is an example for authorities throughout Australia.

The restoration approach has been refreshingly straightforward. The purists might disapprove that only facades and sidewalk verandahs have been included in the programme. Even existing contemporary shopfronts have been excluded.

The inescapable truth is, of course, that a total restoration project would not have been affordable and could have imposed intolerable inhibitions on the housing and shops behind the facades which have been adapted over the years to modern usage. The Burra Charter rules have nevertheless been applied.

A budget has been met and the community now enjoys the rich streetscape architecture of an age past.

Where previous alteration work had vandalised the facades, the costs of intricate replacement have been avoided simply by painting on the facsimiles of missing architectural elements. The architectural rhythm is preserved and those who notice the white lie are amused by its wit.

THE BIG STABLE RENOVATION, NEWMARKET, NSW

TIMOTHY COURT

JURY REPORT

This is a conservation project which may not please those purists who see conservation as an art in which the minute detail of the original building is restored to an almost museum-like quality. The Big Stable restoration by Timothy Court is, instead, a very practical restoration, the kind of restoration which allows significant buildings from the past to remain with us for this and future generations. It is a conservation project which, through the skills and versatility of the architect, has for a relatively minimal cost restored a delightful building from the 1880s to a working building of the 1980s. It has done so in a way that honours the style, is true to the original concepts of the designers and pays great respect to that time and its craft and skill.

This is a building which delights anyone who walks in it, not only for the romantic appeal of the racecourse life, but also because of the way in which it has been executed, its charm and its sheer practicality. If more buildings were given the same chance for a new life through the skilled use of an architect and consultant engineer, then our cultural fabric would be far richer.

The jury was most impressed with the restoration of the stables building, considering the extreme termite damage and the lack of stability generally in the structure. Two things stand out clearly in this building — the ability of a young architect to encourage a corporate client to restore rather than demolish, and the restoration itself, carried out ingeniously and sensitively in a manner that almost adds to the original architecture, and does not detract from the design.

This building is a good example of a sensible and financially feasible alternative to demolition of one of Sydney's unique buildings. It is a sensible conservation, almost minimalist, ensuring that the building maintains its use and place in the racing fraternity. The revitalisation is exciting, and it is remarkable that such a large and regularly used building should have survived with little damage and no evidence of later alteration.

There is some deterioration — the sunhoods are partly rusted away, some door hinges have slipped and many of the posts on the stable doors have been rubbed deeply by a century of horses' necks. All of this character is wisely left for us to see.

The new structural bracing is very neatly integrated inside and out and the whole place has a healthy and cheery atmosphere. It has a utilitarian simplicity and the fact that the conservation allowed it to be retained as a working unit, not condemned to be a museum piece, pleased the jury greatly. The philosophy adopted here would allow many significant buildings, otherwise destined for oblivion, to regain their stature and role at small community cost.

The jury agreed unanimously that this was a first class example of conservation. The owners, William Inglis, should be particularly congratulated on this preservation and the fact that the original purpose of the building has been retained.

The restoration demonstrated an excellent collaboration between architect and engineer. The methods of restoration were dynamic and yet completely compatible with the existing. The architect also interpreted the laws and regulations in a contemporary way without destroying the fabric. The use of steel within the building is identifiable as part of the restoration and yet it becomes integral with the building itself.

The essential difference between this building and some of the previous conservation awards is the acceptance that not everything can be done to restore a building. In this case what has been done has been executed faithfully, but the architect has not allowed the minutiae to dominate his thinking. Instead he has taken an overall approach to save the building, to conserve its style and to maintain its use.

The architect knew when to stop. It will serve the profession well to recognise and reward modest attempts with modest buildings. In this there could be no other finer accolade than to award him the Lachlan Macquarie Award for Conservation.

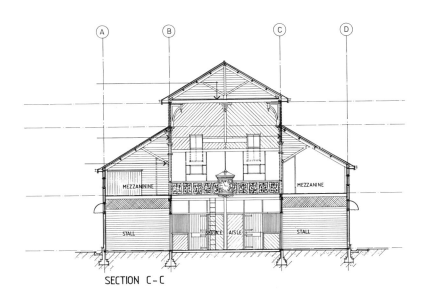

SECTION C-C

JURY REPORT

This is indeed an outstanding working library and archive. An attractive interior has been carefully returned to its original (or later) detail, with the majority of the detail restoration beautifully executed by day labour staff of the SA Department of Housing and Construction.

The insertion of necessary modern services is ingenious and unobtrusive. Any review of a restored building will be influenced by the intrinsic quality of the first design but, even when this is discounted, there is an undeniable excellence in the new work. The architects and users have avoided inserting new furniture, so that with the exception of microfiche readers the interiors are remarkably timeless.

The extensive restoration work included:

• Removal of poorly placed fluorescent lighting and replacement with fixtures characteristic of the first electric fixtures, with wiring fed through the original gas piping.

• New paint colours throughout the library as close as possible to original colours using contemporary paint systems. Original colours were found behind shelving, joinery, etc, or had been covered by cream-coloured paint. The base background wall colour, a blue-grey-green, looks very good and is set off by lighter tones at capitals and with gold leaf accents as originally used.

• Much original furniture has been salvaged. The main desk was re-configured and returned to its earlier position. All of the joinery has been refinished with great control (the architect restraining the joiners from eliminating the patina of wear of the years).

• The architects allowed architectural elements which were later than original if they made overall sense, and used graphics supportive of the character throughout, although there was no evidence of the original signage.

The building has been air-conditioned to archival standards

THE MORTLOCK LIBRARY, JERVOIS WING, SA STATE LIBRARY, ADELAIDE

RON DANVERS, DANVERS ARCHITECTS/P K SHARP AND SA DEPARTMENT OF HOUSING AND CONSTRUCTION

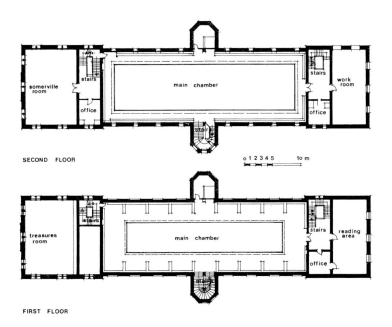

SECOND FLOOR

o 1 2 3 4 5   10 m

FIRST FLOOR

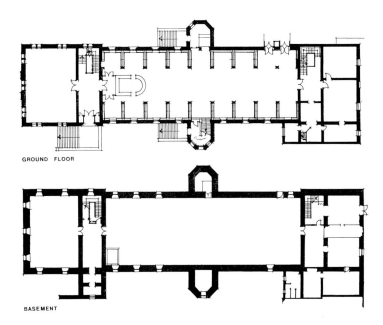

GROUND FLOOR

BASEMENT

without a severe impact on the architectural character. This work was cleverly and appropriately threaded through the existing roof construction and employed well positioned nozzle fittings in ceiling-panels. The overall air-conditioning and fire protection plan was carefully interwoven and supported by the local authorities, although it required several concessions by the Brigade.

The story of the restoration is of interest. Ron Danvers was commissioned to air-condition and repaint the library and was first selected by the department because he had previously shown sensitivity to old structures. Danvers started the work and when the work towards repainting was underway he suggested that they seek the original paint scheme.

That was agreed and so it went through refinishing, shelving if the walls were to be repainted, redo furniture if shelving was to be done, redo lighting and on and on. Carpet on the stairs was chosen to match the original linoleum colour. In effect, Ron walked them through a process towards restoration, always within a yearly budget available for this kind of work. Perhaps not a work of scholarship, but one of excellence.

The main reading room is breathtaking. As a time capsule it presents itself as a space that has been well maintained over the century, when in reality it is a space that has fallen into architectural decay and been brought back to repute. Its greatest quality is that it does not appear to be too new or renewed.

The project shows an appropriate amount of intervention commensurate with restoration and is in its own right an outstanding work.

LACHLAN MACQUARIE AWARD 1988

DUNDULLIMAL HOMESTEAD, DUBBO, NSW

CLIVE LUCAS, STAPLETON & PARTNERS

JURY REPORT

Dundullimal homestead and stables were the subject of an enormous effort in research, with skilful documentation and construction. At the start, the buildings were almost completely dilapidated. All aspects of the restoration process were carried out with great skill and sensitivity, combining restoration of the original character and construction methods, keeping the atmosphere that has been inherited with its great age.

The homestead faithfully displays the unique and charming qualities of the original building. A building of contrasts such as hardwood slab walls combined with highly sophisticated window joinery and a low eaves line, giving a continuous perimeter of shade and shelter. Internally the building convincingly maintains its original character, being carefully restored and furnished.

The sandstone stables are striking and handsome. This is largely due to the building's elegant proportions and the careful restoration of the sandstone walls. Where the timberwork is repaired it is done in an obvious way, avoiding any suggestion that it might be faked or artificially aged.

While Dundullimal is modest when compared to the many larger historic buildings in Australia, it is no less important in the overall national context.

As an example of the farmhouses built by early pioneering Australians, it is a monumental contribution to the country's social and architectural history.

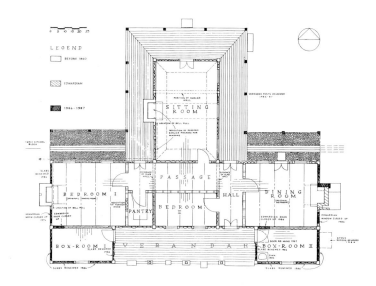

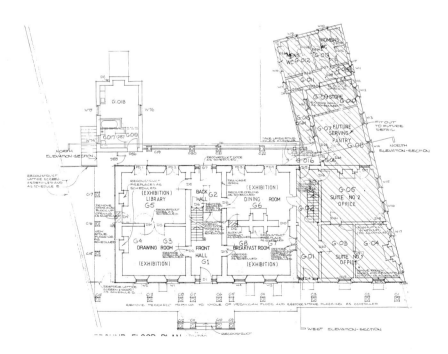

JURY REPORT

Juniper Hall has been sensitively and painstakingly restored to the point where it is now a proud work of architecture, just as it was when first constructed 165 years ago. Originally built in a semi-rural setting, some distance from Sydney town, the building is now surrounded by commercial glitter, high-rise residential buildings, and traffic. Despite this inevitable change in environment, the building has lost little of its intrinsic elegance.

The restoration of Juniper Hall gives the city valuable social and symbolic evidence of its history. From its beginning as an elegant residence, the building has served as an asylum for abandoned or destitute children, a ladies school, a receiving house and a complex warren of flats. In recent times the front gardens were occupied by a row of shops.

In preparing a conservation management plan, the architects have carefully researched the history of the building and grounds, relating the development to the changing occupants and changing functions. Through research it was clear that every aspect of the 'original building' could not be traced and it would be unreasonable to guess at what 'might have been'. A decision was therefore taken to trace individual sections of the building and represent them consistent with the best research and physical evidence available. In the final result, the slight inconsistency is not worrying, indeed it only serves to enrich the 165 year history of the architecture, furnishings and garden.

Juniper Hall is an important example of nineteenth century domestic architecture, and it is highly commendable that the National Trust have elected to preserve it. That the restoration work has been carried out with such skill served to make it exquisite and worthy of special praise. It is for this reason that the jury was unanimous in awarding Juniper Hall the 1989 Lachlan Macquarie Award.
Bruce Bowden

JURY REPORT

The conservation of Lyndhurst is nothing short of a miracle. Built in 1833-36 by John Verge for an important pioneer family, this fine mansion has been resurrected from the wreck it had become.

Having suffered over 100 years of mutilation by fire, damp, vermin, termites and abuse by various owners and lodgers, Verge's legacy in inner-city Glebe seemed doomed for destruction. It is entirely appropriate that Clive Lucas, who chaired the 'Save Lyndhurst' committee in 1972 to prevent the building being demolished for the aborted north-western freeway, was the architect responsible for its restoration.

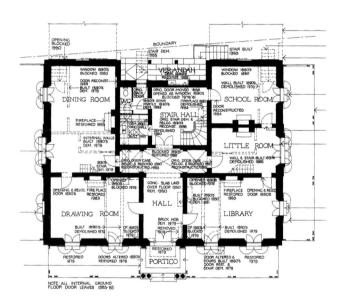

The task involved years of extensive research into Lyndhurst's history and a thorough examination of the building's fabric. This presented enormous difficulties because Lyndhurst had undergone many profound personality and structural changes over time, from a luxurious home with stables set in many acres of gardens to a theological college, hospital, three terraced houses on subdivided land, various factories and a joinery shop.

The restoration allows us to see Lyndhurst in its former splendour, with diminished gardens based upon the original design. Many careful treatments and extensions replace lost, rotted and demolished sections, including chimney pieces, verandahs and porch. Where certain facts were not able to be traced, interpretations suggesting, but not pretending to be, the originals were incorporated. Thus the jigsaw is now complete. The focal point is the grand central staircase, which had been completely demolished for the three terraces. It has been reconstructed superbly, its sweep a gentle parabola.

Respect for Lyndhurst's transformation over the ages in archeological features, such as original sections of plasterwork, location of partitions and layers of ceilings. If only walls could talk. They do at Lyndhurst! Graffiti from its years as a theological college make fascinating reading for Latin scholars. That the building serves as Resource Centre and headquarters of the Historic Houses Trust ensures these elements will be retained for future generations to appreciate.

Lyndhurst provides an important link with early nineteenth century architecture and its progression over 150 years. The jury commends the architects and others involved in the conservation work and unanimously awards Lyndhurst the 1990 Lachlan Macquarie Award.

Helen Wellings and Roger Johnson

COMMONWEALTH BANK HEAD OFFICE, SYDNEY

AUSTRALIAN CONSTRUCTION SERVICES (NSW)

PROJECT ARCHITECT: BARRY MCGREGOR

JURY REPORT

This much-loved Sydney monument has been restored to its former opulence and to a worthy place in commercial life. There have been necessary compromises but nothing of significance has been compromised. The dedication with which the architects have preserved the form of the original public spaces where possible, and the spirit where alteration was inevitable, is remarkable. On the other hand, in returning the working spaces to use, they have not baulked at radical surgery, and the new work is unmistakably new.

Tom Heath

This is a very carefully considered restoration project. Considerable research has been undertaken and a great deal of effort expended to get the restored parts of the building to original condition. As with all restorations that are to be used for contemporary purposes, decisions have been made on boundaries between old and new work. The trick is to carry out the new work in a current idiom, without imitating the old and, at the same time, avoiding unsympathetic collisions between the old and the new. In most cases, the architect has succeeded in this difficult area, inserting an atrium where there was formerly a light well, and in the handling of the main banking chamber. However, some of the office partitioning seemed unsympathetic.

John Morphett

This project is a labour of love and dedication without slavishly complying with historical replication. Old sections are restored faithfully and with skill; new sections within the historic areas are surgically changed appropriately; and new work, whilst overly fussy in wall-glazing systems, is nevertheless successful, climaxing in a new glass-roofed atrium and roof terrace area. The integration of new technological requirements, security and replanning has been very well worked through, recognising always that which is restored and that which is new. The building retains the essence of its earlier period and yet operates now and into the twenty-first century. That is an accomplishment.

Glenn Murcutt

HYDE PARK BARRACKS, SYDNEY

TONKIN ZULAIKHA HARFORD

CONSULTANT CONSERVATION ARCHITECTS: CLIVE LUCAS, STAPLETON & PARTNERS

JURY REPORT

There is often a difficulty, with the judging of conservation projects, in separating an originality of thought and creative design from the somewhat mechanical process of preservation, restoration and reconstruction undertaken in accordance with the principles of the Burra Charter. There has been no such difficulty with this project. A great deal of imagination and creativity has been brought to bear on the revelation and interpretation of the building fabric, throughout its history of many different uses. The new work and fitout have been elegantly designed to touch the existing building very lightly.

John Morphett

The original interior fabric of Hyde Park Barracks has been reconstituted, so that the building itself is revealed as evidence of history as a process, in layers that range, in chronology and effect, from authentic restoration through exposure of various tamperings of time to current interventions that bring a poignant contrast to archaic memories. The distance and the presence of the past are both skilfully conjured with sound tapes, mysterious cut-out silhouette figures, memorabilia displays and archival material, all of which enable the visitor to engage sympathetically in the passage of the building's changing occupancies — architecture mediating with life.

Neville Quarry

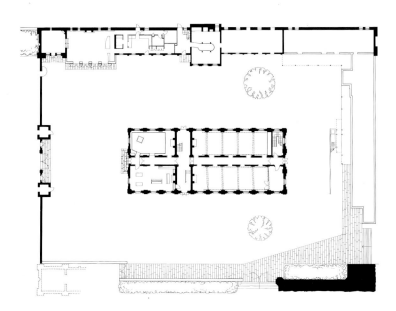

SANDSTONE RESTORATION PROGRAMME, SYDNEY

NSW GOVERNMENT ARCHITECT/HERITAGE GROUP, STATE PROJECTS, NSW DEPARTMENT OF WORKS
PROGRAMME CO-ORDINATOR: ANNE MORRIS, PROJECT ARCHITECTS: ROD CLIMO, VINCE SICARI, JOY SINGH

JURY REPORT

Australia's historical architecture and building is an essential and living part of our cultural heritage. The Sydney stonework programme is an extensive, thorough, sensitive and systematic approach to the conservation of Sydney's public stonework. The visual impact is minimal but the process is appropriate and masterly.
Robert Cheesman

Realising the State's considerable stake in stone buildings and structures, the PWD with government support has developed over several years a very laudable programme of stone repair, replacement, ongoing maintenance and even the commissioning of new work. As the trade of stone masonry had virtually died out in this State, this entailed the creation of a skilled trade.
Anne Cunningham

All areas of this programme draw on the care and complete dedication of all participants so that complex tasks are achieved, resulting in arresting not only the rapidly accelerating ravages of climate and time but conserving irreplaceable cultural heritage.
Glenn Murcutt

This award is not to a single building, nor to a one-off circumstance, but to a total programme. A dedicated band of architects and artisans has carried out meticulous research into the nature of the material, its sources, qualities, methods of quarrying, crafting and maintenance.
Neville Quarry

Only the dedication, skill and passion of those involved in this significant and highly commendable programme could convince this jury member to set aside her healthy hate of heights and scale the scaffolding of one of the buildings blessed for salvation under this programme. I survived, but more importantly, so did the building.
Maggie Tabberer

JURY REPORT

Retention of the old building and its enhancement for today's use contributes to the built environment. Conservation has been consistently undertaken with quality and thoroughness. [However] the new buildings and linkages detract from the quality of the three converted old buildings.
Graham Bligh

From the extensive preliminary research to the detailed documentation, and throughout the works period, an amazingly high degree of scholarship and craftsmanship has been applied to the task of ensuring that this project becomes one of the most significant examples of the process of conservation in the country.
Peter Crone

The conservation work on these three charming, extroverted buildings has been assiduously undertaken. The banking hall, in particular, brings to mind an army of artisans exercising timeless skills. Elsewhere, there is evidence of patient and painstaking labour both in research and execution.
Rebecca Gilling

This is a truly sumptuous conservation, luxurious in colour, decoration and extraordinary craftsmanship. It is astonishing that within this restored magnificence, the present-day banking necessities of electronic information technology and occupational comfort flourish contentedly.
Neville Quarry

A faithful restoration of the three buildings, carried out with great care and thought. The materials are the originals or recreations of the originals. Alternative materials have not been substituted. Modern services have been cleverly concealed.
James Taylor

LUNA PARK, MILSONS POINT, NSW

HASSELL MAHER/PAUL BERKEMEIER AND McCONNEL SMITH & JOHNSON
PROJECT ARCHITECTS: KEN MAHER, PAUL BERKEMEIER, MARK WILLETT
DESIGN ASSOCIATES: PATRICIA GOSLING, EVERARD KLOOTS, ROBIN McINNES, MARK JONES

JURY REPORT

While the restoration of Luna Park remains true to the original, this is no museum piece. There has been conservation of the spirit and history of Luna Park rather than the fabric alone. The architects must be praised for their confidence in not intervening and for resisting the temptation to update the concept of a 1930s fun park — there are no computer games.

There is skill in the integration of modern requirements such as fire control, and the new and the conserved are carefully related. Many mediums (for example, graphics, lighting), not just building skills, are used to achieve deliberate effects — demonstrating the immense versatility and expertise an architect can bring to projects with non-building elements.

The Luna Park restoration is a good example of an increasing trend that architectural firms work in association, combining their skills and resources for a project. The restoration is exemplary in its execution of the conservation process, and the quality of the work (in accordance with the conservation plan) is impressive; for example the architects used oral history as well as documentary evidence.

1985   **THE WHARF, WALSH BAY, SYDNEY**

VIVIAN FRASER WITH THE NSW GOVERNMENT ARCHITECT

1986   **THE ADELAIDE CASINO**

WOODHEAD HALL McDONALD
AND BROWNWELL RANGER

1987   **UNIVERSITY OF TASMANIA CENTRE
FOR THE ARTS, HOBART**

GARRY FORWARD, FORWARD CONSULTANTS
WITH ALEX KOSTROMIN

1988   **POWERHOUSE MUSEUM, SYDNEY**

NSW PUBLIC WORKS DEPARTMENT, ARCHITECTURAL DIVISION
GOVERNMENT ARCHITECT: JN THOMSON
PRINCIPAL ARCHITECT: LIONEL GLENDENNING
PRINCIPAL DESIGN CONSULTANTS: DENTON CORKER MARSHALL

1989   **HYATT HOTEL, CANBERRA**

DARYL JACKSON AND HIRSCH BEDNER

1990   **THE PORT OFFICE, BRISBANE**

KERRY HILL (SINGAPORE) WITH PIE MARRS CLARE

1991   **SAVOY PARK PLAZA HOTEL,
MELBOURNE**

CURNOW FREIVERTS GLOVER PATTEN

1992   **ADDITIONS AND ALTERATIONS
TO WATSON BUILDING,
TRINITY GRAMMAR, MELBOURNE**

CRONE ROSS/PETER CRONE, TOM JORDAN

1993   **ADELPHI HOTEL, MELBOURNE**

DENTON CORKER MARSHALL

1994   **ROCKHAMPTON ROUNDHOUSE,
QUEENSLAND**

ALLOM LOVELL MARQUIS-KYLE ARCHITECTS

1995   **KERRIDGE WALLACE WAREHOUSE
RENOVATION, DARLINGHURST,
NSW**

KERRIDGE WALLACE DESIGN PARTNERSHIP;
PROJECT ARCHITECT AND INTERIOR DESIGNER:
VIRGINIA KERRIDGE

Projects within this category can be any recycled building
which displays a change of use and may be applied to any
class of building under the BCA.
Hence, this may include residential projects, alterations and
additions, refurbishments, and generally not be eligible for the
Lachlan Macquarie Award.

RAIA Awards Rules, March 1991

PRESIDENT'S AWARD

FOR RE-CYCLED BUILDINGS

REMEMBRANCE OF THINGS PAST

Even as they begin to rise from the ground, buildings start to self-destruct. An inevitable wearing-out begins with the moment of construction. Bricks crumble, stone fractures, timber rots, metals corrode, concrete creeps, plastics decompose, glass shatters. Buildings move. The motion may be infinitesimal, but is always happening. Materials expand and contract under changes of temperature, get wet and dry out, bend to the wind, oscillate on their foundations and are abraded by the passage of people. Many of these processes are very slow. They may be accelerated by natural disasters: lightning, floods, earthquakes, spontaneous combustion or by deliberate abuse. Such forces of destruction can be delayed by human intervention: attentive maintenance, repair and rejuvenation. A simple, lazy way of destroying a building is to pay no attention to it. To cause a ruin, do nothing. Let doors sag on their hinges, floors warp, walls buckle, roofs fall, ceilings drop, windows pop, surfaces delaminate, fittings rust, gutters overflow, drains block. Vermin will scramble in — munching, crunching, clogging, splitting. Debris accumulates, accidental fires start or someone engages in a bout of arson. Another development site becomes available. Otherwise, although the cladding might disintegrate, the structure of buildings stays remarkably durable if protected from weather and fire. The plain fact is that buildings can continue being habitable for centuries, or can be recovered from a ruined state by diligent refurbishing and reconstruction. Buildings are the outcome of imagination, energy, labour and capital. It is sensible not to squander that investment. So why do cultural or commercial investors ever let buildings degenerate to the point where they become useless for their intended purpose and are no longer safe to inhabit? There are many reasons. Most of them are not due to physical deterioration of the building fabric, but to a coalition of endemic cultural values, financial greed and fluctuations in notions of social prestige. As population pressures increase — fired by competition and the possibility of more intensive use: more people, more space requirements, more activity, more money — land values inflate. The value of an existing built investment may be less than the future value of a new investment on the same site. A new building, attuned to new uses and therefore more profitable, may be possible only if the old is removed. The commercial rationale is not hard to establish, once the initiating circumstances of an existing building become obsolete.

What could be the point in preserving, for instance, a wool store which no longer stores wool, a wharf to which ships no longer deliver cargo, a parliament house in which political assemblies no longer sit, a governor's mansion in which the representative of the Queen no longer resides, an amusement park which is no longer funny? There is a meaningful relationship between a shelter and its purpose, so that once the purpose is past, the architecture is no longer poignant. How can a new role be assigned to an old fabric without both being compromised? When, say, behind the remnant facade of a low-rise Edwardian office building there is erected a high-rise commercial tower, is not the early facade reduced to not much more stature than fake three-dimensional wallpaper — a curiosity with no integrity?

If every old building were to be demolished when incapable of producing an investment return, would a community suffer? Such a community would soon cease to have common goals, of anything other than expedient economic rationalism. If all old buildings were deliberately retained, how would needs for expansion of space be satisfied? Would all current owners need to be compensated for the loss of imaginable future profits gained by building anew? The offset to forsaking anticipated added value would have to be turned into a tax, or tax relief, of some kind ultimately payable by the entire community. Old buildings may have already absorbed the capital expenditure of their initial construction, but they are not free of charge.

RECYCLING

The discipline of the Lachlan Macquarie Award as a single category could not cover the entire gamut of architectural responses to the regeneration of the inherited building stock. Thus, the President's Award for recycled buildings was established in 1985. If an original building does not remain intact, or an 'authentic' restoration has not been attempted, yet the total project is an example of adaptive reuse, the work falls into the President's Award category. Rehabilitation of part or whole to enable a building's survival with at least a trace of a prior narrative is desirable. Most striking in the quality of the President's Award projects is the ingenuity with which the architects have accepted, to begin with, the challenge of converting sometimes quite unpromising extant material into buildings that are extraordinarily relevant and appealing in their new configurations. Many show such empathy with the original that one would be inclined to expect that if the initial architects were by some mystical rite resurrected into the current age to manage their own adaptations, they might do exactly what their latter day colleagues have done. For example, the Wharf Theatre, adapted from a cargo storage facility, has kept the faith of its crude timber progenitor, and taken it into another realm of unloading the performance arts. The main Adelaide Railway Station, once evocative of the magnificence of train travel, has had its former use shunted into a splendiferous casino in the same decorative mode; run-down hotels in Canberra and Melbourne shift into new gear; a string of classrooms learns contemporary lessons. Bygone architects, if transported into our own time, would be astonished and thrilled to witness the winners in this President's Award category: a Hobart jam factory fruitfully transformed into an arts centre; a redundant powerhouse recharging as an energetic museum; a harbourmaster's office riding the tide into a hotel restaurant; a rag trade factory transforming its cutting edge into a boutique hotel; a steam train maintenance depot in Rockhampton and a carriage repair workshop in Darlinghurst welcoming smart refits as offices. These are genuinely creative acts, worthy of special praise, for they incorporate the bonus of using existing building stock with sensitivity and intelligence — a crucial strategy for a sustainable future.

THE WHARF, WALSH BAY, SYDNEY

VIVIAN FRASER WITH THE NSW GOVERNMENT ARCHITECT

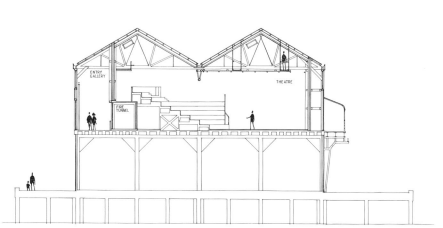

JURY REPORT

This is the first year for the President's Award as the category has previously been part of the Lachlan Macquarie Award.

The obvious difficulties in assessing conservation against recycling projects has led to the splitting of the awards. This award now seeks to commend projects which result in a new life for old buildings which do not necessarily have special historic value. It reflects the concern architects hold for their built environment and shows the way a skilled architect can provide socially and economically practical alternatives to demolition.

The winner of the 1985 President's Award, the Wharf Theatre on Wharf 4/5 at Walsh Bay in Sydney, is an excellent recycling project. The building dates from 1914 and is part of the development that took place in that area after the bubonic plague outbreak in the Rocks at the end of the nineteenth century.

The shore-based end of the wharf is a conventional brick structure addressing Hickson Street. The remainder of the building is of bold timber construction and is clad in timber. The wharf is part of the National Estate.

The recycling is masterful. The full range of facilities for the Sydney Theatre Company, including a major performance theatre and restaurant for the public, now function well, uncompromised by the finger shape of the host building.

Patrons can enjoy all the pleasure of the maritime surroundings and the wharf itself still stands modestly among its neighbours, unadulterated by its new sophisticated use. The challenge set by the length of the building to access and fire escape has been solved without fuss or complexity. The way the new function exploits the wharf and allows it to stand as a part of an historic group of buildings is very clever.

The result is unassuming, uses no gimmicks, is somehow engagingly shy yet confident. No false modesty. Just an air of rightness of purpose and place.

JURY REPORT

This project called for an imaginative re-use of part of the old Adelaide Railway Station. The Adelaide Casino project is an excellent example of the conversion of an old building for re-use and the Casino has become a major part of Adelaide's social fabric.

Heritage items have been preserved, the building has been enhanced with the minimal influence on the facade, and the venture works aesthetically and commercially.

The jury considered it a credit to the design team, the owners, the consultants and construction crews.

While it is true to say that a massive investment of money has helped in this case, there has been a major achievement in creating a spatial experience appropriate to the expectations of the old facades and the new users. The top floor restaurant is particularly successful as a place to relax from the drama going on below.

It is interesting to reflect that this is a building on a grand scale which works hard. The popularity of its bars and restaurants can be seen from the statistics: 2.9 million visitors a year, 16 million glasses of beer, and 290 thousand meals. At any one time 2,800 people can indulge in their gambling activities, yet the building never gives you the impression of such size or crowds. There is a human scale that works well despite the workload and the grand proportions of the building are well used, without creating an overpowering atmosphere.

The building itself dates from 1928 and is of architectural significance. It was placed on the City of Adelaide Heritage Survey in 1982 and is on the State Heritage register.

The jury was delighted with the skill used by the architects in capturing the essential style of the 1920s in the Grand European manner, with the Casino decorated in a classic way.

The owners' requirements for security and special equipment servicing has been handled in a subdued manner, but such devices as catwalks, concealed above the ceiling, for surveillance. This attention to detail was welcomed. Thoughtful use of existing materials, and a selective palette of new materials in harmony with the old, has resulted in a well executed adaptation, respectful of the heritage of the structure and highly enjoyable for the visitor.

DESIGN PHILOSOPHY

The Railway Station for Adelaide was designed in the late 1920s in the Grand European manner with elaborate use of materials and decoration in the classic style.

The principles set by the existing building formed a basis for the design philosophy of the alterations. This was reinforced by the re-use of many elements salvaged from the building and the selection of similar materials to those originally used. A feeling of elegant opulence was required which would enhance the public image of the 'European Casino'.

The aesthetic design philosophy was based on maintaining the impressive external elevations without alteration and adhering close to the elegant detailing of the building or its period for interior design and at the same time creating a functional modern casino operation incorporating state of the art technology.

In view of the heritage listing, it was imperative that the architectural integrity of the building be respected.

Internally, care was taken to restore, replicate or adopt details from or in sympathy with the original architecture. For example, many materials or elements from the old building were reused, refurbished or replicated.

The Great Hall forming the entrance to the Casino was totally refurbished, including new marble flooring and special lighting.

JURY REPORT

Here the task was to take a collection of old buildings in the most historically significant part of Hobart and give them a new lease of life as a creative centre for the arts and education. Never an easy task, it was made all the more difficult in this case by the nature of the buildings.

The structure is a mixture of timber and concrete and contains, we were told, the earliest reinforced concrete building in Australia. As a result of the new use, a considerable amount of strengthening has been required to the old structure. It is the way in which this has been done and the way in which the new uses have been cut delicately into the new building which makes this a fine architectural achievement.

There was a desire to conserve the feel of the old IXL Henry Jones Jam factory complex. Yet the punishment these buildings had seen was incredible. Years of storing hundreds of tonnes of jam had compressed many of the supporting timbers. Cold stores had been relined frequently, with the most unlikely of materials, including seaweed. The results were extensive dry rot, a problem virtually unheard of in Australia. The site lies on what was once a small island. Thus part of the buildings are on rock foundations, parts on very old Tasmanian blue gum stumps and

parts on reclaimed land, in one area reclaimed with fruit pips, a by-product of the jam production.

In addition, much of the original structure was not put together with great care. Posts were often not plumb and seldom in line. Much of the detailed laying out of wall positions had to be done on the site with chalk lines. Thus the design had to be incredibly flexible and avoid the normal practice of including the structure within the walls.

The National Jury's impressions were most favourable. From the outside the centre is quite unprepossessing, the external timberwork consisting almost entirely of painting the timber window panes. The surprise on entering is therefore considerable. The complex is deceptively large.

As will be clear from the photographs, the building contains a wide range of activities. Internally there has been considerable skill used in creating special points of activity. The only weak point of the design at the moment is a new entrance which faces a yet-to-be completed courtyard. Once inside the entrance, however, the user is shown a range of distinct yet related places. Some jolly good fun is evident in

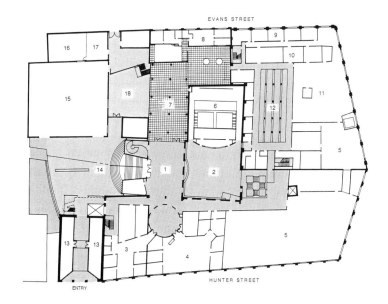

the re-creation of the dome of the Pantheon and in a formal screen to the administration offices. The cafeteria area is also bright and somewhat special, and forms a small village square off the main circulation spine.

A new stair has been inserted in the corner of the major L-shaped corridor. This stair is a finely detailed steel structure, very clearly not rising to the roof and very clearly separated from the old structure by a galvanised steel grid. Throughout all of the detailing and all of the materials used, here is a consistency of approach. This is not a pure restoration at all, but an adaptation of an existing volume to suit new activities. New materials seldom, if ever, touch old materials and where they do, great care is evident. New plasterboard walls have been toothed around old beams, floors and catwalks float through the spaces, and the architects have managed to make a space which is old and new at the same time.

While the new form of many adaptively reused buildings is a creation of what was already there, the Centre for the Arts starts from scratch. Here the change of use is total and has called for an

imagination, inventiveness and skill quite different from that used, for example, in the excellent Queen Victoria Building project in Sydney.

This retrofit is an exemplary example of interior architecture. It is successful because the fine architectural work is supported by the fact that the old building is very well suited to the new use and the architects have capitalised fully on this situation.

Art schools have a reputation for being hard on their buildings. They require immense flexibility, the quiet seclusion for creativity, contrasted with, for example, the tough and noisy environment of metalworking. In this building the whole range of experiences has been achieved frugally and economically.

There is no pretence to recreate a false history. This is a hard-working and economical building which, through the excellent and creative skills of the architectural team, will once more play a vital role in Hobart's cultural fabric.

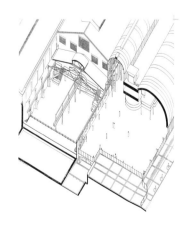 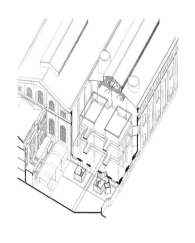 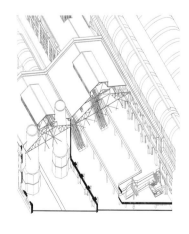 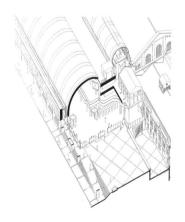

POWERHOUSE MUSEUM, SYDNEY

NSW PUBLIC WORKS DEPARTMENT, ARCHITECTURAL DIVISION, ARCHITECT: J.W. THOMSON
PRINCIPAL ARCHITECT: LIONEL GLENDENNING
PRINCIPAL DESIGN CONSULTANTS: DENTON CORKER MARSHALL

JURY REPORT

This is the first project ever to have been nominated for three categories in the National Architecture Awards, and that says a great deal about its quality and national significance. This project demonstrates clearly why a city's old buildings, even such apparently unusable ones as an old generating station, are not always write-offs. In fact, as this project shows, they can become even more significant the second time around.

The Powerhouse used to generate electricity for the city's tram system and the cavernous space of the old building has been recycled and a major new section added. The result: a great place to visit, to explore and be transported back into a land of memorabilia.

Of course, the jury could have been captivated by the exhibits too but that would have been unfair. After all, how many architects get to use such magnificent props as space craft, trains and aeroplanes as interior modules. The reality is the building will remain a great project, even if all its displays were more mundane.

Being next to Darling Harbour has helped its popularity but the project would have been a success without this help. Architecturally it is interesting because of the skill in converting an old building, because of the fun created with the new building and because of the flexibility and quality of its display spaces.

Perhaps the most impressive aspect of the design is in the way it handles space. The forecourt provides a sense of excitement and anticipation, giving a most appropriate welcome to a building with varied and exciting interiors.

The design of the interior exhibition spaces is exquisite, brilliantly complementing and enriching the architectural spaces while providing a tasteful background for the myriad of exhibits.

The Sydney Powerhouse is exuberant, brash, exhibitionist and, above all, fun. Old and new blend well, but wisely the temptation to copy the old structure has been properly resisted.

Large numbers of people visit the Powerhouse but the planning of interior spaces is an important change from the norm. We are used to museums forcing visitors along rigid routes through an exhibition. The Powerhouse is refreshingly different, even confusing.

The visitor is left intentionally wondering if they have seen everything and thinking that a return visit would be worthwhile. This is a charm seldom found in contemporary work but well loved in traditional museums.

The interiors at the Powerhouse are dazzling. A *tour de force* of form, colour, shape, pattern and texture. Scope remains for change and growth, yet one is never left with a sense of incompleteness.

In an era which demands the separation of architecture, interiors and exhibition design, this project demonstrates that they are very much part and parcel of the same family. The result is stunning. Public acceptance and enthusiasm is overwhelming.

The Sydney Powerhouse is a powerful exhibit, an exhibition and a design centre. It will make a significant contribution to architecture in raising the general design consciousness of all its visitors in an entertaining and memorable way.

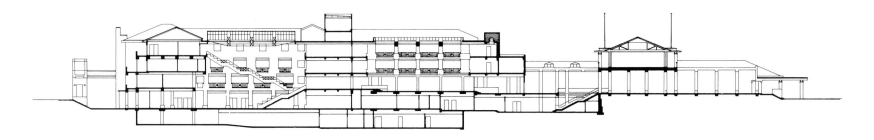

HYATT HOTEL, CANBERRA

DARYL JACKSON AND HIRSCH BEDNER

JURY REPORT

Many significant buildings of the 1920s and 1930s have disappeared, such as the Capitol Cinema in Manuka, ACT. The Hotel Canberra (now the Hyatt) very nearly went the same way. It is to the credit of all involved that it was rescued, and to the architects for re-capturing its original club-like domestic ambience. The new building surpasses the old in practically every respect.

While there is a large measure of successful conservation work in this project, it was given the President's Award mainly for its success in maintaining the original character of the hotel while vastly extending its size and use.

The original pavilion plan of the Commonwelth Avenue side of the hotel has been retained, and only marginal alterations were required to give a fine entry to the new hotel.

The clever aspect of the planning lies in the extension of the central circulation axis which now has greater functional and spatial variety. Particularly effective is the way in which the fall of the land towards the lake has been exploited, allowing an extra storey to be added to the new residential extensions without this dominating the appearance from Commonwealth Avenue.

INTERIOR DESIGN

The interiors of the hotel required a design concept to span the period between the original building and the new extensions, and give the hotel a single unified character. While the historical section retains its original layout and spatial character, the extension is planned with a more internal drama through the use of atrium spaces and internal courts. Careful thought is given to stairway forms, balustrade details and finishes; the employment of a cross-diagonal motif in the details reflects a characteristic of the original building, and provides a recognisable theme throughout.

The colours are warm but unobtrusive, with off-white walls providing a backdrop for carefully chosen artworks and graphics. A touch of drama is intoduced by the use of marble and granite finishes to the bathrooms. The bars and restaurants are treated with restraint, and blend well with the general ambience.

Roger Johnson and Bruce Bowden

THE PORT OFFICE, BRISBANE

KERRY HILL (SINGAPORE) WITH PIE MARRS CLARE

JURY REPORT

The Port Office in Brisbane has been given a fresh lease of life as the foredrop to the Heritage International Hotel. Designed by F.D.B. Stanley in 1878 as Brisbane's port office, this gracious edifice is a focal point amongst a cluster of historic and contemporary buildings in lower Edward Street. Its successful recycling has provided for 'Siggi's', the hotel's principal restaurant on the upper floor, with cellar and shops on the lower level.

The refurbished exterior, with the addition of the originally designed verandah wings, new internal mezzanine, bar, restaurant and well-handled stairs, is a most commendable result. Colours, fittings and furnishings have been chosen with care and produce a lively and inviting atmosphere. Already Siggi's has established a healthy clientele, testimony to the success of the renovation. The colonial theme is carried through to the re-established forecourt gardens.

The jury had reservations about the effect of the dark granite finish of the new hotel, which forms a massive backdrop to the Port Office. Fortunately there are other old buidings around to form a precinct with which the Port Office can be more at ease. This precinct, in turn, leads to a new waterfront of integrated design by the same architects. So, in a sense, the building has an external role to perform beyond being an attachment to the new hotel. As such, the recycled Port Office exudes an independent character and a strong civic presence.

Roger Johnson and Helen Wellings

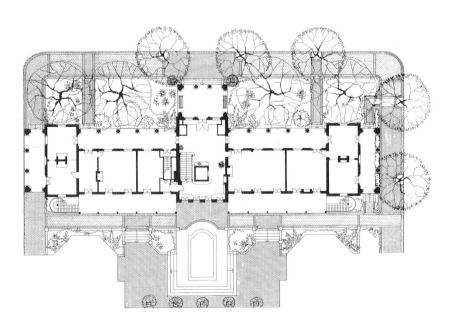

SAVOY PARK PLAZA HOTEL, MELBOURNE

CURNOW FRIEVERTS GLOVER PLATTEN

JURY REPORT

An extremely competent refurbishment of a building of moderate historic interest. The architect's involvement as initiator of the project, then his follow-through, shows that he developed an excellent working relationship with his client.
Robert Caulfield

This building had suffered a number of changes of use and was sadly deteriorated. The architect took an entrepeneurial role, as well as a design role, in its renaissance. The recreation of a dignified and

new, reproduced and invented detail, have been blended without weak concessions to historicism is particularly commendable.
concessions to historicism is particularly commendable.
Tom Heath

This is a sensitively recycled multi-storeyed building from the 1920s, which has been completely gutted and rebuilt. The architect has taken great care in detailing, rethinking the idioms of the 1920s in new ways, expressing the feelings of the times, without resorting to reproduction. The result is a comfortable and inviting atmosphere in both public spaces and guest rooms. Some of the fit-out (not the responsibility of the architect) is a bit 'over the top'.
John Morphett

To have been able to bring this old building back to life, to have been able to meet the regulations and still have the essence, is an achievement. Attention to fire protection, clever air movement holes within doors and window panels and the selection of the old metal windows are all most appropriately designed to achieve a work which is not yet another replica of something else.
Glenn Murcutt

The gutting and reconstruction process took some four years, and enormous problems, such as an exteme advanced case of 'concrete cancer' on the facades had to be overcome. The result is a hotel of considerable style and individuality.
Helen Wellings

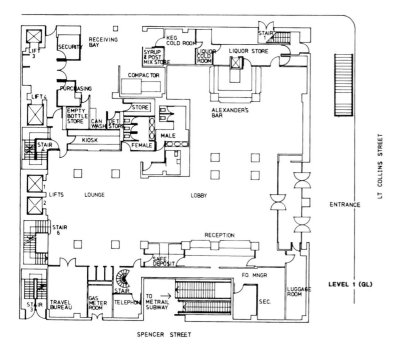

ADDITIONS AND ALTERATIONS TO WATSON BUILDING, TRINITY GRAMMAR, MELBOURNE

CRONE ROSS / PETER CRONE, TOM JORDAN

JURY REPORT

A very clever recycling of a wing of existing undersized classrooms into one with larger, more flexible spaces, and ancillary amenity areas. The design relates the building to the adjacent oval, forming an edge with areas for children to gather and to watch activities on the oval. The detailing is consistent with that of the new and altered work in other areas of the school, giving unity to the otherwise unrelated group of buildings.
Anne Cunningham

The architect has served the school well by providing an elegantly recycled building at much less cost than the alternative of demolition and rebuilding. Existing accommodation has been upgraded and enlarged by the addition of a two-storeyed covered walk which introduces a strong unifying element alongside the junior school playing area. The walkway is anchored by two imaginatively detailed stair shafts.
John Morphett

A clever and sympathetic alteration that saw a very basic school building skilfully restructured to accommodate more space and light, plus (the principal objective) more students.
Maggie Tabberer

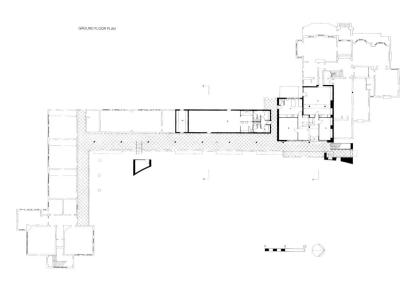

GROUND FLOOR PLAN

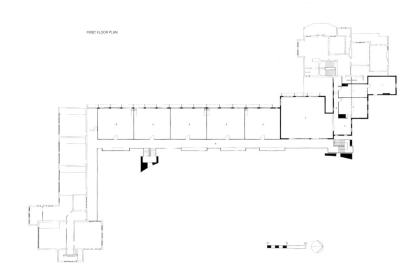

FIRST FLOOR PLAN

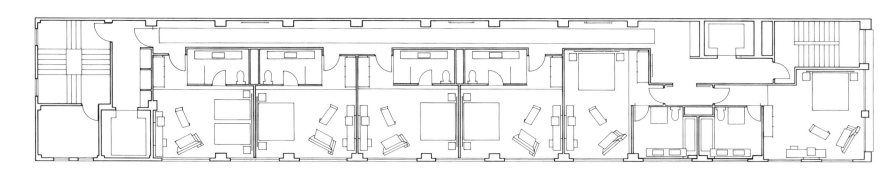

ADELPHI HOTEL, MELBOURNE

DENTON CORKER MARSHALL

JURY REPORT

An excellent location and untidy city street have elicited a sparkling and unique internal environment. Innovative stacking of uses and atypical room planning have allowed the infusion of light, memorable spaces and details, and exciting finishes.
Robert Cheesman

An ambitious and clever adaptation of a solid, unpretentious clothing factory into not just another boutique hotel. Unashamedly modern with more than a touch of Memphis, this hotel offers the opportunity for patronage by those who enjoy good design. While it may be somewhat severe in style, original elements such as the timber panelling on the bedroom floors provide softening.
Anne Cunningham

A superb conversion, maintaining the character of the existing building with the addition of new and old elements... most carefully thought through and beautifully detailed... a joy to experience.
Glenn Murcutt

The design vocabulary is austere, abstract and luxurious, with flashes of the bizarre, all exquisitely detailed to a consistent visual theme which emphasises the inherent material qualities of sheet aluminium, glass, mirror, stainless steel and wood veneers.
Neville Quarry

It's sharp, smart and very seductive. A far cry from the chintzy look favoured by boutique hotels. I have a problem with some of the room details... a coffee table that kills off little toes can take the shine off your stay. But the Adelphi and its designers are courageous trail-blazers.
Maggie Tabberer

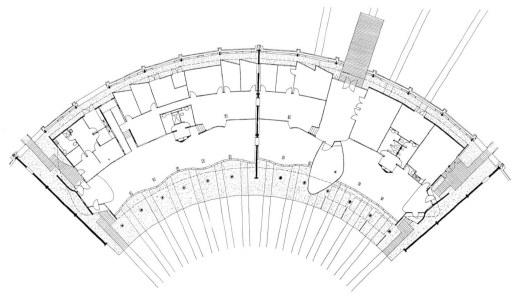

ROCKHAMPTON ROUNDHOUSE, QUEENSLAND

ALLOM LOVELL MARQUIS-KYLE

JURY REPORT

Purposely, the new building is in contrast to the old building but is recessive and complementary. This is achieved in colour, materials and line. The new building is largely concealed until one is quite close. However, the use of vertical venetians inside the new glass wall suggests a sun penetration problem.
Graham Bligh

The sensitive insertion into a portion of one of this country's most important industrial heritage buildings has hopefully ensured the future of the Roundhouse. The new structure of steel and glass sits snugly inside 14 bays of the rusty outer building — the volume between the new and old roof is an efficient ventilation/insulation zone.
Peter Crone

This is a delightful building, displaying an incredible richness of form, texture, light and shade. A large part of the success is in its recognition of the enormous charm and historical importance of the place and its credentials for survival and regeneration.
Rebecca Gilling

A vast annulus, divided into segments with sturdy radial brick walls, a pleated roof supported by a vigorous timber frame, with a corrugated iron cladding picturesquely aged like some antediluvian skin. Within this structure, trim steel and glass offices have been neatly shunted, an intervention that allows the original to retain its identity and offers the promise of renewed liveliness.
Neville Quarry

The original use of the Roundhouse is being respected and incorporated in the overall design. The original building is being brought back (slowly) to its former state and is not dominated by the new functions. It is a magnificently functional building of a bygone era being sensitively restored and recycled.
James Taylor

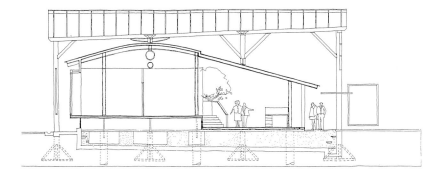

KERRIDGE WALLACE WAREHOUSE
RENOVATION, DARLINGHURST, NSW

KERRIDGE WALLACE DESIGN PARTNERSHIP
PROJECT ARCHITECT AND INTERIOR DESIGNER: VIRGINIA KERRIDGE

JURY REPORT

The result is a success — light, spacious, private and contemporary, it is a residence and office space with individuality related to the architectural language and identity of the original building and its use — curved roofs, sulky shafts as stair handrails and balustrades and recycled floorboards help carry the theme along. The striking colour palette extends the expression of contrast with the past and emphasises the individual forms and wall planes of the new.

The exciting sequencing of spaces, from the rusty front door onwards, is well-orchestrated through understated use of softly curved wall planes. Lyrical new spaces have been created within a very austere urban skin to create joyfulness using colour, form and materials sensitively — in particular the very successful use of plywood.

This old building has become a modern amenity in terms of solar design, light, security and attention to environmental performance with ridge and cross-ventilation. Unexpected balconies and courtyards reinforce the oasis effect in the city.

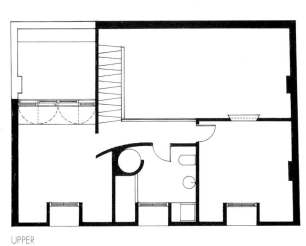

UPPER

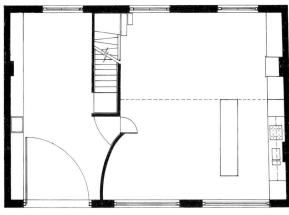

GROUND

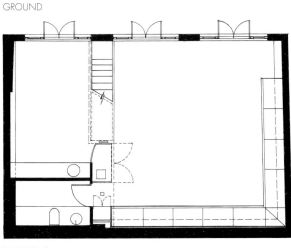

BASEMENT

1988 ONE ADELAIDE TERRACE, PERTH

FORBES & FITZHARDINGE

1989 91-97 WILLIAM STREET, MELBOURNE

DENTON CORKER MARSHALL

1990 HAMILTON'S PORSCHE CENTRE, MELBOURNE

AXIA

1991 SHELL HOUSE, MELBOURNE

HARRY SEIDLER

1992 QV1 BUILDING, PERTH

HARRY SEIDLER

1993 FRIENDLY BEACHES ECOLOGICAL TOURIST DEVELOPMENT, TASMANIA

LATONA MASTERMAN

1994 GOVERNOR PHILLIP TOWER, SYDNEY

DENTON CORKER MARSHALL

KINGFISHER BAY RESORT, FRASER ISLAND, QUEENSLAND

GUYMER BAILEY

1995 SKI N SURF, BLI BLI, QUEENSLAND

CLARE DESIGN/LINDSAY CLARE, KERRY CLARE, JEFF LEE, SCOTT CHASELING, TERRY BRADDOCK

Projects eligible for this category will be those providing generally leased or occupied spaces built primarily for commercial purposes and predominantly falling within BCA Classes 5, 6, 7 and 8 including alterations and additions. These buildings should have been designed for strictly commercial purposes, either for owner/client occupation or occupations by others on purely commercial considerations.
Examples may include an office building for a government, municipal or private/public company accommodation.

RAIA Awards Rules, March 1991

COMMERCIAL ARCHITECTURE AWARD

BUILT INVESTMENT

Because each building is a financial investment, it has a commercial aspect. Those buildings that rate in the commercial category have the special purpose of sheltering activities that themselves are intended to have a commercial output: the workers in the building need accommodation which will induce them to be productive and the building itself may be constructed as a commodity which gains value over time. To have a workplace which induces productivity may sound instrumentalist, like an excuse for unscrupulous reductions in working conditions to the most meagre and mean environment of minimum investment. The realistic situation is more like the reverse: people produce most effectively when their working conditions are invigorating. The totality of working conditions includes management and labour relationships that architecture cannot address, except insofar as the quality of the architectural environment may be indicative of the level of concern of the management for workers' wellbeing. Physically, there must be sufficient floor space, and light, air, acoustic and thermal factors must be suitably safe and comfortable — these are tangible measures which are calculable and controllable, and should of course be met in all buildings, whether commercially inspired or not. Individuals working on their own are special cases. Presumably they arrange their solo workplaces into configurations which are personally compatible, and which may suit no others — these are idiosyncratic concerns, and their internalised critiques are self-justifying. For groups of people working together, the workplace has demands additional to the merely physical. The workplace ought to be a social place, where workers can feel like citizens rather than just cyphers; where they can have the option of being gregarious or reserved; where their environment can serve as meeting place as well as a production line; where if innovation is appropriate, it is inspired; and where boring routine procedures, whether paper shifting or spanner shifting, can be relieved by the pleasure of the architecture of the place. The workforce is a segment of 'the public'. The criteria for a 'commercial' building are no less demanding than those for a 'public' building.

BEST INVESTMENTS

Among the nine Commercial Award winners, two are eco-tourist resorts, two are retail shops and five are large office buildings. Extremely purist conservationists may logically argue that eco-tourism is an oxymoron, since any man-made construction must damage the previous environment. The pragmatic riposte is that an environment that is not perceivable is not appreciated, and that which is unknown to the public is easiest for exploiters to damage. Between the absence and the exploitation lies the reality. Caring for the environment is an attitude that has to be cultivated. Human history suggests people easily slip into being predatory and polluting, and that it takes a deliberate act of will and foresight for them to be co-operative and resource-careful. Resorts which have a small toehold on the edge of a vast ecological territory can demonstrate to large numbers of people, by example and by educational programmes, a realm of knowledge and enjoyment which should lead to environmentally appropriate ways of behaviour. And, by the way, still allow a range of hedonistic pursuits. Danger lurks when the eco-resort becomes successful, and seeks to expand beyond the capacity of the fragile system within which it resides, or when too many resorts begin to dominate the pristine conditions they claim to protect. Friendly Beaches Ecological Tourist Development (1993) and the Kingfisher Bay Resort (1994) remain on the good side of the cusp between controlled conservation and untrammelled exploitation.

There are spectacular differences in both image and actuality between the goods sold by the Hamilton's Porsche Centre and the Ski 'n Surf shop. Their commercial contexts are poles apart. The Porsche is a machine of high technological refinement: exclusive, elitist, immensely expensive and sublimely beautiful. Surfboards, flippers, goggles, snorkels and sea skis are ubiquitous, accessible, relatively cheap and have their own casually functionally determinate grace — which cannot easily be said about the more decorative wetsuits. Each of these buildings responds admirably to its market and each, in its own way, is an architecture entitled to respect.

The office building is a machine for leasing in. The commodity is floor space, and its financial rate is determined by the location of the building and the quality of its corporate facilities and services. For a given building, which once located can hardly change its site, the proportion of rentable floor area compared with total area inclusive of circulation and service spaces is indicative of its likely efficiency in giving maximum rental return per element of construction cost. For whatever reason, if people do not like working in a building — if they avoid it as a workplace — no matter what the efficency ratios say, the building will be a commercial flop. The interior must be attractive and comfortable if an office building is to satisfy the occupants. So much for the inhabitants: what about the external observers, for whom the typical high-rise is more than an avoidable blip on the landscape? The major observable external component is size; then shape, which is a function of plan outline; skyline silhouette and height; the surface quality of the facade; and, most significantly from an urban point of view, the way in which the building meets the ground and mediates with the context of public space.

One Adelaide Terrace, Perth, has a semi-doughnut plan, the hole of which is turned into a glass-roofed atrium, animated by stairs plunging through the space. The exterior: a cylindrical extrusion up to five storeys, windows recessed between the exposed structural frame, and a horizontal sky profile. It sits surrounded by parkland, a suburban public domain. Shell House and QV1 extend the Modernist theme. Their plans have characteristically curvilinear and serpentine elements, extruded to 26 storeys for Shell, Melbourne; 36 storeys for QV1, Perth; in each case with windows set between the structural concrete frame, with an occasional double-height bay, so the facades are richly textured and mobile under sunlight. QV1 adds the encrustations of sun shades tuned to various orientations. Each finishes with a horizontal sky profile. Shell is set back generously on a corner site, but its public space is peripheral. QV1 engages the city deliberately and with affection — a swooping transparent canopy over the main southerly entrance and to the north a public court with palm trees, water in ponds and cascades, retail shops and open-air restaurants. In contrast, the floor plans at 91-97 William Street, Melbourne, and the Governor Phillip Tower, Sydney are austere rectangles, shafting up to ten and 64 storeys respectively. The William Street project has windows like square apertures sliced into a tattooed and pierced skin, with bay window, blade balustrade and string course body decorations. A shallow colonnade addresses William Street in a proper manner. Governor Phillip Tower has a more sombre surface, less highly differentiated, but still quite responsive to light changes throughout the day. Each finishes skywards with a horizontal edge, but the tower is surmounted by a flourish: an intersecting set of stainless steel vertical planes. The tower precinct is more complex, with heritage restraints requiring recognition of the archeologically significant site, preservation of Victorian sandstone terraces and a pedestrian right of way. On its northern plaza, the Museum of Sydney faces a superb civic space, made even more enchanting by the site-specific sound-sculpture 'Edge of the Trees' by Janet Laurence and Fiona Foley. These Commercial Award buildings demonstrate that commercial interests can contribute to the public domain.

JURY REPORT

One Adelaide Terrace is no ordinary office building. It is an expression of corporate identity for Woodside and a positive reinforced unity of purpose within the corporation.

Its internal spaces and circulation pattern create a feeling of sharing, reinforced by a staff bistro that enlivens the atrium floor in the manner of a Parisian café and a staff fitness centre adjacent to landscaped open space.

Yet in spite of this additional consideration for its occupants, it is not an expensive, highly finished building. The architects have demonstrated a remarkable ability to clearly identify, express and implement the essence of the design concept within the confines of a strict budget.

It is important in an urban design sense too. One Adelaide Terrace can be seen as a gateway to the central area and at the same time the point where the city becomes suburb.

The building shape follows the path of the Swan River giving the best available view for most occupants. The spectacular atrium space is flooded with natural light from above. Bridges leap across the open space of the atrium from the lift core to the office areas.

One Adelaide Terrace is an exemplary example of the contribution architects can make to even the most cost-driven commercial building.

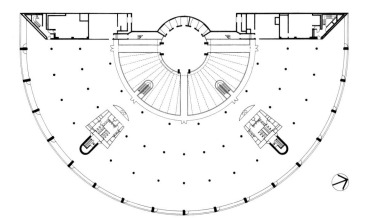

91-97 WILLIAM STREET, MELBOURNE

DENTON CORKER MARSHALL

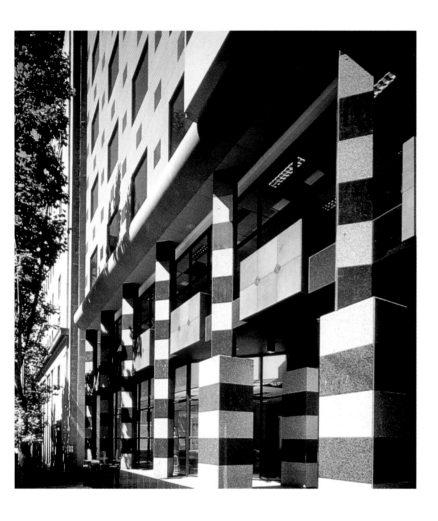

JURY REPORT

This building acknowledges the economic fact that in commercial buildings the facade and the entry lobby usually provide the only opportunity for making an architectural statement. Denton Corker Marshall have experimentally adapted curtain wall technology to insert precast panels and polished stone.

Unlike its mirror glass neighbours, the facade is rendered as a billboard sign for architecture (the architects even go so far as to pull the facade away from the box of offices behind). It has a base, middle, and top, also a cornice, bay windows and columns.

A human dimension is suggested in the windows that locate individual offices, the balcony handrails, and the delicate coloured stone patterning that measures scale. The facade also successfully makes connections with its neighbours in the street. In all, a very urbane, economical, little office building.

Peter McIntyre

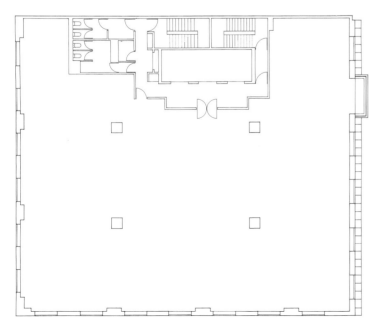

HAMILTON'S PORSCHE CENTRE, MELBOURNE
AXIA

JURY REPORT

A site liberally endowed, not to say encumbered, with historically significant industrial buildings would not be the first choice of every architect. When the buildings concerned date from the early decades of this century and the objective is to produce a setting which will facilitate the sale of technically advanced, luxurious and beautiful cars, the task becomes even more daunting. In designing and overseeing the construction of the Hamilton Porsche and Rolls Royce Centre, Axia have taken the boldest possible approach to these difficulties and have succeeded brilliantly. The new is uncompromisingly new and its glitter, gloss and elegance of detail are entirely appropriate to the new function. The old has been refurbished and adapted faithfully and then incorporated into the fabric as if it were any other significant element of architecture — a stair, say — which has to take its own place in the overall composition. Where the new and the old meet, the new touches the old lightly and respectfully, neither seeking to upstage it nor giving it undue reverence.

The symbolic possibilities of this unusual conjunction have been effectively exploited. The old dining hall, a showpiece of paternalist industrial relations, is a showpiece still, but now shows historic cars. A new kitchen has been installed so that it can again serve, on occasion, for ceremonious entertainment. The ambiguity of complete masonry buildings partly wrapped in glass is played upon with sensitivity and wit to produce a showroom space which is neither 'inside' nor 'outside' but has the best of both.

Like Michelangelo carving David from a block already partly shaped by another hand to another end, Axia have used old elements to generate a new and superior whole.

Tom Heath

JURY REPORT

The use of courtyards and garden spaces at low and high levels creates a variety of retreats from the hustle and bustle of city life. This building shows a superb understanding of spatial relationships and building construction and the commercial requirements of the client.
Robert Caulfield •

The modern office building presents the physical image of bureaucracy. Traditionally the order and restraint which are its natural characteristics relax at two points: where it meets the sky and the organisation becomes human enough to dream or play, and where it encounters the rough intrusion of the outside world, at the street. This one has its palace on the heights and seeks to present a welcoming face to passers-by. But it also provides nests of flying gardens in its austere flanks. Is something changing?
Tom Heath

This head office building is a fine example of the genre which the architect has developed with successive office buildings over a number of years. The curvilinear shape responds well to the site at the corner of the city and terminating Wellington Parade, a major approach road. The odd, wedge-shaped meeting rooms and dead-end lift lobbies are a disappointment, but generally the building design is very professional.
John Morphett

The building goes beyond the regular dreary plan of many high-rise offices through the introduction of two curved forms, curved access ways and simple internal partitioning finished in white plasterboard which augments the apparent geometry of the plan.

Gardens within the building have been well thought out and the roof garden contributes to 'living at the top', if that is what society wants! Structure is clear and generally straightforward, with a whacking column at the entry. From some aspects it reads quite decoratively; within it takes the view away and is a frustration. Shell House looks as though it was efficiently constructed, economical and reasonably scaled in its dress circle location onto the Yarra.
Glenn Murcutt

The sculpture at the Spring Street approach to Shell House invites contact, and the main lobby, featuring a mural by Arthur Boyd, continues this welcoming, friendly, spacious setting. Not so generous and friendly is the public eating area above, which seems gloomy in comparison. Thriving garden terraces provide a relief from the hard surfaces and office humdrum. It is pleasing to note that energy efficiency is an important aspect of the design of Shell House. The most remarkable feature of the design is at entry point — the tapered major support pier which gathers three columns into one support pier below. This pier is on axis with the approaching road, Wellington Parade.
Helen Wellings

LEGEND
1   High Rise Lifts
2   Executive Chairman
3   Meeting Room
4   Executive Directors
5   Secretaries
6   Reception
7   Stairs up to Exec. Conference Level
8   Roof Terrace
9   Covered Terrace

QV1 BUILDING, PERTH

HARRY SEIDLER

JURY REPORT

Perth's QV1 building is an elegant and sophisticated office building of the highest order. Its sophistication is apparent in all aspects, from its structural engineering and building services to the refinement of its architectural detailing. The well-resolved sunshading sets it apart from most office buildings in this country, but QV1 is surely more Australian than they. The ground floor is simple and uncluttered, without the alienating monumentality so prevalent at present, and the complex includes a public garden court whose popularity testifies to the quality of its design.

Jamieson Allom

One is tempted to write 'Harry triumphs yet again!' But it is hard to ignore Seidler's understanding not only of building as an art, but also of building as science. His ability to create interesting plans and volumes both within and without his buildings, and his skilful incorporation of state-of-the-art technology together with flexibility for future change, is generally unmatched in the profession. His response to climatic conditions, in particular the sunshading devices, is a hallmark of his work. In QV1 it is also worth noting the carefully considered handling of service areas and the beautifully designed bridge connecting the main building with the car park across the street.

Anne Cunningham

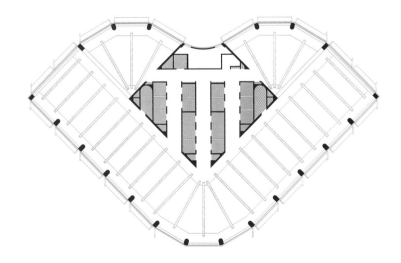

FRIENDLY BEACHES ECOLOGICAL TOURIST DEVELOPMENT, TASMANIA

LATONA MASTERMAN

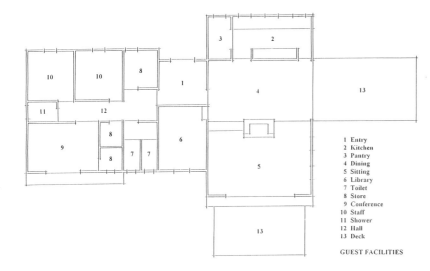

1 Entry
2 Kitchen
3 Pantry
4 Dining
5 Sitting
6 Library
7 Toilet
8 Store
9 Conference
10 Staff
11 Shower
12 Hall
13 Deck

GUEST FACILITIES

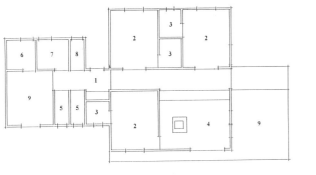

1 Entry
2 Guest Bedroom
3 Dressing Room
4 Sitting
5 Toilet
6 Store
7 Bath
8 Shower
9 Deck

GUEST ACCOMMODATION

JURY REPORT

Tourist developments incorporating architectural excellence, minimal environmental impact and principles of ecologically sustainable development are still to find their place in Australia. Friendly Beaches is a shining example, breathing the serenity and beauty of a coastal bushland setting.
Robert Cheesman

How refreshing it is to reward this commercial venture, which exhibits such a sensitivity to its site and in doing so creates a simple but beautiful group of buildings that even in winter positively entices visitors to seek and enjoy. Using a surprising economy of means and following the Queensland tradition of an inside-out stud wall and an unlined corrugated iron roof, the buildings elegantly tread lightly on this earth.
Anne Cunningham

It works, it feels right and it appears to go a long way towards addressing many of the issues properly argued by the environmental movement. Simple, minimal construction is employed throughout. The clear simple spaces are all made richer by beautifully realised detailing, framed views, flow of spaces, simple but beautiful furnishings.
Glenn Murcutt

This small tourist resort is an exemplary model of an ecologically sustainable environment, commercially viable to the growing demand for eco-tourism and adventure travel. Sites were selected where the buildings would not be observable from the beach and where there had already been disturbance to existing vegetation.
Neville Quarry

It's breathtakingly beautiful because it's so breathtakingly simple. It's both responsible to its environment and sensitive to its occupants, and its tranquility is infectious. Oh that we could all live like that.
Maggie Tabberer

GOVERNOR PHILLIP TOWER, SYDNEY

DENTON CORKER MARSHALL

JURY REPORT

The 'tower' building is a major city form representing the centre of commerce and corporate aspirations. This project is the latest state-of-the-art city building, equipped with all technology facilities, which outsteps competitors in design control/discipline, intellect and street consciousness.
Graham Bligh

This tower succeeds in a number of ways which may be considered as setting a new standard for high-rise design. The strong and consistent structural resolution is expressed from the ground, throughout, and up to the metal clad fins at roof level... the strength of an idea is most obvious.
Peter Crone

Undoubtedly a highly sophisticated and finely controlled work. The glass-roofed foyer feels almost celestial in its vastness. Beyond this however, my judgement is coloured by the fact that, to me, the office tower is an alien beast, the extravagance of which is inimical to sustainability.
Rebecca Gilling

The torso is a tower... which because of emphatic mullions and the banding of three floor heights into grids, shifts character from the relatively bland to the absolutely scintillating during the daily progress of the sun.
Neville Quarry

The structure is highly imaginative. The building has a confident look from close and from afar. The problem of the first 30 metres is well resolved and the combination of structure and aesthetics well resolved.
James Taylor

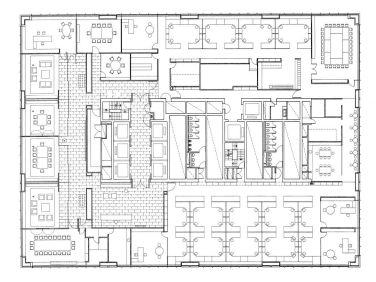

KINGFISHER BAY RESORT
FRASER ISLAND, QUEENSLAND

GUYMER BAILEY

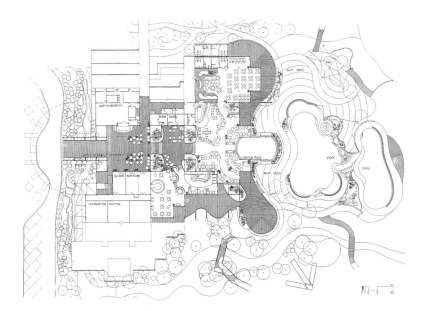

JURY REPORT

The project appears to be well received by the public and was in full occupancy during our visit. The control buildings work well without air-conditioning and low energy use is a factor in the design. The whole project has been sensitive to the peat/swamp nature of the site. All landscaping is native to the site. Effluent is fully treated on site. The only problem in high achievement is lack of cross room ventilation and absence of environmentally active water control.
Graham Bligh

The large, multi-functioned, central space is meticulously detailed with its curved plywood-clad roof planes lightly overlapping and forming clerestorey windows in between. By reducing structural forms to a familiar scale, the architect has achieved an intimacy which is not often found in volumes as large as this.
Peter Crone

This is not a demure work, for it intends to be festive and gathers its character from a deliberate and happy display of architecture as environmental spectacle.
Neville Quarry

The dilemma with a place as pristine as Fraser Island is whether and how much to develop and, while Kingfisher Bay Resort is hardly a tent, real care has been taken to minimise local impact while providing a holiday that combines a high degree of comfort and communion with nature.
Rebecca Gilling

A very good example of a resort hotel using its architecture to enhance the pleasure of staying. Respectful of its environment; it does not try to dominate but reflects the rounded hills in the background. Was obviously restricted to a budget.
James Taylor

SKI N SURF, BLI BLI, QUEENSLAND

CLARE DESIGN

LINDSAY CLARE, KERRY CLARE, JEFF LEE, SCOTT CHASELING, TERRY BRADDOCK

JURY REPORT

The result is a credit to the architect and the building teams — a rapid and confident architectural response to an immediate problem which reflects the needs of the operation for a focus, control point and identity, relating to both large and small numbers of people and well-considered in terms of climate.

It is a most successful solution with open planning and simple materials used superbly. The combination of simple design and structural expression, basic lightness, openness and colour create a casual yet vibrant atmosphere for the visitors, users and employees.

This stunningly simple leisure facility evokes the spirit of indigenous Queensland buildings with a strong emphasis on sparse structural resolution, lightweight cladding and detachment from the ground. The sinuous approach ramp provides an effective transitional element through which the act of arrival is cleverly celebrated. The shed and verandah forms which abut the major curved roof pavilion are located around the perimeter, seemingly growing out of the main volume. Skilful use of materials and colour articulate these forms. User satisfaction is high and the building provides all the amenities required for the commercial operation it houses, including a flexible series of spaces inside and out for day and evening use. The effect is light, lively and efficient, with no sacrifice in the detail or the finish. It demonstrates that a tight time frame and controlled budget need not inhibit an outstanding and environmental solution.

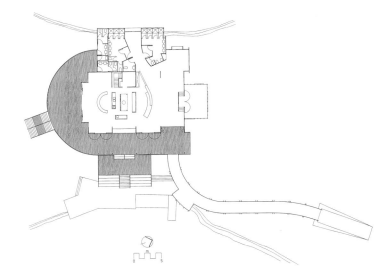

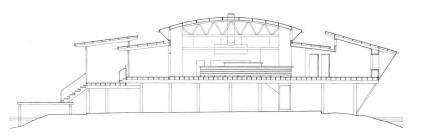

1988 **POWERHOUSE MUSEUM**

NSW PUBLIC WORKS DEPARTMENT,
ARCHITECTURAL DIVISION
GOVERNMENT ARCHITECT: JW THOMSON
PRINCIPAL ARCHITECT: LIONEL GLENDENNING
PRINCIPAL DESIGN CONSULTANTS: DENTON CORKER MARSHALL
INTERIOR DESIGN CONSULTANT: MARSH FREEDMAN
EXHIBITION DESIGNERS: NSW PUBLIC WORKS DEPARTMENT;
DENTON CORKER MARSHALL; NEIL BURLEY & ASSOCIATES;
CAMPBELLS; MUSEUM DESIGN DEPARTMENT

1989 **HYATT HOTEL, CANBERRA**

DARYL JACKSON AND HIRSCH BEDNER

1990 **SHERATON OFFICES, BRISBANE**

CONRAD & GARGETT

1991 **OFFICE EXTENSIONS AND PENTHOUSE, SYDNEY**

HARRY SEIDLER

1992 **FITZROY APARTMENT, MELBOURNE**

PETER ELLIOTT/MICHAEL McKENNA,
RICHARD EDBERG, JOHN TING

1993 **NATION APARTMENT, FITZROY, MELBOURNE**

NATION FENDER

1994 **ALLEN ALLEN & HEMSLEY OFFICES, SYDNEY**

MITCHELL/GIURGOLA & THORP

1995 **COLIBAN FARMHOUSE, LAURISTON, VICTORIA**

ROBERT McINTYRE

Projects eligible for this category will be those completed for a new building or forming part of the refurbishment of an existing building and can be within any BCA Class of building.

However it is intended that the projects submitted have resulted from a separate architectural commission specifically for the interior, and not just be part of the overall architectural commission.

Examples include tenancy fitouts in commercial buildings, separate commission for residential, hotel, restaurant or institutional interiors.

RAIA Awards Rules, March 1991

INTERIOR ARCHITECTURE AWARD

INTERIOR ARCHITECTURE

Excluding monuments and tombs, architecture is experienced from outside and from within. Most architects aim for an ideal fusion between exterior and interior, a continuation of the central concept or guide vision throughout all aspects of the project. Some architects may deliberately aim for the surprise of an internal space disjointed in character from that which is promised by the external evidence. In some buildings, especially those large enough to have separate compartments occupied by different entities, or where there is a later refurbishment, the architect for the overall building may not be commissioned for interiors. It is for such projects that the Interior Architecture Award is appropriate, but it is also available for architects who have designed both exterior and interior of a single project, for to eliminate that possibility would strike at the ideal.

DIFFERENT SCOPES

Three very different apartment interiors illustrate the range of responses: Harry Seidler's Office Extensions and Penthouse is a sweepingly sumptuous sculptural enclosure, generated by the curved shapes of the perimeter walls, and centripetally pinned by a stair spiralling through two storeys, all embracing a panoramic view to the west. Service facilities and bedrooms are planned with reticence so that they do not intrude upon the luxurious internal volume. Bob Nation's apartment strives no less to inject a powerful Modernist image, but the architectonic techniques are opposite to Harry Seidler's. The Nation Office and Apartment develops within the existing orthogonal interior of an old disused factory, whose external walls remain intact and relatively neutral as containment — except where to the east and south-west, glass walls are set back so that some open-to-the-sky space is borrowed. The floor reads like a plateau, on which the kitchen bench sits as an elegant technocratic quasi-altar; the storage space as unfoldable tabernacles and, in one corner, a baptismal bathroom glows behind translucent partitions. The other Fitzroy winner, by Peter Elliott, is also within the rectangular space of an old factory. Not only the walls but also the windows have been retained. An outdoor court, central double-height volume, judicious placement of skylights and sometimes skewed, sometimes enfilade, vistas invoke an exploration of space as sequence, compared with Nation's objects and translucencies and Seidler's curvilinear container. Far removed in location and in state of mind from the urbanites is the Coliban Farmhouse. This is a hand-crafted space, like the inside a piece of pottery, feeling numinous and resilient. Compared to the Nation apartment, it is quite at the opposite end of the spectrum of architectural expression. The similarity of the two office interiors — Sheraton Offices and Allen Allen & Hemsley Offices — is that for client types who are usually surmised to be conservative and rather fearful of full-bore Modernism, neither office refurbishment has receded into nostalgic Historicism. At Sheraton, the interior planning creates a rather orthodox series of rooms, with finishes and furniture of high quality and excellent taste, pleasantly contemporary. Allen Allen & Hemsley share the same meticulous visual values, but are rather more daring in accepting an interior environment of overlapping professional and social spaces. At the Powerhouse (1988) the new use (museum) is entirely different from the old (industrial), and while some of the robust character has been encouraged to persist, the interior is fundamentally new and discrete. At the Hyatt Hotel, Canberra, the architectural heritage and hotel uses were already established and although considerably extended, provide a positive architectural quality which has inspired the new.

As a variation on conventional design methods, inspired by the success of adaptive re-use, some architects have even contemplated imagining first, a hypothetically existing building, which can be adapted for a novel circumstance, while retaining its pseudo-original character. In the imaginary universe of all conceivable buildings one need only search for that example which most suits the brief.

POWERHOUSE MUSEUM, SYDNEY

NSW PUBLIC WORKS DEPARTMENT, ARCHITECTURAL DIVISION, GOVERNMENT ARCHITECT: J.W. THOMSON,
PRINCIPAL ARCHITECT: LIONEL GLENDENNING
PRINCIPAL DESIGN CONSULTANTS: DENTON CORKER MARSHALL
INTERIOR DESIGN CONSULTANT: MARSH FREEDMAN
EXHIBITION DESIGNERS: NSW PUBLIC WORKS DEPARTMENT;
DENTON CORKER MARSHALL; NEIL BURLEY & ASSOCIATES;
CAMPBELLS; MUSEUM DESIGN DEPARTMENT

JURY REPORT

In 1988, the Powerhouse Museum received both the President's and the Interior Architecture Awards — one of only two buildings so far to receive awards in two different categories in a single year.

(The other, in 1989, was the Hyatt Hotel, Canberra, also receiving the President's and the Interior Architecture Awards.)

The jury commentary will be found under the President's Award category, for it is relevant to both awards.

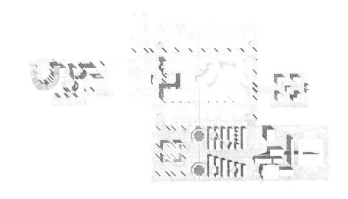

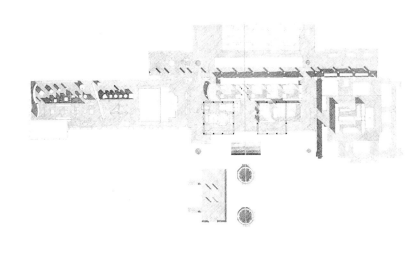

HYATT HOTEL, CANBERRA

DARYL JACKSON AND HIRSCH BEDNER

JURY REPORT

(See also under President's Award for 1989.)

The interiors of the hotel required a design concept to span the period between the original building and the new extensions, and give the hotel a single, unified character.

While the historical section retains its original layout and spatial character, the extension is planned with more internal drama through the use of atrium spaces and internal courts. Careful thought is given to stairway forms, balustrade details and finishes. The employment of a cross-diagonal motif in the details reflects a characteristic of the original building, and provides a recognisable theme throughout.

The colours are warm but unobtrusive, with off-white walls providing a backdrop for carefully chosen artworks and graphics. A touch of drama is introduced by the marble and granite finishes to the bathrooms. The bars and restaurants are treated with restraint, and blend well with the general ambience.

Roger Johnson and Bruce Bowden

SHERATON OFFICES, BRISBANE

CONRAD & GARGETT

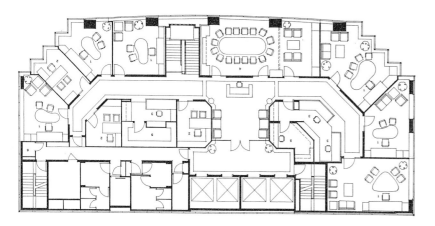

JURY REPORT

Beauty and function are perfecly harmonised in the Sheraton Asia Pacific offices, headquarters of the organisation's Asia Pacific region. In an age when corporate ostentation abounds, it is with surprised delight that one enters this haven of good taste.

Furniture, fittings and floor coverings eschew fashion for solid, timeless looks. Quality is apparent everywhere, from the rose-stained burled walnut veneers, and the specially designed low-energy light fittings, to the restrained carpet. The pale grey fabric wall-covering forms a perfect backdrop for the superb collection of Australian art and carefully selected and lit pots. The desks are kidney-shaped, their soft curves eliminating hard-edged divisions between executives and staff, company and clients.

These elements produce an expansive and relaxed ambience which renders a powerful but not overwhelmingly corporate presence. The design integrity is enormous and one can imagine the problems that had to be solved to produce such a calm interior.

The aesthetics are not marred by noisy, nasty objects which bespeak 'work', such as VDUs, printers and facsimile machines. These are hidden but within easy access when needed. Electrical work is concealed also. In these offices everything has a place to maximise efficiency and minimise stress-producing noise.

Client, designer and joinery contractor have all worked together to contribute to these spaces and it is pleasing to see the high quality of joinery work that can be produced locally. By any standards, the Sheraton Asia Pacific headquarters must be considered one of the most impressive office interiors in Australia.

Helen Wellings and Roger Johnson

OFFICE EXTENSIONS AND PENTHOUSE, SYDNEY

HARRY SEIDLER

JURY REPORT

Maturity and serenity, a governing sense of order which is enlivened by some playful digressions, mark this inner-city apartment. The world is not changing so fast that we need a new architecture every Tuesday. Continuity, reflection and refinement have benefits which are here clearly demonstrated.
Tom Heath

This interior is a very fine example of the mainstream of the modern movement in design. There is great generosity in the use of space with vertical and horizontal interconnections between spaces in the two-level apartment — very well handled. The sweeping curves of balconies and staircase are very effective and, in most cases, justified functionally by the way in which they define and enclose spaces. The architecture is complemented by the use of fine materials, careful detailing and the selection of furniture and artworks of the highest quality.
John Morphett

Early modern reproductions in furniture (antiques in fact!), modern works of art, granite tables and finishes, and a stunning outlook over Sydney Harbour all go to make this one of the most sophisticated apartments in the country — and perhaps one of the most expensive. Although this must be an extraordinarily expensive apartment, it does not become pretentious. The limiting of the working palette of materials, the spaces, light, outlook make for a very beautiful interior.
Glenn Murcutt

From its vantage point at the top of a sandstone cliff, the top two floors of Harry Seidler and Associates' office building offer a magnificent panorama of Sydney Harbour and well beyond. The stark neutral grey, white and black furnishings and fittings offer a perfect backdrop for the vibrant, colourful artworks by Hilarie Mais, Nolan, Stella and others. Extensive glazing requires effective solar control. This has been carefully considered with the installation of fixed vertical concrete louvres on the eastern side and wide overhanging balcony 'eaves' to give shade on the western side.
Helen Wellings

UPPER LEVEL   LOWER LEVEL

FITZROY APARTMENT, MELBOURNE

PETER ELLIOT / MICHAEL McKENNA, RICHARD EKBERG, JOHN TING

JURY REPORT

This is a very seductive interior indeed. The architect has made use of existing large spaces on the first floor of an old warehouse, with minimum intervention and maximum effect. The generosity of the spaces, the effective use of vistas and visual connections between rooms, the careful detailing and use of colour and the elegant fitout combine to make this an outstanding interior.
John Morphett

Unsuspected from the street and from the ground floor, the interior of this first floor apartment is a series of architectural events that are always vivacious, compelling the observer to stay in the particular space and simultaneously enticing further exploration. This is achieved by an artful use of skylights, by large glass doors opening onto the first floor terrace, contrasting with existing aperture-like windows, gradually revealed vistas from one room to another, and some exceptionally innovative detailing of the kitchen, fireplace and storage elements. The meticulous selection and placing of numerous artworks keeps them, and the architecture, integrated into a visual environment which remains physically sparse but aesthetically saturated.
Neville Quarry

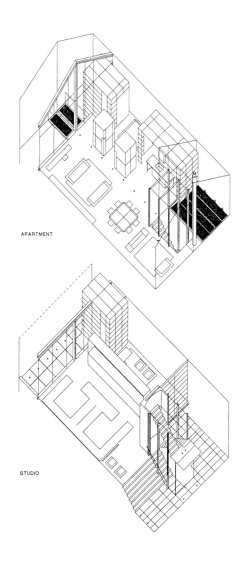

APARTMENT

STUDIO

JURY REPORT

This is a beautifully conceived interior space with exciting use of steel, glass and light. Innovative detailing, concealed storage systems and novel use of glass screens were delightful to discover.
Robert Cheesman

There is a certain irony that this exquisitely detailed office/apartment, housed within an old warehouse, sits across the lane from a housing commission estate. It is unashamedly elitist in its design and use but it does both extremely well.
Anne Cunningham

Whilst this work at first appears simplistic, it is far from it. Detailing generally is exceptional, with experiments in metals few jurors have witnessed. The palette is quiet and monochromatic, allowing ease for adjustment through the placement of sculpture or a change of flowers.
Glenn Murcutt

The facade bears an amalgam of traces of former owners and recent interventions — that is it shows character. The interior character is quite different — new, forthright, uncompromising, monochromatic, wonderful. The characteristic is light — pouring down from transparent roofs and walls, suffusing through translucent planes, scintillating off white steel frames and courtyard surfaces.
Neville Quarry

Outrageously glamorous and indulgent, this architect's own apartment makes no apologies to anyone, and why should it? It's by the man for the man. His love of light steel and glass are perfectly brought to play in one stunning space — and what a space!
Maggie Tabberer

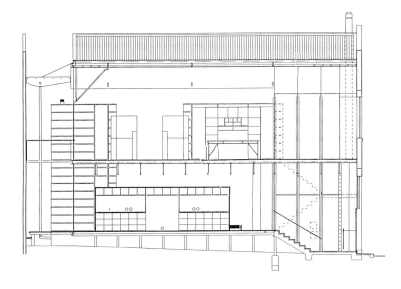

ALLEN ALLEN & HEMSLEY OFFICES, SYDNEY

MITCHELL/GIURGOLA & THORP

JURY REPORT

The adoption of an orthogonal planning matrix set the basis of a functional layout in a floor shape with inherent complexities. Circulation space is open, feels open and is cleverly varied while maintaining discipline.
Graham Bligh

Within an irregular, complex building plan, the architects have tied together ten floors of a major city office building with a combination of sensitive planning skills and a highly inventive resolution of details. It is obvious from the moment of entry that the architects had an informed and enlightened client.
Peter Crone

This project came as a real surprise, so unlike one's expectation of a stuffy, leather-bound legal office... in many respects, a commendably egalitarian approach has been applied to the layout. Offices are on the whole smaller than you would expect, but space has been used so skilfully that there is no sense of cramping.
Rebecca Gilling

Intelligent buildings are usually given that adjective because they contain elaborate electronic technology for communications, security, sound, temperature and humidity controls. These offices qualify on all those counts but go beyond to a higher level of distinctly humane intelligence... interior architecture of fastidious quality.
Neville Quarry

This would have been expensive, however 'cost effective' to client needs. The two floors of public space are generous and set the tone for visiting clients. The work areas are small but with functional office layouts.
James Taylor

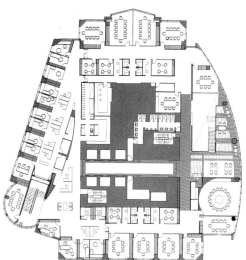

COLIBAN FARMHOUSE, LAURISTON, VICTORIA

ROBERT MCINTYRE

JURY REPORT

There is a timelessness in the presence of the building on its site as it relates to the various interior spaces and exterior views. With its massive walls and cavelike qualities, this interior embodies warmth, security and confidence and celebrates the marriage of architecture, art and sculpture in an often bleak but nonetheless beautiful landscape.

Inside the flow of space culminates in the hearth — heart of the house. The spaces are all handcrafted and consider the placement of specific items of furniture as well as including the design of various fittings.

The most outstanding feature is the consistency and depth of thought which has gone into the creation of different elements in the interior, from wall surfaces to light fittings to door handles to joinery — in some cases purpose-designed and fit for client requirements of furniture and paintings and *objets d'art*; in other cases expressing the integrity of the architectural concepts. The handmade quality of the masonry is complemented at the smaller scale through the wash basins, mirrors, soap holders, door handles and light fittings — all of which were designed and made by the architect — and the spectacular pattern in the bathroom which was designed by the client.

Interior design in this context is more than just the items — it is the linking and flow of the spaces and the creation of sequences of internal spaces which all have different vistas to the outside as you move through the house and get a progression of views across the property, leaving the occupant with a feeling of comfort, protection and livability.

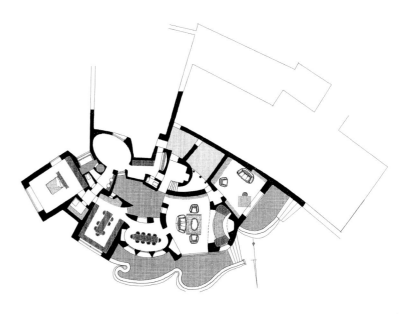

1988   **CIRCULAR QUAY AND MACQUARIE STREET REDEVELOPMENTS, SYDNEY**

NSW PUBLIC WORKS DEPARTMENT
ARCHITECTURAL DIVISION IN ASSOCIATION WITH
ALLEN JACK & COTTIER
CONYBEARE MORRISON & PARTNERS
HALL BOWE & WEBBER
LAWRENCE NIELD

1990   **YARRA PEDESTRIAN BRIDGE, MELBOURNE**

COCKS CARMICHAEL WHITFORD

1991   **WATER FEATURE, DARLING HARBOUR**

ROBERT WOODWARD

1992   **URBAN DESIGN OF THE CITY OF MELBOURNE**

MELBOURNE CITY COUNCIL
URBAN DESIGN & ARCHITECTURE DIVISION

1993   **BELL/BANKSIA STREET FREEWAY LINK, MELBOURNE**

COCKS CARMICHAEL WHITFORD WITH VICROADS

1994   **TYNE STREET HOUSING, CARLTON, MELBOURNE**

WILLIAMS & BOAG

THE ROCKS SQUARE, SYDNEY

TONKIN ZULAIKHA HARFORD

1995   **BUILDING 8, ROYAL MELBOURNE INSTITUTE OF TECHNOLOGY**

EDMOND & CORRIGAN WITH DEMAINE PARTNERSHIP

This Award is for projects of a civic or public nature which have enhanced the quality of the built environment for the general community.
These projects may not be buildings themselves, but must, as elements of urban design, be built work and may consist of courtyards, spaces between other buildings, plazas, fountains etc. and special and significant efforts of a civic nature by an architect.

RAIA Awards Rules, March 1991

CIVIC DESIGN AWARD 1988, WALTER BURLEY GRIFFIN AWARD

FOR CIVIC DESIGN

METROPOLITAN DELIGHTS

The residents of great cities appreciate the same urban qualities as do tourists: local food, entertainment, aesthetic artefacts, indigenous customs and public spaces. For citizens, the appreciation leads to pride in their community, and, as for tourists, sheer enjoyment.

In some older civilisations, urban spaces which are now peacefully enjoyed were once the loci of brutal histories. Some were sites of public executions of people deemed to be anti-social. Some were the places of violent demonstrations of rebellion, or of lavish pageants put on by the established dictatorial cliques: monarchic, municipal, military or religious powers, to divert the attention of the masses and subdue them with extravaganzas. Some plazas even hosted sporting events, like horse racing and skating (these days thought to be undignified or dangerous and shunted off to perimeter zones). In the gentler democracies, perhaps some residual collective memory of all that power display makes civic authorities wary of encouraging the notion of open public spaces in central urban areas, lest civil disobedience be encouraged by the convivial opportunity. Less threatening to the commonweal, the local controllers may be thinking, to establish streets as isolated conduits dedicated to small numbers of people travelling in hermetic vehicles, and to diminish the activities of pedestrians. Those furtive bureaucratic resistances are just my speculations, but I suspect there must be some deeply psychic motivations, other than parsimonious pettiness or imaginative incompetence, which cause city councillors, and sometimes planners too, to refuse to support or incorporate in cities, the sort of public spaces that the public is sure to enjoy. The RAIA Civic Design and Walter Burley Griffin Awards celebrate exceptions to these accusations.

URBAN FABRIC

Every building in a city should contribute positively to the public realm. Facades should vivify the enclosures of streets and courts. The intersection of a building at the ground, where private realm meets public property, should encourage a clear and engaging relationship between the two situations. Opportunities should be available for people to meet, join in a crowd, or avoid others and stay anonymous as *flâneurs*. Moments of concentrated sculptural energy should be invoked — monuments, fountains, vegetation, public furniture — to identify, articulate and bring social meaning to physical places. Cities are trading places — transferring ideas, attitudes, entertainment and knowledge, as well as goods and investments. In

Sydney, Circular Quay and its environs could be expected to lead to an exuberant feast of urbanity. At the harbour edge, business, entertainment and cultural precincts confront each other and mingle. Journeys are completed and transfers are made between ferries and bus, rail and taxi connections. On opposite flanks, the Sydney Opera House and The Rocks are mighty drawcards for citizens and visitors. People swarm between destinations and sometimes just stop in bewilderment. Such a concentration of scenography — natural and built — and activity — purposeful and accidental — transforms Circular Quay into a dynamic civic arena. The characters are always present on stage, but from time to time in this changing theatre of the public, the script falters. In the 1970s, Circular Quay had become, despite or because of its hustle and bustle, a chaotic and ugly mess. Competitions and plans for improvement came and went, to no avail, until with the spur of the imminent Bicentennial celebrations and a coming election, the NSW Government commissioned the Circular Quay and Macquarie Street Redevelopment. In due course the election was lost by the incumbents. Meanwhile an ebullient and creative team of architects from NSW Public Works and four private practices generated a strategy and an accomplishment. Much of the built dross was removed, but the urban dynamic was kept, in a brilliant balance of retention, rejuvenation and innovation. The public rejoiced. That, it seemed, would be that. But demands continue, from politicians and other experts. The situation is never static. East Circular Quay is under commercial redevelopment. Another architectural competition was held, just prior to another State election, which the incumbent party lost. So it goes. By the next election, the next generation of voters may want to retain the Cahill Expressway double-tiered open structure as a sort of proud portcullis keeping commerce at bay and framing the city. Options are always opening up — now that the Governor's house is to be democratised, a grand flight of steps from the Quay to the Royal Botanic Gardens would be possible, as magnificent a processional as the podium of the Sydney Opera House.

Back in 1988, the Circular Quay and Macquarie Street Redevelopment won the inaugural Civic Design Award. The following year, the award was renamed: the Walter Burley Griffin Award for Urban Design.

Transport connections won the 1990 and 1993 Walter Burley Griffin Awards. The Yarra Pedestrian Bridge transforms what could have been nothing more than a drab plank access into a series of progressions and delays, like a hesitation waltz, with bold shapes and a gently humorous structure. Its quality is such that it can even survive, over Christmas, the ultimate kitsch model of Santa and reindeer twinkling across its arch. In Sydney, Darling Harbour's buildings have many critics, perhaps on more socio-political than architectural grounds, but there is no doubting the appeal to the public who throng its open spaces. The most successful element is the awkwardly named 'Water Feature', for which Robert Woodward received the 1991 Walter Burley Griffin Award. A feature it is, but not in the perjorative sense of the word, as established by Robin Boyd. And a fountain it really isn't, if fountains must go skywards. The barest description does not do it justice: a circular hole with water running down in spiral sweeps over corrugated pathways. It is immensely popular, essentially because it is participatory; even the most anxious parents let their children walk in it when it dawns that they won't get too wet or drown. A masterpiece. One would like to see Woodward given a commission to design its inverse — a water mountain.

Cities benefit from coherent planning strategies to guide circumstantial decisions and promote lasting realisations. For doing that exceedingly well, and for bringing to fruitful recognition the Melbourne genre of street grids and greenery, and for specific precinct-making, tree-planting, traffic-calming and other pedestrian encouragements, the Urban Design Strategy of Melbourne prepared by the Urban Design & Architecture Division, Melbourne City Council, won the 1992 Walter Burley Griffin Award. The awards in 1994 and 1995 went to more 'architectural' projects; that is, to inhabited objects rather than concepts. Tyne Street Housing demonstrates that it is possible to continue, in a modern manner, the fine urban grain of an inner-city precinct, by keeping to an intimate scale and the contextual weave of laneways. The Rocks Square conjures genuine and new urban space of comfortable extent, within the existing built fabric, and surrounds it on two sides with new buildings which combine the delightful attributes of pergola, colonnade, verandah, gallery and atrium. The brickwork and timber detailing is robust and the filtered sunlight brings subtle changes throughout the day.

RMIT Building 8 brims with complex allusions and appropriations. The civic design aspect of this building is primarily the facade facing west towards Swanston Street. (The jury didn't mention the back lane, which to me is very Melburnian and urban in an esoteric way.) Certainly this facade brings a brilliance of pattern,

texture and colour, in a rich mixture of humour and bravura, to the walls of the street boundaries. As in Swanston Walk a few blocks to the south, if only in the street here, between Little Lonsdale and Franklin Streets, cars were excluded (trams could stay), what a vibrant urban space that could be! The student population of RMIT, plus readers from the public library could then meander about cafés on the west footpath, enjoying civilisation. Imagine too, the lexicon of east side architecture being argued over: mid-period Bates Smart & McCutcheon, residual John Andrews, rampant Edmond & Corrigan and the bizarre Storey Hall by Ashton Raggatt McDougall. As in ancient squares, one can imagine some dreadful (verbal) executions.

Covered walk to Opera House

CIRCULAR QUAY AND MACQUARIE STREET REDEVELOPMENTS, SYDNEY

NSW PUBLIC WORKS WITH ALLEN JACK & COTTIER, CONYBEARE MORRISON & PARTNERS, HALL BOWE & WEBBER AND LAWRENCE NIELD & PARTNERS

Circular Quay Architects: NSW Public Works Department, Architectural Division; Government Architect: J W Thomson; Assistant Government Architect: Andrew Andersons, in association with:
- For Circular Quay East: Allen Jack & Cottier
- For Circular Quay West: Conybeare Morrison & Partners
- For Opera House Forecourt: Hall Bowe & Webber
- For Sydney Cove Passenger Terminal: Lawrence Nield & Partners
- Macquarie Street Architects: NSW Public Works Department, Architectural Division, in association with Conybeare Morrison & Partners
- Urban/Landscape Design Consultants: Conybeare Morrison & Partners

Overseas Terminal

JURY REPORT

This revitalisation of the Circular Quay and Macquarie Street areas of Sydney is one of the finest acts of concentrated civic effort in Australia. In a short space of time, an area which had for ages been disjointed, both physically and visually, has been brought together as a cohesive whole.

It has consolidated Circular Quay and Macquarie Street in a way that a Sydneysider might say, 'I like being here so much, I can forgive the city any of its frustrations'.

It is the unity of all elements which makes this work. The components that combine to make this commendable project are:

Circular Quay West and refurbishment of the shipping terminal, ferry wharves, railway station and Circular Quay East; Opera House Forecourt; Macquarie Street South and Fountain; Macquarie Street North including the upgrading of Sydney Hospital facade; and Bicentennial decorations to Macquarie Street and Hyde Park.

Sydney now has a cosmopolitan atmosphere which has brought people back to the edge of its beautiful harbour. People who can stroll, stop for a drink or have a meal. These people have revitalised this area. The glass covered way from Circular Quay to the Opera House forecourt has made the best posssible effort to resolve a problem that has no perfect answer.

The Opera House forecourt cleverly develops a dual pedestrian system through changes in level, allowing equal facilities for those casually enjoying the harbour's edge and for those attending a performance.

Macquarie Street always has been a special part of the Sydney city centre due to its relationship with the Botanic Gardens and its many fine historic buildings. With the tasteful upgrading of the paving, streetscape and buildings it has now achieved its full potential.

The addition of the Bicentennial street decorations along Macquarie Street from Bridge Street to the War Memorial in Hyde Park was a difficult task, given that by day the decorations could look awkward and self conscious, and the designers have achieved exciting and memorable results. They improve with every visit. The total project is a work of civic design and social revitalisation that any city in the world could be proud of. Sydneysiders can be glad it belongs to them.

YARRA PEDESTRIAN BRIDGE, MELBOURNE

COCKS CARMICHAEL WHITFORD

West Elevation

East Elevation

JURY REPORT

This bridge represents a most important piece of urban design in Melbourne. The Victorian government has been opening access to the river frontage and has been following a programme of enhancement. Commercial office buildings of high density have commenced to sprout along the southern banks.

Pedestrian walkways have been created on both the north and south banks. This bridge forms the most important link between Flinders Street Station, the heart of Melbourne's public transport system, and the Southbank development, including the new Arts Centre.

To walk across this bridge is to experience a whole set of varying emotions. Firstly the city is viewed from a position never previously experienced by the citizens of Melbourne. It has a serene ambience and brings people closer to the Yarra than they would normally expect. The journey across the bridge can be broken by descending to the two artificial islands, which are so close to the water that one can lean down and dip one's hand in it.

The whole solution results from an extraordinary teaming of architects and engineer. It would be hard to find any major bridge built in Melbourne for which the architect has so obviously had such a profound influence. The design team has been able to overcome the most stringent constraints in relation to flooding and impeding river flow. Brilliantly conceived, the new pedestrian bridge makes one conscious of the space between the planned office buildings and the historically significant railway station. The discontinuity of our urban landscape has been overcome by this linkage.

The opening of access to the river and the completion of this beautiful and elegant pedestrian bridge is an event which should be celebrated by the people of Melbourne.

Peter McIntyre

WATER FEATURE, DARLING HARBOUR, SYDNEY

ROBERT WOODWARD

JURY REPORT

Nothing looks more beguilingly simple or has more power to enchant than a good fountain, and nothing of comparable scale is harder to achieve. Under today's low-maintenance conditions, complex technology is required to get them to work and keep on working; in this case also to make the make the visible pieces. Controlling the water, on the other hand, is a great art in the pre-Romantic sense. It requires long experience and the humility to approach each new task in a spirit of patient and painstaking exploration and experiment. Finally the fountain designer must consult the spirit of the place. Sydney is fortunate to have such a fountain.
Tom Heath

A delightful element in the urban landscape of Darling Harbour. The spiral streams carve their way into a saucer-shaped depression in the paving, with a gentle, natural, burbling sound, creating amazing diagonal weave patterns which sparkle beautifully in the sunlight. The project has been executed with great attention to detail. Every element has been well researched and developed from trial mock-ups. The result is beautiful in its simplicity.
John Morphett

This is a totally involving waterplay element for children and adults alike. It draws one away, in some ways tempts one successfully to pause and stray from one's course. The spiral saucer-shaped depression comprises ten paths for water, two for people, with water emanating at the headers at concourse level and slowly spiralling, rippling over the granite ridges and waves downstream. The waves move across the spirals at an angle and reflect from the opposite edge, making for criss-cross interference patterns which calm the sunlight, glistening lifelike in this carefully orchestrated path to the sink outlet. This pattern of water movement is outside the forms in nature; it is original in its concept and the whole experience makes for a memorable event in a thoroughly memorable environment.
Glenn Murcutt

Testimony to the success of the Darling Harbour Water Feature are the crowds of passers-by who constantly stop to gaze, then become mesmerised by its shallow, spiralling ripples. Designed for participatory and sensory experience, the feature engages people of all ages, inviting them to travel down any one of 12 circuits, two dry, ten wet.

From the centre, the waterplay can be viewed in more detail: the geometric patterns; the criss-cross wave action; the constant repetition of shapes; reflections on a sunny day. The Water Feature's simple and unobtrusive design also provides welcome respite from the more commercial aspects of Darling Harbour. While other structures within its precinct (such as the monorail, exhibition centre, overhead freeways, shopping complex and city scape) cause one to look up, out and into the distance, the Water Feature draws one in and downwards. As such, it is a delightful and worthwhile piece of urban design.
Helen Wellings

WALTER BURLEY GRIFFIN AWARD 1992

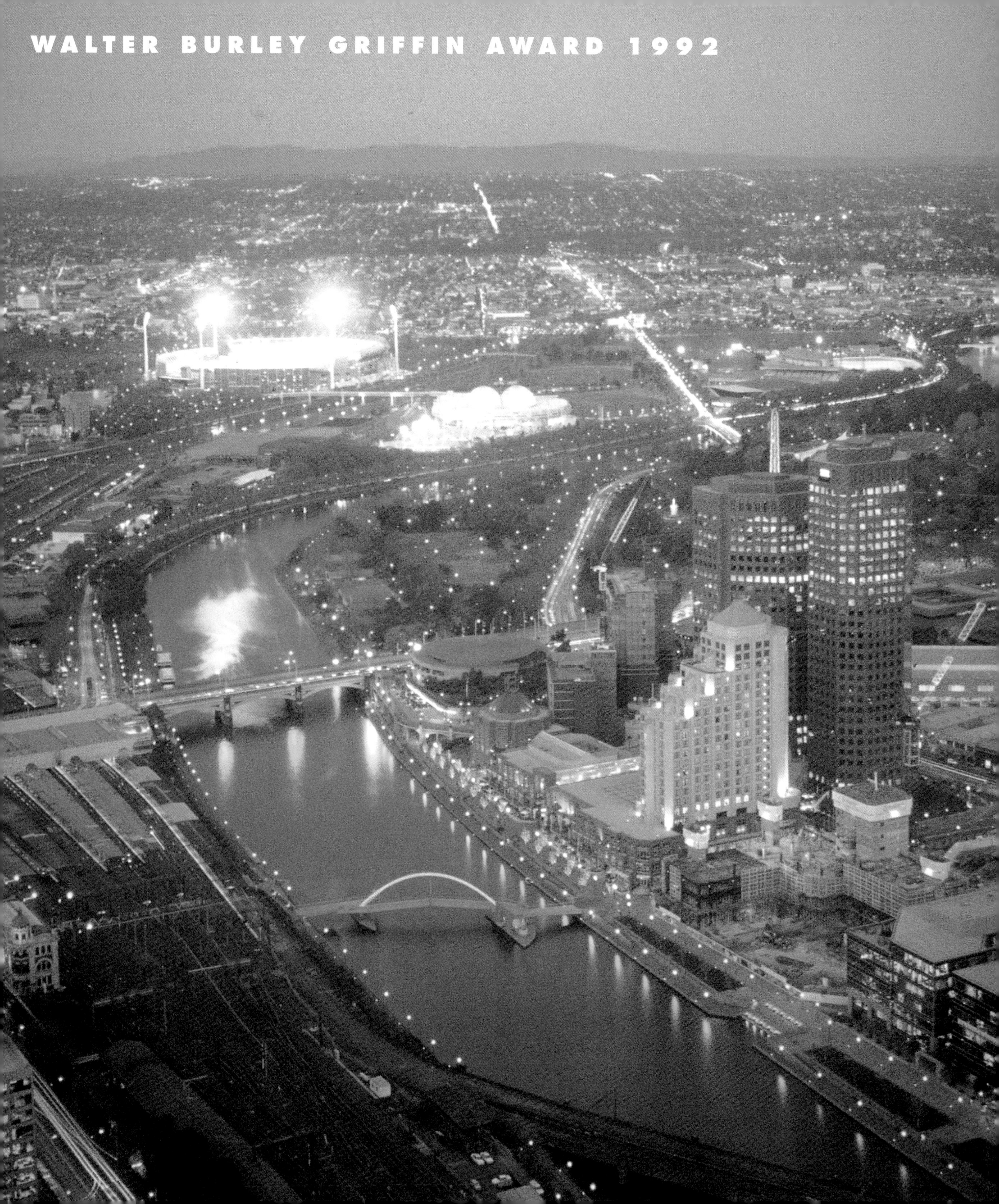

URBAN DESIGN BRANCH, MELBOURNE CITY COUNCIL: ROB ADAMS, MALCOLM SNOW, RON JONES, PETER HORNRIDGE, NATHAN ALEXANDER, IAN DRYDEN, PETER ABRAAM

JURY REPORT

This award is for a strategy plan carried out with dedication and commitment over a period of years. The plan adopts a consistent approach to the implementation of a high quality of urban design throughout the city. Because it has concentrated on economically achievable actions, implementing a set of principles which have been developed out of Melbourne's existing character and urban form, it is achieving considerable success over time. It is hoped that the strategy will continue to be supported.

John Morphett

If it's the little things in life that make the difference; in this urban design it's the many little things that make the difference. It is a commendable project that puts as much good design effort into a street trash can as it has into the larger undertakings, like city malls. All will inevitably enhance the profile of the city.

Maggie Tabberer

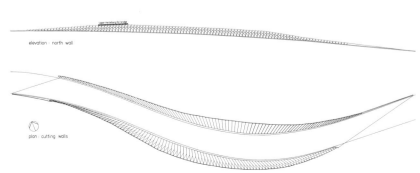

BELL/BANKSIA STREET FREEWAY LINK, MELBOURNE

COCKS CARMICHAEL WHITFORD WITH VICROADS

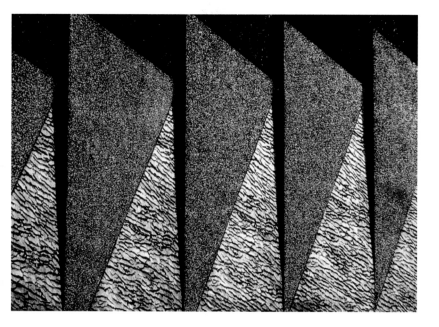

JURY REPORT

Civic design tends to focus on static or slow environments in consideration of character and impact. This design is an excellent response to the speed, curvature, topography and depth of the link. The design solution is essentially an art form which deftly effects a transitional urban space as a unique linking experience.
Robert Cheesman

Instead of an oppressive, graffiti-prone, grey, concrete-lined cutting, we have the opportunity to be visually rewarded in our journey. The experience is particularly enhanced by the different treatment of each side of the cutting, making travel in each direction a different experience.
Anne Cunningham

The design of the walls exploits the variable topography, alignment and spatial characteristics of the cutting with the convex north wall shaded and the concave wall absorbing the movement of the sun.
Glenn Murcutt

To make an incision in the earth can be a profound primeval ritual, the potent marking of a place. To make a cutting in the ground for some cars to pass through can be a mundane act, concerned only with achieving an appropriate curve and gradient. To give some magic to such a profane and ordinary event is not usual in roadway works, but this particular connection manages brilliantly.
Neville Quarry

I'm bowled over by the spirit and achievement of his project. What is basically a cutting to reduce traffic congestion has been treated to a spirited new urban design concept. It has enormous visual appeal with its vast, unmatched walls. It addresses safety, maintenance and graffiti and seems to win on all fronts.
Maggie Tabberer

TYNE STREET HOUSING, CARLTON, MELBOURNE

WILLIAMS & BOAG

JURY REPORT

The layout follows the street pattern and provides for public pedestrian access through the site without loss of privacy or security. The internal planning provides for small, home-based business, so continuing the exciting mixed use and meeting the growing trend. Internally, the units make good use of space, daylight and accessibility.
Graham Bligh

The architects have created an innovative group of buildings which demonstrate how good contemporary design can successfully integrate with an historical precinct without resorting to the often used stylistic gimmicks. The attention to scale, variation of form and colour compliments the older building stock.
Peter Crone

Despite the impositions of a small sensitive site over a public car park, this project makes a considerable contribution to current thinking about medium-density housing. A higher than average concentration is achieved, while maintaining spaciousness, variety and integration — both within the development and with its neighbours.
Rebecca Gilling

This is an exemplary model of high-density, low-rise, compact private housing, with a fine urban grain, tight pedestrian network and gently scaled buildings. Externally, the project meshes easily with and extends the respected Carlton typology of shared wall housing, avoids extraneous or coy elements.
Neville Quarry

An excellent example of what can be done on an inner-city site by mixing council requirements with a private developer. A highly successful project has been achieved.
James Taylor

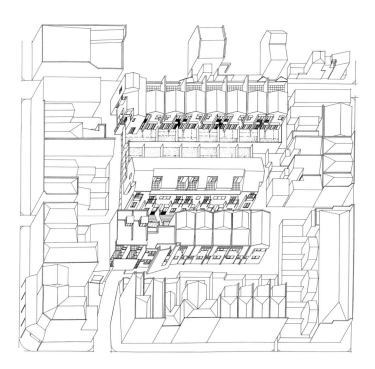

THE ROCKS SQUARE, SYDNEY

TONKIN ZULAIKHA HARFORD

JURY REPORT

It would apear that the project is environmentally responsible, particularly in its main thrust of recycling space. It is climatically sensitive. It would appear to be cost-effective, simply through re-use, simple intervention and high use. The whole blends well and lifts the overall quality. The open area is revitalised.
Graham Bligh

An urban zone of great delight. The sensitive use of brick, steel and timber combine to produce a softness which enhances the atmosphere of the precinct and creates an environment that is a delight to occupy.
Peter Crone

A rare thing in the heart of the city. The new works marry well with the existing fabric while maintaining their own integrity. No attempt is made to upstage the surroundings. The result is a harmonious whole made up of manifold corners of activity.
Rebecca Gilling

In an area noted for its nostalgic character, tourist orientation and sometimes sentimental overtones... this Rocks Square engages the historical context by being architecturally robust, sympathetic and yet unmistakably a modern contribution. It engenders a real focus for the wandering pedestrian and the observer of programmed or casual happenings.
Neville Quarry

A sensitive development of existing buildings which moves the adjacent road into an urban square. There is a simple, direct layout of shops at two levels and housing at three. The new two-storey glass roof structure ties the project together and gives the public shelter and a focus.
James Taylor

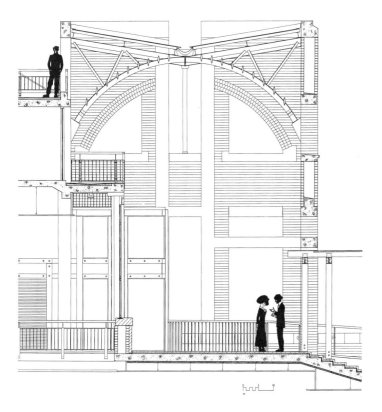

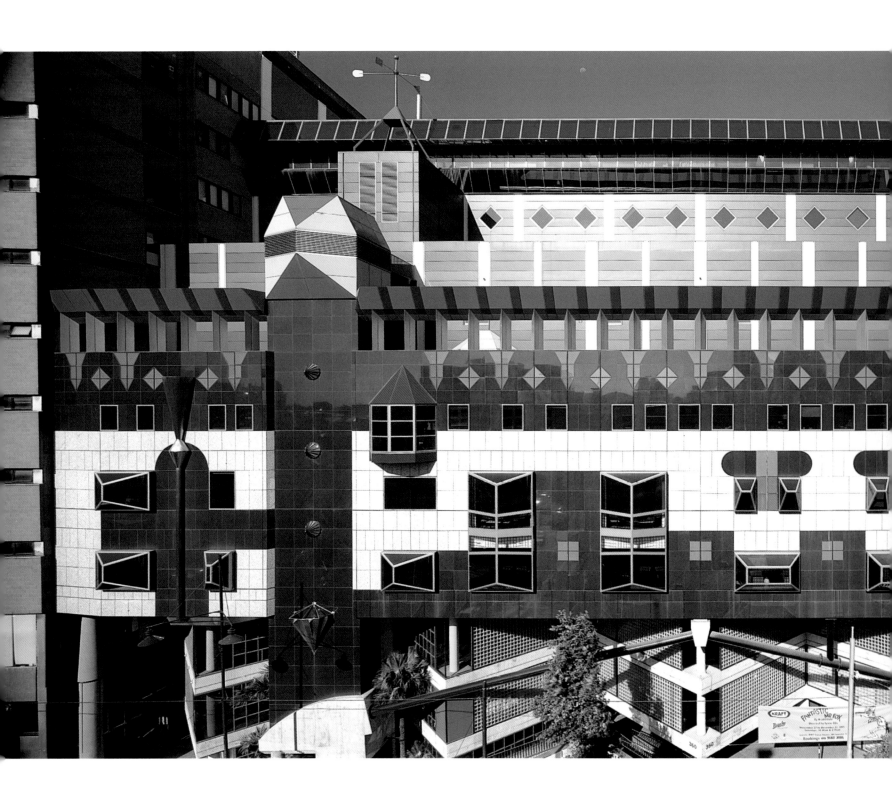

BUILDING 8, ROYAL MELBOURNE INSTITUTE OF TECHNOLOGY

EDMOND & CORRIGAN WITH DEMAINE PARTNERSHIP

JURY REPORT

It draws the city into the university and the university into the city both physically and metaphorically — it doesn't just look across the road at the building opposite but sets up vistas and frames views of a myriad of cityscapes. The facades enable the students and staff to reflect on the surrounding city from many levels and provide a visual link to these via the external balcony spaces...

Stairways, bridges, openings and pathways coincide to give new life to previously leftover spaces including rear alleys and lanes. The jewel-like facade enhances the civic nature of Swanston Street. Links with other buildings work at every level.

There is evidence of a driving philosophy which has succeeded where a similar challenge in lesser hands may have failed. The values of streetscape are acknowledged as the project makes its presence felt in the bustle of the CBD. Yet it shows that good urban design is not just limited to streetscape but considers circulation routes, entrances, courtyards etc. Building 8 creates a landmark precinct which demonstrates the ability to achieve better urban design through brilliant architectural resolve which is extended beyond the building skin into the city.

1991   **AUSTRALIAN CHANCERY COMPLEX, RIYADH, SAUDI ARABIA**

DARYL JACKSON MELDRUM BURROWS COLLABORATIVE

1992   **AUSTRALIAN EMBASSY, BEIJING, CHINA**

DENTON CORKER MARSHALL

1993   **AMANUSA RESORT, BALI**

KERRY HILL

MUANG THONG THANI INDUSTRIAL CONDOMINIUMS, BANGKOK

NATION FENDER

1994   **THE DATAI, LANGKAWI, MALAYSIA**

KERRY HILL WITH AKITEK JURURANCANG (MALAYSIA)

1995   **MERIDIEN BANK, ZAMBIA BRANCH OFFICES, LUSAKA, ZAMBIA**

WALTER DOBKINS AND ANDERSON & ANDERSON

Ultimately, the RAIA International Award exists so that work overseas by Australian architects can gain acknowledgement for outstanding accomplishment. This Award category should be read in its own context — that of international publication and the promotion of the worthiness of Australian architects. There is a less obvious but nonetheless relevant implication — that architectural education in Australia, if not necessarily responsible for, at least does not prevent, those who are accepted domestically, from shining internationally.

The process is imperfect, but when the ground rules are understood, it is a legitimate and valuable form of recognition.

INTERNATIONAL AWARD

WHY LOOK ABROAD?

The RAIA International Awards are controversial. To some people, the adjective 'international' might convey the misleading impression that these awards are made after the whole global realm of architecture has been considered. Of course this is not so. In pedantic fullness, the award title would read 'Awards given by a jury appointed by the RAIA, for architectural work done by members of the RAIA, constructed outside Australia'. In instances where an Australian firm has collaborated with another, it must be clear that the Australian firm played the dominant design role, for the project to be eligible for the award.

Documentary evidence of projects is submitted directly to the RAIA. No pre-award vetting or preselection happens. Because the international works are inevitably distant, there is neither the time nor the financial resources available for the jury to visit the locations (jurors have often been heard to offer to sacrifice their personal time if only their air fares were paid!). The jury is thus dependent entirely upon the evidence submitted by the architects — photographs, drawings, text. Skill in public relations presentations is no handicap. Of course, we know that the international reputations of some overseas architects have been established from work which only a few have seen in any reality other than photographs. Much under-graduate architectural education has to rely upon the surrogate presentation of examples that the student has not yet met.

ACCUSTOMED AS WE ARE

The appreciation of images unsubstantiated by direct encounter is part of the normal communication experiences of architects, deficient as it is in many respects. To assess via media messages is now a commonplace event. On the other hand, many architects will recall the disappointment or exhilaration that can happen at their first 'live' encounter, on visiting a building previously experienced only photographically. Errors of judgement are undeniably possible. Architecture that presents a powerful photographic image may, in situ, seem out of physical or cultural context. Giving an award without the reality of visiting the building breaks the necessity of the essential sensory experience from which architecture is perceived. For that reason some architects refuse to participate in assessing the International Awards category. Actually, architects are constantly in the habit of making judgements of work that they have not seen in the flesh — and they do this in full awareness of the dangers of misrepresentation. Architects continue to make remote assessments because if the architectural discourse were to be limited only to 'seen' works, the ambit of the discussion would be too narrow. Architects use photographs as evidence from which architectural qualities are inferred — and so long as the limitations of such inferences are admitted, I see no reason to censor discussion, or not to make judgements on the basis of what is clearly not the entire repertoire of picture, story and surroundings; provided of course that the basis of the judgement is overt and that deliberate distortions in the cause of art or propaganda are brought to the attention of the viewer. (Who but a person already culturally acclimatised can assay cultural relevance anyway, and for how long and under how many different circumstances must a building be experienced before a durable evaluation can be made? A very long time — and in this sense awards should perhaps be made only after a decade or two. Not surprisingly, architects like their awards when the building is still fresh and hot.)

Pragmatically, many national architectural organisations give certain awards for overseas works that may not have been seen directly but are of an already established reputation by publication. Who would negate, for instance, the influence of Frank Lloyd Wright in Europe, early this century, not through Europeans visiting Oak Park, but by the Wasmuth Edition of drawings of his work, published in Holland? Another instance: the Barcelona Pavilion, by Mies van der Rohe, reached heroic status almost entirely on the basis of photographs and hearsay. Indeed the pavilion was only intended to be temporarily used, for the Weimar Republic of Germany at the Barcelona Exposition of 1929. Architects agreed this little building to be of such exalted significance that it was reconstructed near its original location in 1986.

AUSTRALIANISM

The possibly unique 'Australianism' of Australian architecture is like the mirage of an oasis in the desert. Wonderful in appeal, the mirage disappears when approached too closely.

Fundamentally, the characteristics of a work of architecture are perceived through the physical sets of material that are used and the arrangement of those materials in extent, distribution and sequence. How much of what material, where, and in what order, are the instrumental decisions which architects make or assent to. When a group of architects make similar decisions about the physical sets that inform the character of the buildings they design, we may interpret these resemblances as a common approach — a school of thought or a visual style.

A school or a style of architecture may arise from a set of material commonly deployed, a set of arrangements consistently appropriate to a constant climatic or landscape condition, or a set of aesthetic or cultural values held in concert.

The Australianism of Australian architecture may be conjectured as evident in the use of certain materials: corrugated iron, tapestry brick, terracotta tiles, cement render or timber framing. But use of these materials is not unique to Australia. Architectural forms like barrel vault roofs, stiffened sails or slanted diving boards are not seen only in Australia.

In the outback and tropical zones of Australia, weather conditions and availablity of materials have furnished a gloss on the Australian ethos. In the suburbs, the single family house on a large block, semi-detatched and terrace houses have each evolved as a distinctly Australian type. In the cities, the forms of commercial and industrial buildings fuse domestic interest and international influences.

The impact of migration into Australia with people of cultures other than Anglo-Celtic has already become evident in food, fashions and cultural festivals. This multicultural influence is scarcely evident in Australian architecture. In a few pockets of concentrated migrant settlement, some recent buildings for special community purposes owe much to their overseas antecedents.

Generally, however, multiculturalism emerges as a collage — precast concrete 'Classical' balustrades between aluminium 'Victorian' verandah columns, beside arched garage doorways, overlaying brick veneer bungalows with tile roofs — not usually pretty but undeniably Australian.

Australian architecture still draws more upon international precedents for its inspiration than upon domestic cues. We have yet to arrive at that fusion of cultures and physical elements that generated the hybrid architectural glories of enchanted places such as Venice, Granada, Colombo or Los Angeles.

EXEMPLARS

The first two RAIA International Awards were given to buildings for Australian diplomatic services representing Australia abroad. Should such diplomatic buildings on foreign soil somehow represent Australia architecturally? Is it a creditable phenomenon that a particular artefact can signify an entire nation or even some part of it? Is a diplomatic building also a message of propaganda? Is it imaginable that a building could be so cleverly configured that any onlooker would immediately say 'That's obviously an Australian building'? Is there any diplomatic responsibility to present, architecturally, the architectural traditions of the host country? Is it conceivable that an Australian, seeing a televised image of an Australian Embassy, might say 'That's obviously a building in China, (or wherever) designed by an Australian'? Is it possible that a building could manage to have multicultural signals incorporated harmoniously within its singular form? Would the result be a clumsy hybrid? Quite possibly. Lest we forget: in history and contemporaneously, hardly any cultures are pure and unchanging. Neighbouring, invading or dominating foreign cultures always have an impact. No culture can exist for long without interaction with another. All extant cultures are contaminated by infections from others. Attempts to maintain 'purity' or 'authenticity' are futile. Multiculturalism is the norm of civilised existence, even when it is manifest in the antagonisms of war and terrorism. No culture is an island anymore.

In true Australian style, the Australian Chancery in Riyadh has a bet each way on state of origin and state of location. The hot, dry climate and the vibrant red earth of Riyadh suggest similarities with that of central Australia. Saudi Arabia has a lengthy urban tradition of architecture which has large areas of plain wall, small window apertures, shaded by lattice screens and double-height volumes, deep and dim within the interior, with subtle presences of water, which has not yet developed in Australia's hinterland. The Chancery in Riyadh uses these regional architectural devices, but tactfully eschews any attempt at indigenous ornament and, thus undecorated, would be not out of place in any arid zone in any country. The swimming pool, with the squash and tennis courts, give a sporting accommodation which is indubitably Australian. Paradoxically, this unusual Australian export to an exotic place has tangible architectural messages which would adapt sensibly in similar climates in the home country.

The colours of the city of Beijing (except for the Forbidden City) are like the Miesian palette — black, white, and shades of grey. The Australian Embassy in Beijing sticks to this sobriety of colour. The building contains a chancery, head of mission's residence, 33 staff apartments and recreational facilities. Denton Corker Marshall aimed to create a 'contextual container' that respects traditional Chinese city development, planning philosophy and local materials and skills, while exhibiting Australian qualities in landscaping and building materials, and reflecting the Australian lifestyle in the residential areas of the building.

Because of the double-coding that is fundamental to the function and imagery of embassies, the cultures and aesthetics of the guest and of the host countries, there is a large spectrum of design possibilities. There are analogous programmes and problems with tourist resorts, in which two possibly conflicting motives abound: the need to satisfy the tourists' urge to experience a different culture and exotic set of appearances, and the need to give the tourists sufficient comfort and respite from the unfamiliar, to enable them to feel relaxed, reassured and prepared to spend money to benefit the local economy.

The Amanusa Resort, Bali, and The Datai, a resort in Langkawi, Malaysia, have some common approaches. Dramatic sites with spectacular views have been chosen. Then the design imagination comes into play: architectural progressions over and between stone walls, under thatch or timber shingle roofs, steeply pitched with generous overhangs, through walls open to air flow and closeable with shutters — all this making theatrical and practical sense in a tropical climate. In such locations, intensive manual labour is a more appropriate construction method than high technology, and more economical. So it is perhaps inevitable that this expediency of selection and adaptation to locale and climate results in an architecture that has many of the characteristics of the traditional vernacular — which has of course itself been the consequence of responding to many similar design optimisations; except for the inhibition of having to house wealthy foreign tourists. There is much rationale behind this process and its realisation, rather than the simplistic sentimental notion of determining to 'reflect the traditional'. Very likely, if the distinctive cultural clues of local artworks, ornaments and staff uniforms were erased, an observer would be hard pressed to identify which resort was in Malaysia, which in Indonesia.

These resorts deliver architecturally excellent versions of a building type — the *luxe-primitif* tropical resort. This paradigm, or exemplary model, is subject to local declensions which enable adjustment to the uniqueness of sites and specialities of particular customs. Although a type, the pavilion resort is always capable of indigenous or imported enrichment. The use or non-use of air conditioning is a paradoxical indicator of the status of a resort — the cheapest and the most expensive resorts use it least. The public areas in many of the most luxurious establishments use natural ventilation, unimpeded by walls and assisted, if need be, by overhead fans. There is usually the option to invoke air conditioning if there are storms or the humidity or temperature goes beyond the endurable. If a place can afford to be abundant in space, it doesn't need to be profligate with continuous energy use. Middle rank resorts air condition everything except the poolside. For locals, backpackers or overnight passengers dumped by international airlines, the 'budget' hotels air condition nothing. The feel of real air on the skin is often refreshing, even if it is warm, humid, and carries the trace of unfamiliar odours. To paraphrase an epigram of Gertrude Stein: When you get there, there's plenty of there there. What about the question of a resort 'authentically' reflecting local culture and specifically local architecture? The notion of a 'uniquely traditional architecture' begins, upon analysis, to deconstruct itself. Only traditions which have already atrophied do not change. Living traditions are never totally untransformed by other traditions — they continuously absorb, adapt, alter and respond. 'Authenticity' as a concept readily diminishes into a mockery of the tradition that it is supposed to sustain. In *Tropical Architecture and Interiors: Tradition-Based Design of Indonesia, Malaysia, Singapore, Thailand*, architect and critic Tan Hock Beng suggests resorts may be construed as secluded enclaves — environmental symbols of excessive affluence. Resort architecture carries with it the inferred prestige of elitism and wealth. Pastiches of cultural stereotypes and picturesque symbols, one must agree, are often beguiling, increase local income and stimulate

moribund traditions. The award-winners avoid aesthetic trash, are not overwhelmed by nostalgia, and have the prospect of becoming an important source of inspiration for other, more modest, local works.

The Muang Thong Thani Industrial Condominiums, Bangkok, Thailand, are multi-storey, deep floor plate, flatted factories, for lease in the manner of high-rise office buildings. Each of the eight identical towers has a gross floor area of 65,000 square metres and includes ground floor loading and unloading areas, public spaces, a first floor car park for 140 vehicles, eight floors subdivisible into self-sufficient tenancies and a roof recreation club, with tennis courts. Whether this turns out to have been a superimposition of imperialist capitalism or an opportunity for better working conditions is yet to be demonstrated when the project is fully occupied.

The Meridian Bank, Zambia. According to a report in *Architecture Australia*, this project "includes offices, a banking hall, car parking, ancillary areas, training facilities, staff flats, a 'nsaka' which functions as a conference and entertainment facility, a public café and shop, a library/auditorium, boardrooms and a multi-purpose exhibition area leased to the United States Information Service. This was the group's first consolidated headquarters and the brief offered an opportunity to incorporate its collection of artworks by Zambian painters and sculptors. The architectural challenge was to provide a low-key and friendly landmark in a regional style appropriate to Zambia". Judging from the photographs, this is a vigorous work; a courageous attempt to fuse the imagery and customs of two distinct cultures.

As Tan Hock Beng writes: "how to become modern and to return to sources, 'how to revive an old, dormant civilisation and take part in universal civilisation'", is the paradox. How to partake, and evolve with dignity, is the challenge.

AUSTRALIAN CHANCERY COMPLEX, RIYADH, SAUDI ARABIA

DARYL JACKSON MELDRUM BURROWS COLLABORATIVE

JURY REPORT

The red soil and cubic form of Middle Eastern architecture are reflected in this fine building. The architect has shown that he can separate himself from the influences of modern Australian architecture and address the character of a foreign environment.
Robert Caulfield

Rob Mallet-Stevens, in his early essay on the influence of film on architecture, welcomed the notion of architecture as a well-lit stage for the human drama but warned against the superficial image-making which could follow. Embassies have a similar problem. The slightly fantastic courtesies of diplomacy have to be embodied and made credible. As well as one can judge from several thousand miles away, this building skates deftly over thin ice.
Tom Heath

This award was judged on impressions gained from drawings and photographs.

It appears to be a very romantic building, with beautiful references to traditional Arabian architecture. It sits well in the landcape and is impressive, without imposing an Australian aesthetic on the Riyadh landcape. The detailing is well-executed, with some delightful touches in gates, screens, etc.
John Morphett

AUSTRALIAN EMBASSY, BEIJING

DENTON CORKER MARSHALL

JURY REPORT

It does not descend to the kitsch representation of identifiable Australian icons, or borrow Chinese elements indiscriminately, but reflects an Australian way of life respectfully carried out in a Chinese city. This is done by the provision of both the more formal north-south axis and formal front to the compound, together with an east-west axis ending in the relaxed informal courtyard, and the provision of openings piercing the external wall, exhibiting an openness and interactiveness characteristic of the Australian way of life. Like most of DCM's work, the embassy exhibits beautiful and creative detailing.
Anne Cunningham

The Embassy complex exhibits qualities which are direct references to traditional Chinese architecture and planning. These qualities — such as the organisation of the plan, the spatial sequences and the use of enclosing walls — are interpreted in a very sophisticated way. The result is very far removed from the twee nationalism of so many embassies; here is a fine embassy of the modern world.
Jamieson Allom

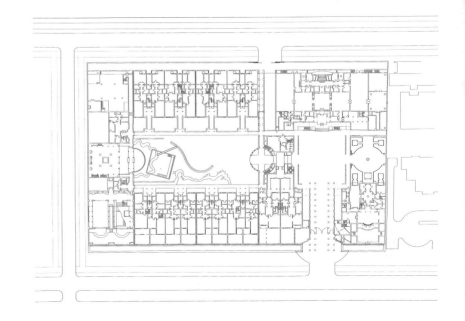

AMANUSA RESORT, BALI

JURY REPORT

This is, without doubt, a luxurious situation. It has often been the case that economic gluttony has led to aesthetic indigestion, but not so here. The architectural elements are relatively subdued, but fundamentally enriching. A number of tectonic schemes and devices are skilfully and vigorously manipulated. There emerges a strong sense of mass, platform and canopy, structural legibility and strength, clear proportional relationships between solid and void, some lovely conjunctions of materials — thatch, stone and water — and throughout, the ordering of spatial sequences, of steps, gateways, walls, courtyards, water and plant foliage, that encourage inhabitants to gain architectural enjoyment from their serendipitous journeys.
Neville Quarry

MUANG THONG THANI INDUSTRIAL CONDOMINIUMS BANGKOK

NATION FENDER

JURY REPORT

All of this is a huge step forward from the sometime degraded conditions of sweat shop cubicles in narrow alleyways, that was once the workers expectation in Asia. The MTT development is directed towards functional servicing and commercial viability, together with worker health, safety and amenity improvements. As an architectural statement, the industrial condominiums are simple and forceful: the cubical block is essentially a layer cake of strip windows and concrete spandrels, with concentrations of strong colour on the lift towers, around entrances and signage. The car access ramp to the first floor is expressed as a cylindrical drum, engaging one corner of the block. Ranks of suspended metal mesh platforms, currently empty but casting lively shadows, await the installation of air-conditioning packages by lessees.

Neville Quarry

THE DATAI, LANGKAWI, MALAYSIA

KERRY HILL WITH AKITEK JURURANCANG (MALAYSIA)

JURY REPORT

The project appears to bravely address the steep slope and forest in a respectful manner, though it is a major intervention. There is a synergy.
Graham Bligh

The openness of planning, relationship to the forest and well-sequenced spaces are skilfully arranged so as to heighten the effect of this picturesque theatrical concept.
Peter Crone

A resort of lip-smacking luxury and elegance, it has been sensitively positioned away from the beach to reduce its environmental impact. A harmonious relationship with the site and context using massive walls of local stone and towering tree trunks salvaged from clearing operations.
Rebecca Gilling

Given the evidence of photographs and on-site observations of architect-visitors, it is clear that this is a meticulously controlled work of architecture. From the hints of a local vocabulary of grand sheltering roofs on tall columns, this modest vernacular is transformed into a splendid set of forms and spatial sequences that are obviously luxurious and tantalising, yet serene in their extravagance.
Neville Quarry

A tasteful, exciting building using its site to the maximum by the use of stairs, paths, etc. The use of large timber components gives depth to the spaces and colour.
James Taylor

MERIDIEN BANK, ZAMBIA BRANCH OFFICES
LUSAKA

WALTER DOBKINS AND ANDERSON & ANDERSON
PROJECT ARCHITECT: WALTER H. DOBKINS

JURY REPORT

The building acknowledges precedents set by earlier colonial models in its celebration of humanising elements through inventive detailing of sills, screens and doorways. The cleverly articulated form appears as if it is a building within a building — a crisp, white, modernist object within a red, fragmented shell. The red responds to the colour of the local earth, while the associated use of black responds to the strong image of black-limbed trees in a vast, dry landscape. An innovative roof truss system has been adopted, using timber members with steel junctions; all finished in the bank's colours of dark blue and yellow. Another successful innovation is the integration of a natural ventilating system within the banking chamber. This is an example of an architect working sensitively within a local culture and construction environment. While other large commercial offices in developing countries often ignore or at best pay lip service to local traditions, this building embraces indigenous crafts and techniques, works with the climate and seeks to attract passers-by rather than exclude them. The architect's solution demonstrates ways of bringing indigenous culture together with current international banking requirements. This approach deals with the two most important aspects of architecture — the cultural environment and the natural environment. The result is strongly rooted to its site and regional conditions and ought to be a model for environmental performance, particularly where electricity and water supplies are not reliable.

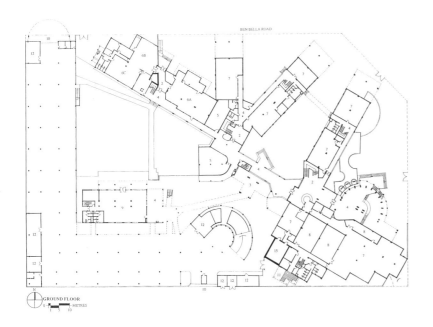

GROUND FLOOR

1982   EDMOND & CORRIGAN

FOR ARCHITECTURAL THEORY, RELEVANT TO THE AUSTRALIAN
REGIONAL CONTEXT

1983   MINISTRY OF HOUSING, VICTORIA

FOR INNOVATIVE DEVELOPMENTS IN PRACTICE IN
AREAS OF COMMUNITY INVOLVEMENT

1984   NO AWARD

1985   EDWIN CODD

FOR INNOVATION IN ARCHITECTURE

**1986   COMMONWEALTH DEPARTMENT OF
HOUSING AND CONSTRUCTION,
ANTARCTIC DIVISION**

FOR ANTARCTIC CONTAINERISED BUILDING MODULE

**1987   DAVID ALLEN OF CULPIN
PLANNING UK**

FOR THE ISMAILIA DEVELOPMENT PROJECTS, EGYPT

ACI Award 1982-87
The ACI Award was introduced in 1982 as a result of the generosity
of Australian Consolidated Industries International Limited and their
desire for an award to recognise new ideas in architecture.

ACI AWARD

THE ACI AWARD

According to RAIA President, Peter Johnson, at its 1982 inception:

Unlike the other awards, the ACI Architecture Award is not for an individual building but for a contribution by an architect or firm to architectural development in a specific area. The area nominated will vary from year to year and this first year it is to be awarded to 'the architect or architectural firm making the most outstanding contribution to the development of architectural theory expressed in completed buildings, having particular relevance and significance to the Australian regional context'.

In the first year of the ACI Award, the criteria related to the notion of being relevant and significant in some 'Australian' way, and embedding that quality in buildings. The buildings which Edmond & Corrigan had completed to that date certainly had qualities which were not characteristic of any other country and not like most other Australian buildings. No one has yet satisfactorily defined Australianism, except in retrospective terms — that which is done in Australia, by Australians, for Australians, surely must be Australian? Peter Corrigan had, since student days, argued for an approach to architecture that would grow from an acceptance of the primacy of Australian culture, independent of imported ideas. But this did not mean a retreat into isolationism. Corrigan began with the obvious: the Australian condition of suburbia, which intellectuals, aesthetes and social planners seemed set upon disparaging, but which the inhabitants perversely chose to enjoy. Edmond & Corrigan were no doubt heartened that they received in 1982 both the inaugural ACI Award and a Commendation for a house they designed in Kew (there being no Robin Boyd Award given in that year). Despite this early apparent acceptance into the canon of the establishment, and despite many awards subsequently from the RAIA Victorian Chapter, it was not until 1995 that Edmond & Corrigan won another national award — the Walter Burley Griffin Award for their RMIT Building 8. During this time, Edmond & Corrigan have continued to be active in practising what they preach. And what, exactly, is that? Their mode of thought is not just some local scrap of larrikinism. It has a legitimate heritage. Before Modernism had congealed into the orthodoxy of the International Style and succumbed to pseudo-scientific determinism, there were some devotees, like Haering and Mendelsohn, who sought a more soul-searching expressionism, rooted in a belief about people and opposed to functionalist dogma. It is this sort of belief in an 'other' architecture which is heritage for Edmond & Corrigan. It is an idea which has had international currency, but which emphasises the inspiration of cultural locality. Aristocratic refinement is its antithesis.

The painter Jean Dubuffet was another 'other' who valued the marks of human character more than sublime beauty. In 1945 he outraged fine art connoisseurs with his grotesque thick-pigment portraits and statements like '...people who have a star or a shrub or a map of a river basin across their faces interest me a lot more than Greekeries and I don't think a little oak sapling is necessarily prettier than an aged oak, and a little numskull of a regatta yacht doesn't interest me as a dirty trawler full of cod does'. In 1957, Dubuffet declared: *'I cannot help feeling that the things closest to us, the most constantly before our eyes, are also the ones that have at all times been the least perceived, that they remain the least known and that, if we try to find the key to things, we are likely to discover in those that are the most copiously repeated'.* Edmond & Corrigan looked at what was closest to them, Melbourne populism. Encouraged philosophically perhaps by the continuity between high and low culture that was being noted by people like the sociologist Herbert Gans, the complexities and contradictions advocated by architect Robert Venturi, and the appreciation of suburbia by Australian academic Hugh Stretton, Edmond & Corrigan developed, from these anti-conventional premises, an individualist vocabulary from commonplace elements, collected into unique architectural arrangements. Rather than aiming for pedantic composure, Edmond & Corrigan promote an expression of cultural activity, diverse and hectic.

In 1983, the ACI Award was to an architect or architectural firm making the most significant contribution in the period 1980-83 to innovative developments in practice in areas of community involvement, having regard to the quality of service and the architectural quality of completed projects, whether in new buildings or in changes of existing buildings. The Ministry of Housing, Victoria made the following strategic statement, and received the award:

The essential means of achieving the Ministry's objective is in its community involvement in the housing process. This enables the clients to express their needs and priorities, and to have greater control over their living environments ... small scale projects which allow more individuality and user input. The Ministry is utilising a wide range of private and in-house architectural expertise. Some of that expertise is illustrated with projects such as Kay Street, Carlton, and Caroline Chisholm Terrace, Keysborough, Edmond & Corrigan architects; St Georges Road, North Fitzroy; Norman Day architect; Station Street, Carlton, Peter Crone architect; Nelson Road, South Melbourne, Robert Pierce project architect, and Emerald Hill rehabilitation, Adler and Engel project architects.

The Ministry selected bright young architects for this enlightened approach to housing and the courage of their choice has been rewarded. It is evident that these projects have an unusually vital and cheerful collusion with popular taste and enthusiasms. In retrospect, maybe some of the flamboyant forms owe as much to young architects' flirtations with post-modernism as they do with the unprejudiced exuberance of the suburbanites. That quibble aside, this was a public housing approach that genuinely brought architects and people together in common objectives, without the architect being the aristocratic dictator.

The year 1983 was surely a high point for community involvement and innovation. Architect Brian Klopper received a Commendation for his work on projects which utilised recycled materials, and seemed also to succeed in recycling opportunities for people on the edge of despair. Other worthy nominees in 1983 were Chris Johnson and Philip Rose, NSW Government Architect's Branch, particularly for their concept of user involvement in school building design; Roger Johnson in the ACT and Barry McNeill in Tasmania, for their separate contributions as practising architects and as insightful teachers in their own regions; and the Aldgate Primary School, South Australia, which kept community use in mind, for example in the design of the activity hall to incorporate canteen, toilets and covered outdoor area for general social occasions. Unfortunately, all these community concerns have to be put in the past tense. Now that governments are driven by economic rationalism rather than by notions of the common good, this sort of adventurous, co-operative and healthy stimulation seems to have disappeared from the State's agenda.

Perhaps overcome by the surfeit of brilliance in the previous year, in 1984 there was no award. Too much to expect of course, that innovation would submit to an annual routine.

No single person can claim to have invented the structural principle of the space frame. Edwin Codd, winner of the 1985 ACI Award, by compellingly shrewd rethinking of the configurations of members and joints, was able to manufacture a new version, with speed and economic advantages in production and assembly. Wisely he kept the concept, the realisation and the subsequent commercial company, within his personal control. Eddie's practical, imaginative and managerial abilities have turned his invention into the basis for an international business, an export initiative that makes its own success. In a 1996 update on progress, Codd writes:

Architects are in the best possible position to be at the leading edge of building technology. There is very little competition since research and development undertaken in the building industry, other than that carried out by building materials manufacturers, is minimal. The best use of materials and components is entirely in the hands of the architectural profession.

The 1986 ACI Award was for another technical triumph — a containerised building module for use in Antarctica. Peter Magill, Acting Chief Engineer, Australian Antarctic Division, Department of the Environment, Sport and Territories, brings information up to the present in reporting:

I believe the award was given for the ANARESAT buildings at Casey and Mawson. This was a single module building to house satellite communications systems. Subsequently, multi-modular buildings were built at Casey and Mawson to house the emergency power houses. With all the modular buildings the majority of the fitout was done in Australia and the units were transported and installed as a near-completed building on prepared foundations at the stations. Our standard insulated (cold room) panels were fitted to the exterior. There are about another 12 buildings at each of the three stations which are built with the standard AANBUS system (steel portal frames, insulated, lined and fitted out on site).

In photographs, the bright blue container module with its attendant Radome twinkling beside, on a gaunt terrain of grey rock and white snow under a neutral sky, is the epitome of surrealism — an abstract high-tech object in a realistic but improbable landscape. (I am reminded of Andre Lautremont's definition of Surrealism: The chance meeting of an umbrella and a sewing machine on a dissecting table.)

The 1987 ACI winner, Culpin Planning UK, with a team led by Australian architect David Allen, in their Ismailia Development Projects in Egypt, produced not designs for buildings, but an inspirational community system for empowering a deprived population by enabling people to secure land and build their own homes.

Since the end of the 1970s, Australian architects and architecture schools have not concerned themselves much with schemes for housing the dispossessed, whether in other countries or domestically. Refusal to engage with the imperialist mode may be felt to underlie the gesture, or maybe it was just plain self-satisfied apathy, but the impetus faded. For instance, with few exceptions, built projects destined to improve the housing situation of the Australian Aborigines have not been successful. To encourage a community to reach its own objectives and achieve self-determination is a social rather than design skill. Could it be that architects have too much of a professional inclination to focus on physical outcomes rather than community processes and objectives?

ACI AWARD 1982
FOR ARCHITECTURAL THEORY RELEVANT
TO THE AUSTRALIAN REGIONAL CONTEXT

JURY REPORT

The work of Edmond & Corrigan has provoked wide discussion in the architectural profession and has polarised attitudes of approval and disapproval. Often those who disapprove have seen only illustrations of the buildings (which they have not visited) and have failed to understand the context of suburban Melbourne in which the buildings are placed, the close relationship the buildings have to their context and the strong theoretical base and stronger convictions which lie behind the buildings.

The National Selection Committee had no doubts that there was a structure of ideas in the body of work for which this firm is responsible which is clearly and firmly related to the Australian regional context, albeit to a particular part of that context — suburban Melbourne — which fully merits the giving of the ACI Architecture Award.

The Selection Committee believes that the work is of considerable significance and that there is already evidence of the ideas generated by Edmond and Corrigan in the work of other, mostly younger, architects now producing work in this country, especially in the Melbourne area.

The approach taken however, has wider significance and will influence thinking about architectural problems in other places.

The following extracts from a statement submitted by the jury of the Victorian Chapter's nomination of Edmond & Corrigan to support the Chapter's nomination of Edmond & Corrigan for the ACI Award:

The completed buildings of Maggie Edmond and Peter Corrigan have stimulated ideas and provoked debate on the nature of architectural form and method in Australia.

In their architecture Edmond & Corrigan have provided new alternatives to that architecture which draws upon inspiration from the international style or from colonial and rural vernacular. They have become central to a movement involving debate, writing and design by younger artists.

In their approach to regional context, their work is notable for its renewed exploration of Australia's urban landscape, in particular its response to the ordinary architecture of the suburbs.

Edmond & Corrigan carry their exploration into a range of building types: houses, schools, churches, parish buildings — money for which has been mostly very limited. They have built low budget buildings which explore and develop everyday building techniques, putting together familiar elements in ways which challenge the suburbs while acknowledging them, giving suburban forms new meaning. The domestic elements employed in Edmond & Corrigan's three churches are an example. They have also explored dynamic plans in which complexity of function is accepted and expressed.

Edmond & Corrigan have widened the sources from which an Australian architecture can find strength and a sense of place. They have, as Jennifer Taylor has observed, provided 'the first mature example' in Australia of an architectural method which includes rather than excludes, which adds rather than reduces. In their expression of function and the recognition of regional context, Edmond & Corrigan accept that their work expresses the 'difficulty' in their explorations of Australian activities, needs and surroundings, seldom expressing 'easiness'.

Their distinctive view of an Australian architecture as expressed in buildings and in Peter Corrigan's writing has prompted a response in architectural debate by a number of writers both in Australia and overseas (in *Architecture Australia*, *Transition*, *A + U*, *Process*, *Architectural Review* and *Domus*). The significance of their work has been recognised by the following awards: the RAIA Victorian Chapter Bronze Medal for the Resurrection School and citations for the Resurrection Church, Caroline Chisholm Terrace and the McCartney House.

Edmond and Corrigan's work was chosen for the Australian Perspecta exhibition and for the Paris Biennale.

ACI AWARD 1983
FOR INNOVATIVE DEVELOPMENTS
IN PRACTICE IN AREAS OF
COMMUNITY INVOLVEMENT

JURY REPORT

The ACI Architecture Award 1983 was a difficult task. Within the National Selection Committee, a great deal of discussion took place on the significance of the public architect acting within a bureaucratic framework producing buildings to fulfil public expectations, considered in contrast with the private practitioner risking financial stability and reputation for the sake of architectural experiment or innovation.

Two significant aspects were considered in the decision to make the award to the Ministry of Housing, Victoria. Firstly, the Ministry's action in re-evaluating its approach which produced anonymous public housing, in redefining the nature of public housing and the role of the Ministry, and the conscious restructuring of its philosophies. The methodology of user participation, one which had proved successful elsewhere, was adopted as the basis of the new approach. Secondly, the architecture produced as a result of the re-evaluation is considered to be of high quality, and stands as an indication of the success of user participation in design.

The award is given in recognition of the success of the Ministry's role redefinition, and the decision to act in the public interest rather than in the pursuit of architectural expression.

JURY REPORT

A special jury of three was appointed for the ACI Award for Innovation. Like the National Jury, it went through a process of elimination, a process of visits and investigation, followed by a second conference to pick a winner.

The task facing the jury was a difficult one, and the large number of entries was very pleasing. It reflected very different views on just what is 'innovation in architecture', and left the jury with some hard decisions.

The unanimous verdict was for the highly innovative space frame concept from architect Edwin Codd. The jury was very impressed with this deceptively simple solution to a complex problem. It would be possible to pass this one over as it looks so easy.

It is not the use of the space frame itself which is new — it is the use of the continuous chord and the simple, even ordinary, way the parts are joined which is the innovation. Through decades engineers across the world have wrestled with this problem and come up with some good, even brilliant solutions. Eddie Codd's innovation eclipses them all and must have left a lot of engineers wondering why they hadn't thought of it.

Architect Edwin Codd comments:

The idea of being able to build a variety of structures from a kit of parts has appealed for a long time, but complex engineering and production have normally resulted in structures which are more expensive than traditional portals. This is not the case with the new system.

I have been involved in the development for four years and it now appears certain that the product will be marketed internationally because of the low cost, simplicity and the use of appropriate technology.

Just as in the fifties and sixties truss roof construction gave way to portal frames, it is possible that portals with their one way spanning limitations will succumb to this structural system.

Because the structural system uses cold rolled steel it is appropriate to construction in under-developed as well as developed countries. It uses less weight of material than conventional portals which will result in considerable economies as production levels are increased. As simple as the system appears, it is unique. All other space frames cut material to module lengths and use complex node connectors.

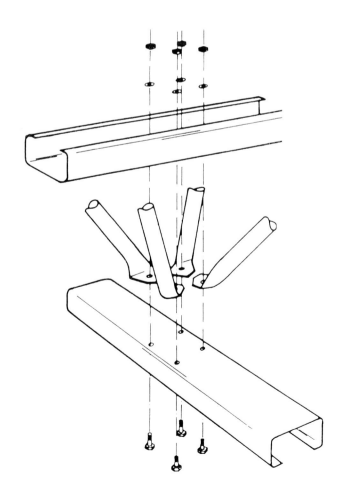

COMMONWEALTH DEPARTMENT OF HOUSING AND CONSTRUCTION (ANTARCTIC DIVISION)

JURY REPORT

The Antarctic is the coldest, windiest and driest continent on Earth. While this lonely continent is still pristine, hardly scarred by mankind's waste and pollution, it is also the most hostile. Unless suitable shelter is provided, research teams and explorers perish quickly.

To provide that shelter requires ingenuity and tenacity — ingenuity in conceiving new and more efficient ways for shelter and tenacity for applying those ways in the demanding local conditions. Transportation is limited to a few months of the year when specially designed ships can make their way to the edge of the ice-coated continent. Once there, there is no margin for error. This is no place to forget the bolts or bring the wrong sized spanner! Time is of the essence if shelter is to be completed by the first blast of a long dark winter.

Faced with these problems and a wealth of experience in the construction of Antarctic bases, it was thought opportune to look hard at future directions for construction. The ideal would be a system with minimal skilled installation requirements, impervious to the elements, and easily transported.

The solution was shelter in the modular scale of an international container, specially designed and manufactured for human habitation rather than for international trade. By using the standardised measurements and fittings, the modules could be easily transported — even with internal fitout — and required little work on the Antarctic mainland to convert from transport storage to workshop, dormitory or laboratory.

Preparation of the site requires no more than concrete footings with suitable locking pins for the modules to be lowered onto. In this way, a series of container modules can be linked to form a single building. The ability of the containers to stack also permits multi-storey construction which until now has not been a practical possibility.

Links between modules are provided by temporary wall areas, removed once the units are in place and sealed. Additional insulation is added externally, following the pattern of insulation systems already in use in Antarctica.

The jury was taken by the simplicity of the approach and the architectural ingenuity shown by the development team. The first practical application of this design resarch work will be the 12-module Upper Atmosphere Physics Building at Davis Base.

ACI AWARD 1987
FOR THE ISMAILIA DEVELOPMENT
PROJECTS, EGYPT

JURY REPORT

The jury was delighted to receive such a detailed and informative submission for the 1987 ACI Award for Architectural Innovation. The quality of the submission reflected the immense work which went into this project to house so many who have so little. This would be a worthy winner in any year, but in this International Year for Shelter of the Homeless (1987), it is even more appropriate.

This is essentially a story about housing. Through the skills of a small and dedicated team of architects and planners, many thousands of very poor people, who have lived in temporary shelter, have been able to build and own their homes at minimal expense. The efforts and leadership of the team and the hard work and dedication of the people of Ismailia have created a city to give pride and self respect to the poor.

The lessons learnt here in Egypt can be applicable throughout the developing world. This team, lead by Australian architect David Allen, has shown that there is every reason for these people to have hope and a sense of purpose and place in this world.

Three specific areas were considered by the jury to be particularly innovative.

Firstly there is the sheer persistence and tenacity shown by the Culpin team in producing the goods. Between 1978 and 1982 more than 5000 plots of land were created for residential purposes in Hai El Salaam, in Egypt. To do this in Melbourne or Canberra would be difficult enough; but in this case it would have been far harder. Before any plots could be released, extensive surveys were undertaken, a plan created and people convinced of the value and benefit of spending precious resources on this project. Negotiations with financial institutions must have been daunting even with the support of a government that set an interest rate of 3%.

All of this had to be carried out harnessing the informal skills of a workforce rather than a traditional design and construction process more familiar to us in Australia. These sorts of projects may be going on all over the world, but rarely have they been so clearly or so effectively carried through to an intermediate or final conclusion.

The second area of innovation is in the extension of the boundaries of architecture (as is normally seen in National Awards) into a wider realm. The architects and others in this scheme have gone behind the normal design process and looked at the provision of housing as a practical activity for people with little ability to house themselves unaided.

At El Hekr, 87% of the population live below the urban poverty threshold set by the World Bank. All of the work had therefore to be relevant to these very low income groups. It had to understand local situations; it had to be capable of being managed without

sophisticated materials and finances; and it had to be capable of being modified to suit a wide range of real human needs. An important part of the scheme included the training of local managers. This was so successful that since 1982 the project agencies have been managed without expatriate technical support.

Thirdly, the schemes have been both realistic and creative. While some might have grand schemes for high-quality housing, these are seldom appropriate for such poor people and obviously mean far fewer people are housed. Others would exercise less control and merely oversee the construction of just another slum.

The Governor of Ismailia shared this concern for relevant quality but was farsighted enough to encourage a scheme which took a whole new approach. As a concession to such fears the plan discourages the use of second-hand or temporary materials.

This happens to coincide with the feelings of the settlers that new materials are preferred, and some happy compromise seems to have been achieved.

The breakdown of costs provided with the submission is also heartening. Of a total project cost to 1982 of some 93,000,000 Egyptian pounds only a small proportion seems to have been paid to the consultants. This represents very good value for money.

The concept is brilliant and like many good ideas is simple, or in retrospect appears simple.

This is a perfect example of architecture at grass roots level, and was carried out largely as an act of love by the consultants rather than for commercial profit. The project is filled with 'humanity' and this is why the dilemma of the people concerned was understood so well and such a satisfactory resolution achieved.

It takes some effort to understand the poverty and the level of crisis involved here. We tend to apply our own definitions to words such as 'low income' etc, but they have a different and more acute meaning in such an environment.

This project may seem very remote from the high-profile technologically advanced towers that many associate with today's architecture, but architecture is much wider than that. It is important to recognise that even in academic terms the work measures up as serious and intelligent architecture for real people.

It is quite appropriate and possible immediately. It also provides a strong foundation for future growth and improvement as the social and economic situation is consolidated. It is a rare and positive work which sets out as a major objective the goal of self-help and self control — one in which the consultant's role is to start the process and allow the local people to take over — a professional act of very high standards.

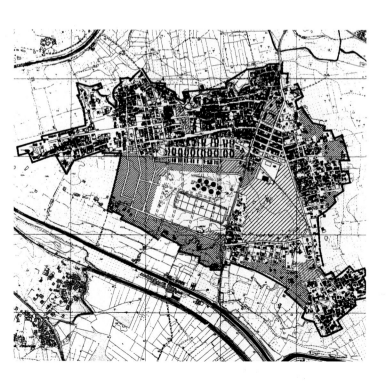

1992   CONTRIBUTION BY TROPPO ARCHITECTS TO ARCHITECTURE IN NORTHERN AUSTRALIA

TROPPO

1993   31ST SQUADRON CHAPEL RECONSTRUCTION, NORTHERN TERRITORY

ARCHITECT UNKNOWN. RECONSTRUCTION BY STAFF AND STUDENTS OF THE FACULTY OF ARCHITECTURE AND BUILDING AT NORTHERN TERRITORY UNIVERSITY

1994   MARIKA/ALDERTON HOUSE, GOVE, NORTHERN TERRITORY

GLENN MURCUTT

Special Jury Award 1992-94
The 1992 Jury, feeling that the existing categories were inadequate for the due recognition of some activities which did not quite fit within took it upon themselves to accept the responsibility for inventing a category which did not seem to have existed before. In fact the objectives were quite similar in approach to the ACI Awards — to recognise and dignify special achievements which did not fall into the standard categories. The 1993 and 1994 Juries continued this innovation.

SPECIAL JURY AWARD

As a member of the three consecutive juries, 1992, 1993 and 1994, which initiated and continued the Special Jury Award, I know how and why this category was introduced. We were looking at the Northern Territory nominees in the usual categories and along the way kept coming across buildings completed by the firm of Troppo Architects (Phil Harris and Adrian Welke). We all felt that here was a body of work which deserved to be more widely known and appreciated. Individual projects didn't quite fit the category awards, but the accumulated corpus of Troppo seemed to be having a ripple effect in raising and realising expectations of good architecture. Since no category suited, the solution was to invent one. We saw no reason why a jury could not exercise its own sense of discretion and innovation. The top levels of the RAIA hierarchy did not oppose the move.

Again in the Territory, the next year's jury were induced, as a side trip, to visit the incredible 31st Squadron Chapel, reconstructed. Because the former materials had all eroded or been eaten by termites, the new building could hardly be called recycled. For the original timber posts, steel had been substituted, so authentic replication could not be claimed. The original architect, if there even was one, remained unknown. The chapel demonstrates an adroit expediency of materials, a wall system well-suited to the wet tropical climate and an architectural form that, not shrinking from the obvious and the practical, makes some more sophisticated urban attempts at Minimalism look overwrought. But it was not material or climatic compatibility alone that moved the jury. Here was, we felt, a monument in the best meaning of the word. The remoteness and very occasional use as a reunion venue for the celebration of a tragic history only adds to the feeling of exquisite pathos.

There must be something about the Top End which drives awards juries to what some might call eccentric behaviour and which others might call insights of penetrating wisdom. Of course a lot of the architecture in this region is an appalling caricature of attitudes and appearances conditioned by milder climates and dimmer minds. Some set of unique conditions in the Northern Territory prompts architects to respond in exceptional ways — unusual causes leading to special effects.

The 1994 Special Jury Award to the Marika/Alderton house recognises the obsessive dedication of the client family, their architect Glenn Murcutt, the foresight of the Yirrkala Aboriginal community and the commitment of constructors and suppliers, all of whom co-operated to bring this remarkable venture to such a brilliant outcome. The late 1930s Darwin houses of architect Beni Burnett may be noted as inspirational precedents, with their woven bamboo shutters, high ceilings, and roof vents; their living and sleeping zones on the plan perimeter, on an elevated floor. Murcutt has moved the model much further in response to an extraordinary site and unique client needs. The main planning concerns were privacy, flexibility of occupancy and weather adaptability. The structure was prefabricated in New South Wales and transported to Gove Peninsula. The house is connected to local mains water, sewer and electricity, boosted by solar panels. External walls are generally fully openable plywood shutters, with pneumatic stays as in a light aircraft door; floors are slatted for air flow. The house is an intricate and sophisticated contraption for climate modification and imaginative dwelling. But above all, it goes beyond its acerbic, intelligent rationality, to reach a magical conceptual resonance with client and locale.

CONTRIBUTION BY TROPPO ARCHITECTS TO ARCHITECTURE IN THE NORTHERN TERRITORY

31ST SQUADRON CHAPEL RECONSTRUCTION
NORTHERN TERRITORY

ARCHITECT UNKNOWN, RECONSTRUCTION BY STAFF AND STUDENTS OF THE FACULTY OF ARCHITECTURE AND BUILDING AT
NORTHERN TERRITORY UNIVERSITY, HEAD OF DEPARTMENT: RICHARD LUXTON, ASSISTED BY ANDREW SCHULZE, MARK SMITH, MARK CHRISTIANSON

JURY REPORT

Its simplicity, fundamental functionalism and delicate disposition in the scrub give it a special quality. The reconstruction by students and architects is worthy of special recognition.
Robert Cheesman

For three main reasons, this building is worthy of an award: the original design is an inspired response to climatic, functional and contextual requirements, pariculary considering the paucity of materials and money available in 1943; secondly, for the research undertaken by the students and graduates and thirdly, for the very competent reconstruction.
Anne Cunningham

Once in a while, there comes to a jury's attention a building which does not fit easily into the nominated categories but which has a uniqueness that deserves recognition and celebration. Such a building is found, if directions are carefully followed, down the bitumen south of Darwin to a point known as 55 Mile, and then off into the bush along a barely distinguishable track into terrain that is now a cattle station... an ecclesiastical shed with rough bush poignancy.
Neville Quarry

This is an odd work to be considered... yet to fail to acknowledge the care and effort in making a work so light, frail almost, and appropriate to spirit, spirit of place, light, shade, ventilation and connectedness to nature, would deny the joy one feels.
Glenn Murcutt

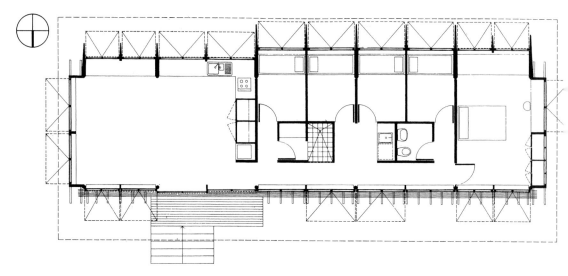

JURY REPORT

It looked to be a high cost level but that was probably in relation to neighbouring dwellings. The building was practical, though, and not excessive in any way. Everything seeems to have been considered. It is like a machine to serve the occupants, recognise cultural constraints and use the climate.
Graham Bligh

Not so much a house in the normal concept, this would more appropriately be called a 'dynamic shelter' which provides the ability to vary the internal environment from a totally enclosed container through varying degrees to a roofed, open, elevated platform.
Peter Crone

The convergence of three powerful intellects has resulted in this lively, light building; a fresh response to Aboriginal housing; one that acknowledges not just the physical character of the location but its spirit. The consequence is not necessarily a model to be slavishly adhered to, but a cornucopia of ideas and possibilities.
Rebecca Gilling

The house is an intricate and sophisticated mechanism for climate modification and imaginative dwelling, but above all, it goes beyond its acerbic, intelligent rationality to reach a magical conceptual resonance.
Neville Quarry

This is more than just a building. This project takes into acount Aboriginal culure and beliefs. Totally natural ventilation. The cowls on the exhausts to the bathroom are an innovative answer which works well.
James Taylor

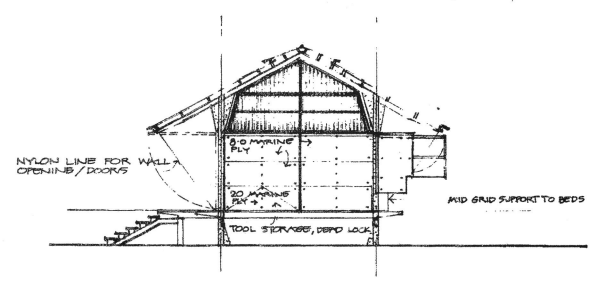

NYLON LINE FOR WALL OPENING / DOORS

8.0 MARINE PLY

20 MARINE PLY

TOOL STORAGE, DEAD LOCK

MID GRID SUPPORT TO BEDS

ENVIRONMENT CITATION

1994 ADVANCED TECHNOLOGY CENTRE, NEWCASTLE, NSW

JACKSON TEECE CHESTERMAN WILLIS

ACCESS CITATION

1994 AQUATIC SCIENCES CENTRE, WEST BEACH, SOUTH AUSTRALIA

SACON; DESIGN ARCHITECT: CARLO GNEZDA

ENVIRONMENT AND ACCESS CITATIONS

1995 DESIGN FACULTY, UNIVERSITY OF NEWCASTLE, NSW

STUTCHBURY & PAPE WITH EJE ARCHITECTURE

CITATIONS
ENVIRONMENT AND ACCESS

BEYOND THE ARCHITECTONIC

All buildings, as a matter of course, ought to respond to their environmental implications, and provide access for people other than those who are normally able. Any building which ignores such considerations should not be eligible for an award in any category. Juries do take this into account when deciding upon winners.

Those buildings which receive Environment and Access Citations have made contributions beyond the ordinary, and in some special ways have demonstrated a thorough appreciation and application of the principles that underlie these issues.

ENVIRONMENT

The RAIA has a very detailed policy on the Environment and there are formal Australian Standards relating to access for the disabled.

The RAIA Environment Policy declares five specific principles:

1. Maintain and, where it has been disturbed, restore bio-diversity.
2. Minimise the consumption of resources, especially non-renewable resources.
3. Minimise pollution of soil, air and water.
4. Maximise the health, safety and comfort of building users.
5. Increase awareness of environmental issues.

The RAIA Environment Policy goes into some detail in recommending particular design actions. For example, under the heading of 'Minimising Pollution' there are recommendations such as: "Encourage a reduction in the need for energy by maximising passive thermal comfort using renewable energy and by re-evaluating design comfort criteria" and "Avoid using insulation or furniture or packing foams that use CFCs in manufacture".

Architects may well agree in principle but dispute the detailed solution. (The notion of renewable energy, for instance, is scientifically impossible.)

Some architects argue that for window frames, the most environmentally benign choice is plantation timber. Others argue that because introduced plantations overwhelm indigenous environments and because the preservation treatment of timber involves poisonous chemicals, the choice of high energy-embodied, long-lasting, aluminium may be environmentally defensible, despite being the product of an extraction industry.

The appropriate choices are not always obvious. Careful scientific analysis and auditing is not always available, or may be equivocal. Clearly however, the first step is to accept that environmental issues must be addressed by every architectural project.

ACCESS

Between the statutory requirements of the Building Code of Australia and the Australian Standard AS 1428 relating to access for the disabled, there is no excuse why any building and its immediate environment should not fulfil these responsibilities. Fulfilling to the letter is one thing, and not difficult to do, although it is still surprising how many buildings do not even manage that. Fulfilling to the spirit is another matter, not always evident. The frame of mind within which the designer must operate is not to so blatantly provide disabled access that it becomes special and segregating, but to weave it into basic design premises so that the access provision is expedient and comfortable for everyone. After all, for everyone, the real architectural experience is an accessible journey.

ADVANCED TECHNOLOGY CENTRE, NEWCASTLE, NSW

JACKSON TEECE CHESTERMAN WILLIS
ENVIRONMENTAL CONSULTANT: TED HARKNESS

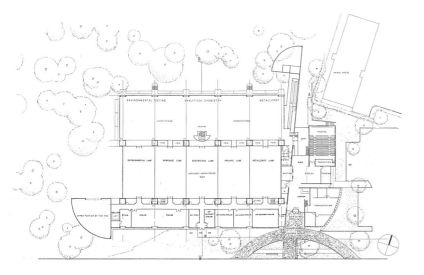

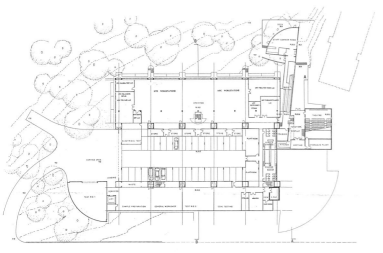

JURY REPORT

All architects consider environmental issues in their approach to design. The aim of the Environment Citation is to acknowledge projects which take as many measures as possible to achieve ecologically sustainable design and which are outstanding in their special integration of these factors into the building.

The Advanced Technology Centre, designed by Jackson Teece Chesterman Willis, is a joint-venture research facility within the University of Newcastle. An essential ingredient in the brief was to design a building which demonstrated the efficient use of electrical energy together with solar efficiency and protection of the natural bushland areas which adjoin the site.

Designed for a power company, the building is an accomplished reflection of Pacific Power's commitment to responsible energy use.

It demonstrates a high degree of sensitivity to its immediate environment, both in the building process and ongoing operation. Landscaping is disciplined and in accordance with the surrounding bush.

Internal spaces are well ventilated and bathed in natural light. The use of light shafts to illuminate internal spaces is effective, while externally, an extensive fixed sunshade system restricts summer sunlight. Multiple air handling systems respond to varying needs and a computerised building management system minimises energy use.

Other measures adopted by the designers include a deep floor plan, incorporating skylights, giving a low wall-to-floor area ratio and a compact building footprint; lightweight cladding panels of high thermal performance; life-cycle costing to guide system selection; automatic sensors turn off perimeter lighting when daylight is sufficient; night flushing with fresh air to pre-cool the structure in summer; and a system of dilution tanks, silt traps and waste water disbursement to control potential damage to bushland from site runoff.

Many of the environmental requirements addressed by this project, and which might be considered a restriction to the creative process, have been used to advantage through careful research and investigation to produce a highly efficient and attractive building.

AQUATIC SCIENCES CENTRE, WEST BEACH, SOUTH AUSTRALIA

ARCHITECT/ENGINEER/QUANTITY SURVEYOR/LANDSCAPE DESIGN: SACON; PROGRAM MANAGER: DEAN MILLARD;
PROJECT MANAGERS: IAN TRELEAVEN AND TREVOR HARRIS; DESIGN ARCHITECT: CARLO GNEZDA; JOB CAPTAIN: BRENTON ELLIS;
SOME DOCUMENTATION BY RAFFEN MARON ARCHITECTS

JURY REPORT

All architects comply with appropriate Australian Standards in their approach to access to people with disabilities. The aim of the Access Citation is to acknowledge excellence and imagination shown in design for access and the seamless integration of these factors into the building.

The South Australian Aquatic Sciences Centre, located in West Beach, Adelaide, provides South Australia with the most comprehensive marine and freshwater biological and fisheries research capability in Australia.

The building makes a statement on its provisions for access and embraces them in a positive way. More than simply doing what is required, it is exemplary in the way it uses access for people with disabilities to aesthetic advantage.

Externally, a bridge makes a dramatic entrance and internally, the focus is on a spiralling ramp which hugs a curved glass brick wall and provides general access to a lower floor, with views to interesting spaces along the way. The ramp is a major architectural achievement and generator of form, providing strong visual orientation around the lecture theatre and foyer areas.

A finely detailed, sculptural building, it celebrates accessibility by highlighting the circulation system.

Wide corridors, excellent natural lighting and a high proportion of circulation space appear a natural part of the building fabric, rather than regulatory inclusions within this cleverly planned facility.

DESIGN FACULTY, UNIVERSITY OF NEWCASTLE, NSW

STUTCHBURY & PAPE WITH EJE ARCHITECTURE

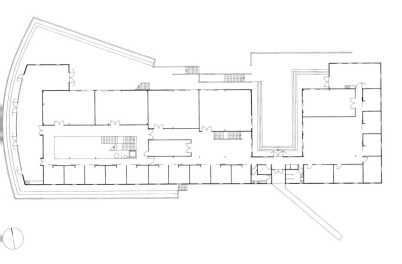

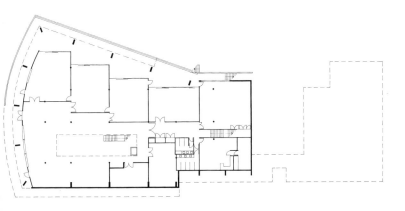

JURY REPORT
ACCESS CITATION

The beauty of this building's solution to disabled access is its understatement. A bridge over a dry creek bed provides an elegant and low-key entry for all users.

This simple and honest approach is carried through in the circulation and access features of the building. Wide corridors linking major spaces appear as a natural component of the building fabric rather than as forced, regulatory conclusions — circulation routes are clearly expressed and celebrate functionality. All major spaces have direct access to verandahs and courtyards. The 'bare bones' nature of the state-of-the-art disabled lift is entirely in keeping with the industrial tone expressed throughout.

ENVIRONMENT CITATION

The architects have demonstrated their attitude to environmentally friendly work through maximising passive solar opportunities, reducing running costs through sensible use of resources such as light and heat, use of low-energy materials, reducing building maintenance, sensible orientation and natural systems of control for light and ventilation.

Built to a tight budget, the building is commonsense and low-tech. It does not have air conditioning but adopts a passive system to effectively provide ventilation — in order to provide thermal comfort, the occupants are required to open and close windows, shutters and roof vents.

The building successfully encourages winter solar gain to the main spaces and uses convection and cross-ventilation cooling in summer. Mechanical ventilation is limited to service and workshop spaces.

The building minimises intrusion onto its natural bushland site and successfully demonstrates the ability to regenerate the surrounding landscape with new planting which respects the retained stands of eucalypts. The containment of stormwater runoff in ponds for later re-use and to enhance the landscape is particularly laudable.

LOCATION, LOCATION, LOCATION

Doing some geographic analysis, I was astonished to discover that two States, New South Wales and Tasmania, had never been the location of a Sir Zelman Cowen Award winner. The smallness of the output in Tasmania might account for that. But New South Wales, the State with largest population (5,716,244), largest RAIA Chapter membership (approx 3,000); no awards for public buildings? Extraordinary. Even more so because for decades the NSW Government Architect's branch was generally recognised as the best public service architectural department in Australia. Many excellent buildings were produced under its auspices. A large number of young architectural talents were nourished there, before they fled the roost to set up practices on their own or to join, at senior levels of responsibility, prestigious private firms. Victoria has been the location of four Sir Zelman Cowen Awards. Queensland and the ACT, three each; West Australia, South Australia and the Northern Territory, two each; New South Wales and Tasmania, nil. Ironically, one notes that four New South Wales practices, Cox Richardson and Taylor, Ancher Mortlock and Woolley (with the Department of Housing and Construction), Harry Seidler and Glenn Murcutt (with Troppo) have been the architects for winners in other States and Territories. There is not much to conclude from this record, except perhaps to be reassured that National Awards juries have not been dominated by NSW members out to boost their home-State products. Unbiased coincidence, unmotivated by regional preferences, is the most likely explanation for the lack of correlation of size of population with number of awards. However, when a tally is made of awards in all other categories, the results correlate more with expectations.

HONOURED PRACTICE

From 1981–1995, 98 awards and four citations have been made, but not to precisely 102 architects, for some have won more than once, and some several in associations of two or more architects.

Denton Corker Marshall have participated in seven awards: 1988 President's and Interior Architecture (as Principal Design Consultants), 1989 Commercial, 1992 Walter Burley Griffin and 1992 International, 1993 President's and 1994 Commercial.

Daryl Jackson, as principal or in association with other architectural firms, has participated in six awards: Sir Zelman Cowen Awards in 1981 (with Evan Walker), 1984 and 1992 (with Tompkins Shaw & Evans), 1989 President's Award, 1989 Interior Architecture Award (with Hirsch Bedner) and 1991 International Award (Daryl Jackson Meldrum Burrows Collaborative).

Clive Lucas has participated in five awards: Lachlan Macquarie in 1983, 1988 and 1989, 1990 (Clive Lucas, Stapleton & Partners) and 1992 (with Tonkin Zulaikha Harford).

The NSW Government Architects' Branch has five awards: 1982 and 1993 Lachlan Macquarie, 1988 President's, Interior Architecture and Civic Design (with Allen Jack & Cottier, Conybeare Morrison, Hall Bowe & Webber and Lawrence Nield).

Lindsay Clare has four: 1990 President's (Kerry Hill with Pie Marrs Clare), 1992 and (Clare Design) 1995 Robin Boyd and 1995 Commercial.

Glenn Murcutt has four: 1981 and 1985 Robin Boyd, 1994 Special and 1994 Sir Zelman Cowen (with Troppo Architects).

Harry Seidler has four: 1987 Sir Zelman Cowen, 1991 Commercial, 1991 Interior Architecture and 1992 Commercial Awards.

Kerry Hill has three: 1990 President's (Kerry Hill with Pie Marrs Clare); 1993 and 1994 International.

Troppo have three: 1992 Special, 1993 Robin Boyd and 1994 Sir Zelman Cowen (with Glenn Murcutt).

Ten firms have each participated in two awards:

Allom Lovell-Marquis Kyle	1994 Lachlan Macquarie and President's
Cox Carmichael Whitford	1990 and 1993 Walter Burley Griffin
Edmond & Corrigan	1982 ACI 1995 Walter Burley Griffin
Forbes & Fitzhardinge	1988 Commercial 1993 Sir Zelman Cowen
Peter McIntyre	1983 Robin Boyd 1987 Sir Zelman Cowen
Mitchell/Guirgola & Thorp	1989 Sir Zelman Cowen 1994 Interior Architecture
Nation Fender	1993 International 1993 Interior Architecture
Geoffrey Pie	1986 Robin Boyd 1990 President's
Tonkin Zulaikha Harford	1992 Lachlan Macquarie 1994 Walter Burley Griffin
Ken Woolley	1986 Sir Zelman Cowen 1987 Robin Boyd
Australian Construction Services	1988 Sir Zelman Cowen 1991 Lachlan Macquarie

Receiving one award, alone or with others, were 44 firms: Robin Gibson, Cameron Chisholm & Nicol, Philip Cox Richardson & Taylor, Bligh Robinson, Greg Burgess, Raffen Maron, Louise St John Kennedy, Alex Tzannes, Don Watson, Alex Popov, Gabriel Poole, Dale Jones-Evans, Gordon and Valich, Lyon Jenkin & Salter, Bud Brannigan, Craig Rossetti, Axia, Latona Masterman, Guymer Bailey, Eugene Kneebone, Timothy Court, Ron Danvers, SA Department of Housing, Peddle Thorp, Vivian Fraser, Woodhead Hall McDonald and Brownwell Ranger, Garry Forward, Curnow Freiverts Glover Patten, Peter Crone, Kerridge Wallace, Allen Jack & Cottier, Conybeare Morrison, Hall Bowe & Webber, Lawrence Nield, Conrad & Gargett, Peter Elliott, Rob McIntyre, Robert Woodward, Melbourne City Council Urban Design & Architecture Division, Williams & Boag, Victoria Ministry of Housing, Eddie Codd, Commonwealth Department of Housing and Construction, and David Allen of Culpin Planning UK.

Citations have been awarded only recently. Stutchbury & Pape scored a double in 1995; Jackson Teece Chesterman & Willis, and Carlo Gnezda of SACON each received citations in 1994.

In the entire RAIA National Awards programme, 66 firms have been named in the awards and citation lists.

CHAPTER BALANCE

In all categories except the ACI, International Awards and Citations, the total is 87.

By geographical location the subtotals are: NSW 26, Victoria 24, Queensland 14, Northern Territory 6, ACT 6, Western Australia 5, South Australia 3, Tasmania 2.

To expect an exact correlation between State population and number of awards would be unreasonable. The growth rate of Queensland, the Commonwealth expenditure on major buildings in Canberra and the exotic opportunities in the Northern Territory would seem to vindicate the relative balance along predictable lines. The numbers are still too small a base upon which to make significant generalisations, but there appears to be no extraordinary emphasis on one zone or another.

FORMAT

The RAIA National Awards Jury reports generally conform to one of three patterns. The report is credited to the jury as a whole; a single report on each awarded building is made by one or two jurors on behalf of the jury, or each juror reports individually on each building. The individual jurors' snippets of applause are easy to read, and the reactions of different jurors interesting to observe, although sometimes repetitive, and often too short to be little more than opinionated responses, presented without supportive argument. The longer 'whole jury' reports have more scope to develop some rhetorical substantiation of the particular award. However, few of even the longer reports really approach the level of being a critique. On the occasion of an award, destructive comments are not called for, but some earnest evaluation surely is appropriate. James Grose's report on the 1984 Sir Zelman Cowen Award winner is an example of the critique without malice. Whichever format is followed is not a policy imposed by the RAIA but the result of each jury's decision. Like all professions with any claims to scholarship and social relevance, architecture needs to be constantly invigorated by informed discussion from within its ranks. Ironically, the anxious spasms of a few power-prone architects, who have sought to protect themselves from negative criticisms by threatening litigious action, has served to inhibit discussion and made publishers wary of printing anything at all about architecture except news bulletins about imminent projects, and usually then without bothering to mention the architect's name.

FAVOURITES

In the RAIA National Awards jury reports from 1981-95, the choices of individual words and collective figures of speech give an indication of the priorities behind the jury judgements. There are provisos, however, as to the accuracy of this correlation between words and concepts. Limited (as everyone is) by the vocabulary of their vocational education and the patterns of speech of professional practice, jurors may not always find precisely the perfect word to convey the meaning intended, and resort to easy clichés and platitudes as a convenient means of quick expression. But even this sort of choice can be revealing. Out of the vast vocabulary of the jury reports, some frequently occurring words include simple, delightful, charming, seductive, gracious, joyful. Favoured phrases of applause: well-detailed and keeping to a limited palette of colours. These rather genteel comments tell us the spontaneous response but do not advance our understanding of the architecture, only of the viewing jury. We may empathise with the viewer's emotional state, but have no way of knowing, simply from reading the words, whether we might share the same response.

As another example of opinion without vindication, the jury reports often mention that a particular building 'responds to the site'. What is the nature of a 'response', and in what sense may one response be more appropriate than another? On a greenfields site, a building may, by snuggling in like a wombat, be scarcely noticeable in the landscape. Another building may prance over the site, as light and overt as a dancer. Yet another may be part embedded, part emergent, like a moth exiting from a chrysalis. Which of these metaphorical states appeals depends upon deeply personal concepts of landscape and human habitat which, in turn, are profoundly linked to myth, memory and ingrained social custom. Such themes are complex and often subconscious, so not easily abandoned, nor dredged opportunely into an architectural critique. Architects seldom have their own fundamental rhetoric codified and ready to discuss; indeed generally they shy away from such intimate exposure, for construction, not introspection, is their professional habit. So the philosophical assumptions go undistilled into the architectural brew, retaining their underlying, if unidentified, potency. Architectural principles elude clarification, because each layer of analysis unveils values which are not primarily architectonic. It is hardly possible to isolate purely abstract architectural content from projects that have an inexorable connection to social and political narratives: say, to compare and differentiate on architectural quality alone, a casino, a gaol, a mosque and a municipal swimming pool.

EXTENDED MEANINGS

It is not the role of the awards jury reports to go deeply into architectural theory. The reports might, however, take the opportunity to consider the extended meanings of notions which have become platitudinous. Simplicity, for instance, is not an easy concept, for it has complex possibilities of meaning. There is crisp simplicity of architectonic form disassociated from representation, such as happens with collections solely of rectangular prisms in Cartesian array. There is another kind of perceptual simplicity, when the observer appreciates the building instantly, at a single glance, no matter how complex the composition. Originality gets no mention in the jury reports, perhaps because originality is an attribute that soon fades under inspection. In a pedantic sense, every building is original in that it did not exist before. For every building there can be found a precursor, a precedent or a seminal influence, if enough scholarly detective work is pursued, so absolute innovation is absolutely impossible. Good detailing, which all architects love to appreciate, is easy to recognise as good design intentions carried out with fine craftsmanship — but difficult to codify. Detailing of say, the junction between adjacent panels, may choose from techniques of butt, gap, lap, or strap joints — there is no necessary hierarchy involved, only that the detailing consistently establishes and contributes to the architectural themes of the entire concept.

IDEOLOGICAL POSTURES

Ideology is not a subject which the jury reports take up, and maybe in static cultures it might be thought unnecessary to do so. Yet in the multiple culture of Australia, can ideology be avoided? In Beijing, in 1973, I came across a quite different cultural interpretation of the significance of architectural conservation. Cruising the Forbidden City, I asked a Chinese official guide why the Communist government was so proud of this architecture of temples and palaces, imperial furniture, jewellery and costumes, which surely must be identified with a class which the revolution had overthrown. He explained to me that I was missing the thrust of the tribute, for all of these artefacts had been made by the artisan and working classes, so that it was the fruits of their labour which should be admired and conserved, despite being commissioned by decadent emperors.

RECOMMENDATION

My view is that, in future, two kinds of report should be published. The short bright accolades from each juror, as personal animated responses should continue to appear. At the same time, the RAIA should publish a more profound essay, from the jurors as a whole or their nominee, which would develop a discourse concerning the attributes and embedded values of the award-winning architecture of that year. Over a decade or so, the accumulation of such discourses could be the basis of some further informed comment on the evolution of architectural attitudes. The canon of built work would have, in parallel, a canon of criticism. The makers of the culture of architecture deserve lavish exposure, deep introspection, robust debate and wide publication.

Some juries in the past listed awards finalists, some made commendations to projects which just missed an award, but were deemed worthy of mention. Some gave multiple awards in a single category. This approach is regarded as too *ad hoc* by some critics, who would rather only one award be given in each category, and no commendations. While this would preserve the speciality of the award-winners, the consolation and the possibilities of debate that a secondary list provides would be lost. There is not space in this book for photographic coverage of all the runners-up, but the list is given for the historical record. For those who know many of the buildings, the fineness of the choice will often be arguable, and some Chapters, loyal to their local projects, may find it incomprehensible that their own favourites did not feature in the awards list, or did not even rate a vist from the jury. Any awards process, whether in architecture, film, literature or social service, is bound to carry acrimony as well as applause, and the saga continues.

REPRISE

The RAIA National Architecture Awards celebrate the achievements of excellence in works of architecture, they give accolades to the architects of those works, they serve a public relations purpose by spreading awarness of high-quality architecture, and they have a didactic function — to lead the community of users and observers into a more discerning appraisal and appreciation of architecture. The RAIA awards juries are not infallible in their judgements, but they represent the opinions of groups that have been selected because of their experience and perscipacity. The awards programmes contribute to the culture of architecture.

SIR ZELMAN COWEN AWARD

Commendations and Finalists

1982   American Express Tower, Sydney
John Andrews International.

1983   Territory Insurance Office, Darwin
Stapledon Architects.
Museum and Tourist Infomation Office, Kempsey, NSW
Glenn Murcutt.

1984   Parklea Prison, NSW
NSW Government Architect.

1985   Parliament Station, Melbourne
Peter McIntyre Partnership.
Singapore High Commission, Canberra
Daryl Jackson, Alastair Swayn, Peter Rees.
No 1 Collins Street, Melbourne
Robert Peck YFHK & Denton Corker Marshall.
Queensland Cultural Centre, Brisbane
Robin Gisbon.

1986   IBM National Headquarters, NSW
Devine Erby Mazlin.
Administration Building, Defence Force Academy, Canberra
Department of Housing and Construction, ACT Region.
Corbould Park Race Course, Sunshine Coast, Queensland
Down and Neyland.

1987   Fountain at Queensland Performing Arts Complex, Brisbane
Robert Woodward.

1988   National Tennis Centre, Melbourne
Peddle Thorpe and Learmonth with Philip Cox and
Partners.
Powerhouse Museum, Sydney
NSW Public Works Department; Denton Corker
Marshall, Principal Design Consultants.

1989   Dandenong College of TAFE, Victoria
Edmond & Corrigan and Ministry of Housing and
Construction.
NSW Exhibition Centre, Darling Harbour, Sydney
Philip Cox Richardson Taylor & Partners.

1990   Adelaide Tropical Conservatory
Raffen Maron.

1991   Box Hill Community Centre, Victoria
Greg Burgess.

1992   Googong Dam Amenities Block, ACT
Ric Butt, Strine Design.

ROBIN BOYD AWARD

Commendations and Finalists

1982 Kew House, Melbourne
Edmond & Corrigan.
Point Lonsdale House, Victoria
Falk & Gurry.
Applecross House and Duplex, Western Australia
Peter Overman, Overman & Zuideveld.

1985 Knox Schlapp Housing Development, Victoria
Peter Elliot, and Lindsay Holland, in conjunction
with the Victorian Ministry of Housing.
Goetz House, Buderim, Queensland
Lindsay Clare Villari.

1986 Ellerslie Place Apartments, Hobart
Architecture & Urban Design Partners.

1987 House at Little Swanport, Tasmania
Ray Heffernan; Eastman Heffernan, Walch & Button.
Badley Residence, Nightcliff, Northern Territory
Steven Ehrlich/MTE Architects.

1988 Swift House, NSW
Terry Dorrough.
House in Bassendean, Western Australia
Howlett & Bailey.
Nankervis House, Paddington, NSW
Allen Jack & Cottier.

1989 Pittwater House, NSW
Alex Tzannes.
Corryton Gardens House, ACT
Addison Associates.

1990 Toorak House, Melbourne
Synman Justin Bialek.
Armadale House, Melbourne
Cocks Carmichael Whitford.

1992 Walk-up apartments, Adelaide
Raffen Maron.
Newman house, Balgownie, NSW
Grose Bradley.
Magney House, Paddington, NSW
Glenn Murcutt.
Residence at St Andrew's Beach, Victoria
Nonda Katsalidis.

1995 Israel House, Avalon, NSW
Stutchbury & Pape; Design architect: Peter J.
Stutchbury.

LACHLAN MACQUARIE AWARD

Commendations and Finalists

1982   Cataract Gorge and Cliff Grounds, Launceston
City Architects Department, Launceston City Council.
Werribee Park, Victoria
Alan Nance.

1985   The Restoration of the Brisbane School of Arts Building
Ron Baker, Design and Construction Branch of the
Department of Health and Community Services,
Brisbane City Council.

1986   Minister's Office, Lands Department Building, Sydney
NSW Public Works Dept; Government Architect J.W.
Thompson; Project Architect T.G. Morris.
Commandant's House, Port Arthur
Clive Lucas.

1987   Lanyon Homestead Museum, Tharwa, Canberra
Howard Tanner.
The Hermitage, Camden, NSW
Clive Lucas/Ian Stapleton.

1988   Belgenny Farm Group, Camden, NSW
Howard Tanner.
Cunningham Residence, Brisbane
Robert Riddel.

1989   The Windmill, Brisbane
Allom Lovell Marquis-Kyle

1990   Princess Theatre, Melbourne
Axia; Conservation: Allom Lovell.

PRESIDENT'S AWARD

Commendations and Finalists

1985   83 Salamanca Place, Hobart
Forward Consultants.
Esprit de Corps, Melbourne
Daryl Jackson.
The Alma Redevelopment, Abbotsford, Victoria
David Sainsberry of McKeever Smith Architects.

1986   Western Australian Maritime Museum, Fremantle
Building Management Authority of Western Australia.

1987   Queen Victoria Building, Sydney
Rice Daubney/Stephenson & Turner.
Mt Lofty House, Crafers, South Australia
Ross Sands.

1988   St Peter's College Chapel, Adelaide
Brown Falconer Group.
Armoury and Barracks, Adelaide
SA Department of Housing & Construction.

1989   Newcastle Regional Museum, NSW
Suters Architects and Planners.
Earl of Spencer Inn, Western Australia
Trevor Saleeba & Associates.

1991   Polo Club, Brisbane
Bruce Buchanan.

COMMERCIAL AWARD

Finalists

1988   Apple Headquarters, Sydney
Allen Jack & Cottier.
Office and Warehouse, Maroochydore, Queensland
Lindsay Clare

1989   Central Plaza 1 & 2, Brisbane
Kisho Kurakawa & Associates,
Peddle Thorp & Harvey, Peddle Thorp & Walker.
222 Exhibition Street, Melbourne
Denton Corker Marshall.

1990   Lake Crackenback Village, NSW
Bligh Robinson.

INTERIOR ARCHITECTURE AWARD

Finalists

1988   Deutscher Gallery and Residence, Victoria
Katsalidis & Partners.
Emery Vincent Offices, Melbourne
Denton Corker Marshall.

1989   Beneficial Finance, Adelaide
Ranger Design.
David Ellis Gallery, Melbourne
Ivan Rivajec.

1990   Cherry Tree Hotel, Melbourne
David Edelman and Tom Kovac.

Commendation:

1993   Perraton Apartment, Sydney
Stephen Varady.

COMMENDATIONS AND FINALISTS

ACI AWARDS

Commendations and Finalists
1983   Brian Klopper, Perth
        (also nominated: Chris Johnson and Philip Rose,
        NSW Government Architect's Branch; Roger
        Johnson, ACT; Ministry of Housing, Victoria; Barry
        McNeil, Tasmania; Aldgate Primary School, SA)
1984   (Victoria only) Robinson Chen.
1985   House at Wilston, Queensland, Russell Hall.
        Design for a Community Rehabilitation Centre for
        Aborigines, Glenn Murcutt.

INTERNATIONAL AWARDS

Commendation
1994   Kuching Waterfront, Malaysia
          Conybeare Morrison & Partners

From 1981-85, awards were made by the National Selection Committee, on which there was a representative of each Chapter of the RAIA. Such a large jury was expensive to manage, especially for site inspections which could range over the whole of Australia. In 1986 the number on the jury was reduced to five, and so it remains.

1981   Andrew Metcalf (chair), Alistair Angus, Roger Johnson.

1982   Peter Johnson (chair), Jennifer Taylor, Graham Brawn, John Dalton, Geoff Nairn, Tony Brand, Bruce Goodsir, Greg Deas, Andy McPhee.

1983   Danny Nutter (chair), Bruce Eeles, Hal Guida, Neil Evans, Bevan Rees, Jack McConnell, Tony Brand, Eddie Dias, John Morton.

1984   Richard Young (chair), Richard Thorp, Richard Apperly, Ron Mutton, Greg Berkman, John Schenk, Jamieson Allom, John Denton, Vin Davies.

1985   David Jackson (chair), Rhys Beames, Robert Bruce, John Ancher, Ken Frey, Bill Macginley, Stefan Pikusa, Christine Young, John Lidbury.

1986   David Jackson (chair), Edwin Codd, Peter Miller, Roger Pegrum, Geoffrey Summerhayes.

1987   Graham Hulme (chair), Hal Guida, Brian Mathieson, Roger Pegrum, Geoffrey Summerhayes.

1988   Bob Hall (chair), Hal Guida, Bruce Bowden, Brian Mathieson, Geoffrey Pie.

1989   Dudley Wilde (chair), Bruce Bowden, Roger Johnson, Peter McIntyre, Geoffrey Pie.

1990   Ron Bodycoat (chair), Tom Heath, Roger Johnson, Peter McIntyre, Helen Wellings.

1991   Robert Caufield (chair), Tom Heath, Glenn Murcutt, Helen Wellings, John Morphett.

1992   Jamieson Allom (chair), Anne Cunningham, John Morphett, Neville Quarry, Maggie Tabberer

1993   Robert Cheesman (Chair), Anne Cunningham, Glenn Murcutt, Neville Quarry, Maggie Tabberer

1994   James Taylor (chair), Graham Bligh, Peter Crone, Rebecca Gilling, Neville Quarry.

1995   Louise Cox (chair), Graham Bligh, Peter Crone, Rebecca Gilling.

REFERENCES

Birrell, James. *Walter Burley Griffin*. University of Queensland Press, St Lucia, Queensland, 1964.

Blake, Peter. *Architecture for the New World: The Work of Harry Seidler*. Horwitz, Sydney, Wittenborn, New York and Karl Kraemer, Stuttgart, 1973.

Boyd, Robin. *Australia's Home: Its Origins, Builders and Occupiers*. Melbourne University Press, Melbourne, 1952.
Boyd, Robin. *The Australian Ugliness*. FW Cheshire, Melbourne, 1960.
Boyd, Robin. *The Puzzle of Architecture*. Melbourne University Press, Melbourne, 1965.
Boyd, Robin. *The Great Great Australian Dream*. Pergamon Press, Sydney, 1972.

Butler, Graeme. *The Californian Bungalow in Australia*. Lothian Books, Melbourne, 1992.

Cox, Philip and Park, Andy. *Yulara*. Panda Books, Sydney, 1986.

Dobney, Stephen. *Cox Architects*. The Images Publishing Group, Mulgrave, Victoria, 1994.

Drew, Philip. *Leaves of Iron: Glenn Murcutt, Pioneer of an Australian Architectural Form*. The Law Book Company, Sydney, 1985.

Evans, Ian. *The Federation House*. Flannel Flower Press, Yeronga, Queensland, 1986. Reprinted 1990.

Farrelly, Elizabeth. *Three Houses. Glenn Murcutt*. 'Architecture in Detail' series. Phaidon Press, New York, 1995.

Frampton, Kenneth. *Riverside Centre*. Horwitz, Sydney and Karl Kraemer, Stuttgart, 1988.

Frampton, Kenneth, and Drew, Philip. *Harry Seidler*. Thames and Hudson, London, 1992.

Freeland, John Maxwell. *Architecture in Australia: A History*. Cheshire, Melbourne, 1968.
Freeland, John Maxwell. *The Making of A Profession*. Angus & Robertson, Sydney, 1971.

Freeman, Peter. *The Homestead: A Riverina Anthology*. Oxford University Press, Melbourne, 1982.

Fromonot, Françoise. *Glenn Murcutt; Works and Projects*. Thames & Hudson, London, 1995.

Hamman, Conrad. *Cities of Hope: Australian Architecture and Design by Edmond & Corrigan*. Oxford University Press, Melbourne, 1993.

Harrison, Peter. *Walter Burley Griffin: Landscape Architect*. National Library of Australia, Canberra, 1995.

Howells, Trevor and Nicholson, Michael. *Towards the Dawn*. Hale & Ironmonger, Sydney, 1989.

Irving, Robert. *The History and Design of the Australian House*. Oxford University Press, Melbourne, 1985.

Jackson, Daryl. *Daryl Jackson: Architecture, Drawings, Photographs*. Macmillan Company of Australia, South Melbourne, 1984.

Jahn, Graham. *Contemporary Australian Architecture*. Craftsman House, Sydney, 1994.

Johnson, Donald. *Australian Architecture 1901-51: Sources of Modernism*. Sydney University Press, Sydney, 1980.
Johnson, Donald. *The Architecture of Walter Burley Griffin*. Macmillan, Melbourne, 1977.

McGregor, Craig. *Australian Built: Responding to Place*. Design Arts Board of the Australia Council, Sydney, 1985.

Marquis-Kyle, Peter, and Walker, Meredith. *The Illustrated Burra Charter*. Australia ICOMOS, Sydney, 1992.

Metcalf, Andrew. *Thinking Architecture: Theory in the Work of Australian Architects*. Royal Australian Institute of Architects, Red Hill, ACT, 1995.

Ogg, Alan. *Architecture in Steel: The Australian Context*. RAIA, Red Hill, ACT, 1987.

Paroissien, Leon, and Griggs, Michael. *Old Continent, New Building*. David Ell Press and Design Arts Committee of the Australia Council, Sydney, 1983.

Pegrum, Roger. *Details in Australian Architecture. Volume 1*. RAIA Education Division, Red Hill, ACT, 1984.
Pegrum, Roger. *Details in Australian Architecture. Volume 2*. RAIA Education Division, Red Hill, ACT, 1987.

Royal Australian Institute of Architects, *Australian Architects Series*:
Pegrum, Roger, David Saunders. *Philip Cox*. RAIA, Canberra, 1st edition 1984, 2nd edition 1988.
Taylor, Jennifer, and Harold Guida, Philip Cox. *Ken Woolley*. RAIA, Canberra, 1985.
Beck, Haig, and Jackie Cooper, Neville Quarry, Alex Selenitsch, Greg Deas. *Denton Corker Marshall*. RAIA, Canberra, 1987.
Quarry, Neville, and Roger Johnson. *Australian Government Architects*. Australian Government Publishing Service, Canberra, 1988.
Keniger, Michael. *Rex Addison, Lindsay Clare and Russell Hall*. RAIA, Canberra, 1990.

Seidler, Harry. *Houses, Interiors, Projects*. Associated General Publications, Sydney, 1954; 2nd edition, Horwitz, Sydney, 1969.
Seidler, Harry. *Towers in the City*. Edizioni Tecno, Milan, 1988.

Serle, Geoffrey. *Robin Boyd: A Life*. The Miegunyah Press, Melbourne, Victoria, 1995.

Sharp, Dennis. *Sources of Modern Architecture*. Granada, London. 2nd edition, 1981.

Sowden, Harry. *Towards an Australian Architecture*. Ure Smith, Sydney, 1968.

Stretton, Hugh. *Ideas for Australian Cities*. Stretton, Adelaide, 1970.

Tan, Hock Beng, *Tropical Architecture and Interiors: Tradition-Based Design of Indonesia, Malaysia, Singapore*. Page One Publishing, Singapore, 1994.
Tan, Hock Beng, *Tropical Resorts*. Page One Publishing, Singapore, 1995.

Tanner, Howard. *Architects of Australia*. Macmillan, Melbourne, 1981.

Taylor, Jennifer. *Australian Architecture Since 1960*. The Law Book Co, Sydney, 1986.

Towndrow, Jennifer. *Philip Cox: Portrait of an Australian Architect*. Penguin Books, Ringwood, Australia, 1991.

ACKNOWLEDGEMENTS

My most important acknowledgements are to the architects –
recipients of the awards – for their achievements and for co-operating
so readily in my quest for information; and to the RAIA juries, for
judging with dedication and tolerance.

Also I acknowledge:

The constructors and consultants, without whom the projects would
not have been realised;

The clients, the private and public inhabitants, for whom the projects
have purpose;

The photographers, for helping to make the award buildings better
known, and for providing essential material for publication;

The Royal Australian Institute of Architects, for supporting the book
with a seeding research grant, and to the many sponsors of the RAIA
National Awards programme;

Davina Jackson, Peg Quarry and John Phillips for perceptive
critiques; Margaret Shaw, Chief Librarian, National Art Gallery,
Canberra, to whom is entrusted the curatorship of the Peter Johnson
Archive of architects' original submissions to the RAIA awards
programme;

Ian Close, publisher, for access to information first published in
Architecture Australia;

Students of architecture, for their constant stimulation; and anyone
else I have otherwise neglected to name, but who diligently or
unwittingly contributed to the enterprise.

Neville Quarry
Bondi Beach
1996

ASSISIS, SARSHID
42, 43, 44, 45, 212, 213.

BALFOUR, TOM
30, 31.

BLUNK, REINER
78, 79, 82, 94, 95, 256, 257.

BODDY, ADRIAN
174, 175.

CARTER, EARL
162, 163 (EARL CARTER/BELLE), 202, 203.

DUPAIN, MAX
22, 58, 59, 66, 67, 70 (RIGHT), 102, 103, 112, 113, 114 (SIERINS-DUPAIN), 116, 117, 118, 119, 132, 133, 166, 186, 187.

EASTWOOD, RICHARD
136, 137

FOX, TREVOR
50, 51

FRANCES, SCOTT
72, 73, 76, 120, 121.

GOLLINGS, JOHN
20, 21, 26, 27, 28, 29, 34, 35, 38, 44, 45, 48, 49, 62, 63, 104, 105, 138, 139, 140, 141, 148, 149, 150, 151, 160, 161, 164, 165, 170, 171, 180, 181, 182, 183, 188, 189, 190, 191, 192, 193, 201, 214, 215, 222, 223, 224, 225, 228, 229, 238, 239.

GRIFFITH, TIM
210, 211.

HYATT, PETER
46, 47, 146, 147, 262, 263.

KENNY, SIMON
152, 153, 168 (TOP).

KOS, FRITZ
24, 25, 64, 65, 158, 159.

LIM, ALBERT
230, 231.

LUCAS, CLIVE
115.

LUNG, GEOFF
77.

MAJIORANA, BART
264, 265, 266, 267.

MEIN, TREVOR
40, 41, 80, 86, 87.

MILES, WAYNE
88, 89.

NICHOLSON, MICHAEL
90, 91, 126, 127.

NICHOLSON, SANDY
194, 195.

PHILLIP, GRAHAM
172, 173.

QUARRY, NEVILLE
254, 255

QUIRK, PHILIP
227.

RAD, PETER
208, 209.

SAUNDERS, MARTIN
92, 93.

STRINGER, RICHARD
36, 37, 68, 69, 74, 75, 142, 143, 184, 185.

TAN, HOCK BENG
226.

TROPPO ARCHITECTS
252, 253.

TWIGG, D
244. AUSTRALIAN ANTARCTIC DIVISION, PWD.

WILSON, RICHARD
168 (BOTTOM).

WOODWARD, ROBERT
204, 205.

WOOLLEY, ROBERT
204, 205

WOOLLEY, KEN
70 (LEFT)